BOUNDARIES OF OUR HABITATIONS

And God made from one every nation to live on all
the earth, having determined allotted periods and
the boundaries of their habitations. (Acts 17:26)

SUNY Series in Religious Studies
Harold Coward, editor

BOUNDARIES
OF OUR
HABITATIONS

Tradition and
Theological Construction

DELWIN BROWN

STATE UNIVERSITY OF NEW YORK PRESS

Published by
State University of New York Press, Albany

© 1994 State University of New York

All rights reserved

Printed in the United States of America

No part of this book may be used or reproduced
in any manner whatsoever without written permission
except in the case of brief quotations embodied in
critical articles and reviews.

For information, address State University of New York Press,
State University Plaza, Albany, N.Y., 12246

Production by Cathleen Collins
Marketing by Dana Yanulavich

Library of Congress Cataloging in Publication Data

Brown, Delwin, 1935–
    Boundaries of our habitations : tradition and theological
construction / Delwin Brown.
        p.   cm. — (SUNY series in religious studies)
    Includes bibliographical references and index.
    ISBN 0–7914–1965–7. — ISBN 0–7914–1966–5 (pbk.)
    1. Tradition (Theology)   2. Hermeneutics — Religious aspects —
Christianity.   3. Theology — Methodology.   4. Postmodernism —
Religious aspects — Christianity.   5. Christianity and culture.
    I. Title.   II. Series.
BT90.B76   1994
230' .01 — dc20   93–27411
                                                                CIP

10 9 8 7 6 5 4 3 2 1

For our daughters
Terri, Kimberli, and Kristen

Contents

WHAT THEOLGIES ARE AND DO
THEOLOGY'S CONSENT

Preface

This inquiry into the nature of tradition and the relationship of tradition to theological construction has at least four motivations. One is programmatic, one philosophical, one frankly political in relationship to the academic theological enterprise, and the fourth motivation is "socio-ecclesiastical." I should perhaps explain them in reverse order because that, it seems to me, is their order of importance.

Liberal religions, liberal theologies, and liberal Western culture generally are "imaginations which have no . . . traditions to give them character."[1] They have lost their pasts and badly need to find them. But if the pasts recovered are wrongly construed, or the recovery is wrongly conducted, the cure could be worse than the disease. I shall argue that viable societies and viable traditions are genuinely innovative and genuinely conservative and that they are most playful precisely in the process of conservation. Further, they are playful, innovative, fluid because of what they conserve, because of the character of their pasts—when, at least, they take their pasts seriously as they are, not as their dogmaticians pretend them to be.

The second motivation of this study, academic politics, is more parochial but still important, at least to theologians. I believe the narrative or postliberal approach to theology is likely to dominate theological discussions for a significant time ahead, and I think this viewpoint is extremely right and extremely wrong. It is right about the crucially constructive role of the past in theology, in religion, and by implication, in culture for the viable conduct of human life. It is wrong, in my judgment, about the nature of the past and the way the past contributes constructively to the future. I write to affirm what is valuable in the postliberal approach, without the stifling and ultimately untenable repristination of the religious heritage that I take to be inherent in its program.

The philosophical motivation is the conviction that the distinctively American tradition of philosophical empiricism— what is sometimes called *radical empiricism* and was developed in the work of Peirce, James, Dewey, and the immigrant, Whitehead—is more adequate than the Kantian perspective that now dominates theological analysis. Radical empiricism does not provide all the analytical tools one needs by any means, and certainly it has not always been adequately articulated, but its employment can be shown to help us avoid a host of deleterious dualisms that always reappear whenever Kantian tools are used to understand human life individually and in relationship to the larger social and natural circumstance. This judgment will be substantiated once again, I believe, in the present attempt to understand the nature and function of religious traditions within cultural processes.

The fourth impetus for this book is a problem I uncovered some years ago in an article on the nature of biblical authority.[2] There I developed and defended the view that the authority of the Bible for the Christian is not its normativeness but its formativeness, its capacity continuously to "author" personal and corporate identity. The problem this proposal left was two-fold: how to conceive of the power of a canonical text to author human identity effectively but creatively, and how to understand this function of a textual canon in relation to the rest of the religious tradition that is often much more prominent in the life of the adherent. In order to address these questions my approach has had to become, in a sense, less Protestant and more Catholic than it once was. Indeed, the fact that I even write on tradition is already evidence of that.

This book is also motivated by the encouragement and assistance of a number of students and colleagues who either share my concerns and views or who respect them enough to think they should be heard and discussed. Among the students over the years to whom I am grateful for help I want to mention in particular Harold Anderson, Joseph Gorman, Diane Mac-Donald, Marie Vandenbark, and Carroll Weaver, as well as Wendy Wilbanks, my research assistant, and William Kenneth Cooper, who prepared the Index. Iliff colleagues in fields other than my own who read all or portions of the manuscript are Donald Messer, David Petersen, Jane Smith, and Thomas Troeger. I am indebted to them, too, for their valuable contributions. I am also grateful to friends and scholars elsewhere who devoted considerable time to reading my work and offering very important critical comments on it or who in other ways served as valuable resources. They are Linell Cady, John Cobb, Sam Gill, Conrad Hyers, Creighton Peden, William Power, Norbert Schedler, David Griffin, and William Dean, especially the latter two who critiqued the entire manuscript. The anonymous readers who reviewed the manuscript for SUNY Press also offered a number of valid criticisms and helpful suggestions, which I sincerely appreciate. The most significant contribution to this project came from my friend and Iliff colleague in theology, Sheila Davaney. Her analytical care made a quite substantive difference to my discussion at a number of points, but especially in the analysis of the negotiability of canonical boundaries and in the emphasis on the destructive as well as the positive potential of canon. Needless to say, however, none of my readers found, or would even now find, everything in my argument to be entirely satisfactory, so I shall save their reputations by acknowledging that the views presented herein, finally, are my own responsibility.

My greatest debt is to my wife, Nancy Brown, with whom I share the challenges of working in the academy, the beauties of living in the mountains, and the joys of many years together, one of which is our daughters. We dedicate this book to them.

Introduction

CICERO'S CONSENT: THE PROBLEM
AND PROCEDURE

THE PROBLEM

Cicero once said that tradition is rather like our second nature.[1] His apparently comfortable consent to tradition has seemed dubious at best since the Enlightenment, for various reasons. In the late seventeenth century, at the dawn of the Enlightenment, consent to tradition was judged unwise and unnecessary. It was thought unwise because the vast variety of inherited beliefs and practices was taken to mean that the past could offer no uniform guidance in the present. It was deemed unnecessary because methodical reason alone was thought capable of ascertaining truth. What good, then, was the past to the present? Hence Descartes resolved to strip himself of "all opinions and beliefs formerly received"[2] and to create truth claims on his own, much as a spider spins a web from its own substance.

We today, at what some call the twilight of Enlightenment "modernism,"[4] are less sure that the past can be stripped away (perhaps because we have reflected further on the source of a spider's substance), but we are not on that account any less suspicious of tradition or, therefore, of consent to it. Again, there are reasons. Cicero's attitude seems oblivious to the destructive capabilities of inherited ideas, actions, and structures. It appears indifferent to the right, indeed the obligation, to transform and even transcend what has gone before. It sounds inconsistent with the need to subject everything, including the past, to critical examination. For such reasons the modern period throughout has been prejudiced against prejudice, as Hans-Georg Gadamer says,[5] and thus, very largely, it has been an anti-traditional tradition.

In the last three or four decades, however, the suspicion of tradition inherited from the seventeenth and eighteenth centuries has begun to moderate.[6] In religious studies and even in academic theology, attention increasingly is given to the hypothesis that in important ways humans are inescapably traditioned and traditional beings, and to the claim that this hypothesis, if true, has positive as well as negative potential.[7] Ironically, this attention to the meaning of tradition is in fact a logical development of the Enlightenment's own critical spirit as it came to be historicized and introduced into liberal theology in the nineteenth century. This is so because an investigation of tradition is an extension of the inquiry into the nature of human historicity, and in the West historicity was "discovered" and its examination begun by nineteenth century liberals like Harnack and Troeltsch and those who followed them, such as the Roman Catholic modernists and the theologians of the early Chicago school. It might be true that our current interest in tradition is motivated in part by the resurgence of religious and cultural conservatism, but, whatever its immediate cause, attention to the meaning of tradition is a task inherent in the questions bequeathed to us by nineteenth century liberal theology. What does it mean to be historical? How are we shaped as historical beings, and how do we shape our histories? What is the past to us? What should it be? These questions about human historicity require an examination of the nature and function of tradition.

Attention to tradition is also implicit in the topic of hermeneutics, which dominates the contemporary critical discussion in theology. How can we "understand understanding" if we do not explore the complex dynamic of inheriting and inheritance that forms and partially constitutes understanding? Clearly it is not enough to understand and take seriously a particular past or a variety of pasts. Nor is it sufficient to analyze an event of understanding as if it were isolated, a happening without a heritage. We must also ask how canalized pasts become ⌐ constitutive in present understanding and how present understanding appropriates its pasts. We must ask what pasts are and what they are for. Thus, whether we address the topic of historicity, which is the broader construal of the modern problematic, or hermeneutics, its more immediate form, the nature and function of tradition must be examined. ⌐

Current theological affirmations of tradition, therefore, are intrinsic to the agenda of modern Western reflection. In some respects, however, I think they are significantly misguided. Owing particularly to deficiencies in the Enlightenment vision that they perhaps unwittingly continue, they foster truncated understandings of tradition. Some of them locate the reality of tradition too narrowly in language. In this they continue the Enlightenment's virtually exclusive preoccupation with the human, now, specifically, with human linguisticality. Their "linquisticism" minimizes tradition's power; it neglects the fundamental efficacy of tradition at the level of bodily feeling, especially in ritual. Other contemporary espousals of the past reduce the function of tradition primarily to its role as norm. They continue the Enlightenment's quest for certainty, often transmuted into a Protestantized portrayal of Scripture. This "normativism" neglects tradition's creativity; it underestimates the capacity of tradition to create novelty and author new forms of life. The argument of this book, I believe, will show that these and related ways of recovering the importance of tradition are inadequate.

The alternative to such inadequacies, however, is not a retreat to pre-modernist, pre-Enlightenment conceptions of tradition. Much can be learned from more "traditional" understandings of tradition, as we shall see. In particular, we can learn to think again of a tradition as a continuously reformed and formative milieu, as a dynamic stream of forces in which we live (or die), move (or stagnate), and gain (or lose) our being. But whatever the failings of the Western intellectual tradition since the seventeenth century, we cannot rescind its commitment to open inquiry and thus we cannot return to a premodern notion of a tradition as a repository of privileged data and specially protected criteria. One purpose of this book, therefore, is to seek an adequate understanding of tradition after the advent of modernism.

The ultimate task of this book, however, is to clarify the role of tradition in the practice of religion and, more specifically, in theology. Formulated in terms of Christianity, the book seeks to answer the question: What is the proper contribution of the Christian theological inheritance to Christian theological construction today? But this question, though evidently theological in character, will not be addressed exclusively from a theological standpoint. The examination of tradition and its relationship to religious and theological reflection undertaken here will draw upon extratheological resources, specifically those of philosophy and the social sciences, religious studies, and the history of religions. The assumption underlying this approach is that what theology says about tradition and the relationship of tradition to the theological task must make sense in terms of the actual phenomena of Christian and other religious traditions, as these phenomena are delineated by other humanistic fields of scholarship.

To conduct the discussion in this way obviously reflects a judgment about how theology ought to be done and, in particular, the criteria to which theological claims are obligated. My judgment, in a word, is that theology, even specifically Christian theology, is answerable to canons of critical inquiry defensible within the various arenas of our common discourse and not merely within those that are Christian.

THE PROCEDURE

Christian theologies today, it has been said, are developed according to either of two evolving methodological models.[8] One model is said to assume with the Enlightenment that there is some kind of universal—a common human experience, a common set of limiting questions, a group of necessary truths— in terms of which theological claims can and must be validated. In this view theological claims, like any other, are to be governed by these general principles of rationality operative in open, public discourse. The second model maintains that there are no universally applicable criteria of judgment and evaluation. Hence, theology must be strictly intrasystemic, obligated only to the "criteria internal to the Christian faith."[9]

Neither of these models as stated, if in fact they properly describe the theologians with whom they are commonly associated, seems adequate.[10] Although it is presumptuous to announce categorically that there are no universals to which all theology is and must be obligated, it is quite defensible to conclude that no candidate has yet arisen that belongs indubitably to the category of transreligious, cross-cultural, universal norms.[11] If so, the conclusion that there are no universal "rules" for theology can be taken as an appropriate working judgment. But from the working hypothesis that there are no universal norms, it does not follow that all criteria are always strictly local, entirely intrasystematic. Whereas it may be the case that no criterion is universal—common to all theological quests, for example—many criteria are common to sets of varied perspectives. Criteria are seldom if ever the sole possession of a single perspective; perspectives seldom if ever possess utterly distinctive criteria. Criteria overlap some standpoints—disciplines, cultures, religions, and so forth—even if no criterion overlaps them all.

Whether there are overlapping criteria is crucially important. Reasons can make a difference intersystematically only if they may appeal to intersystematic criteria of adequacy. Therefore, if no criteria are acceptable beyond the boundaries of a tradition, the giving of reasons beyond the boundaries of a tradition is impossible. But if there are intersystematic criteria, intersystematic reason giving is possible; and if we are obligated to give reasons whenever we can, it follows that providing warrants for our views, in theology as in all other forms of inquiry, is a cross-contextual obligation.

I assume that theology is obligated to give reasons whenever reason giving is possible and that only in so doing can its claims gain credibility. Therefore, I conclude that what is said in theology, as in other inquiries, must be tested in the varied arenas of contemporary knowledge and experience—across disciplinary divisions, across religious lines, across cultural boundaries, across the lines of race, class, and gender. At each point of testing, *none* of the competing perspectives is intrinsically privileged and *each* is a rightful participant in discussions as to the nature of appropriate discussion, the nature of appropriate criteria, and the process of their proper application.[12] No theology will ever be tested in all relevant alternative contexts. But no theology is entitled even tentatively to the claim of credibility if it is not tested in relation to at least some alternative perspectives.[13] Hence, as I say, the examination of tradition offered in this work will involve the resources of philosophy and certain of the social sciences, religious studies, and the history of religions. Other alternative contexts are also valid testing grounds for what will be said about tradition and theological construction, but I hope it will become apparent in the discussion why these particular conversation partners are especially fruitful ones.

Fundamental to the current inquiry is the development of a theory of tradition in terms of which the employment of tradition in current theological constructions can then be examined and evaluated. Thus the first four chapters investigate and theorize some of the apparent behaviors and elements of religious traditions as these are delineated by nontheological fields of investigation. From more descriptive or empirical accounts of traditions (Chapter 1), the discussion moves through a philosophical analysis of the dynamics of cultural traditions (Chapter 2), to (in Chapters 3 and 4) a theory of tradition.[14] In light of this theory of tradition, the fifth chapter assesses the understandings and uses of tradition in contemporary theology and proposes an alternative view of theology which I call *constructive historicism*. The concluding assessment, I should perhaps add, is critical in varying degrees of the entire spectrum of mainline and "professional" theology today. The criticism offered, however, is positive in tone and purpose. For one thing, it identifies and affirms developments of value, with respect to an understanding of tradition, that are rather widespread in contemporary theology. More important, its intent is to help find a way beyond the biases of modernism that have restrained us, through the liberal-conservative, narrative-revisionist, and deconstructive-constructive impasses that now befuddle us, toward a more adequate integration of inheritance and imagination in theological reflection . . . and, thus, I believe, toward a form of theological thinking that is culturally and religiously more effective.

❧ 1 ❧

TECUMSEH, TORAHS, AND CHRISTS

THE DATA OF TRADITIONS

Theology, its detractors say, has little to do with "real" life. The categories of theological analysis seem connected to the world we observe, whether commonly or through our several disciplines of specialized inquiry, only vaguely and haphazardly if at all. Theology, on this view, does not inform the concrete, "empirical" dimensions of our lives, nor does it show much evidence of being informed by them.

This charge can be countered in several ways. For one thing, the concrete modes of existence to which specific theologies relate are frequently unknown to outside observers. More traditional theologies, such as those that reflect the hierarchy of medieval Europe or the social differentiation of Islam, may appear to us disconnected from life simply because we are unaware of the life to which they are connected. Second, a theology may seem divorced from experiential "givens" because its critics have a different view of what is given. Thus, the language of Protestant Christians about sin and guilt will to the Confucian seem hopelessly removed from experience, as removed as Confucian talk of "li" will seem to the Protestant. Third, sometimes theological talk is thought inapplicable to observable realities because its application is not made clear. Theological discussions of the reality of God, for example, might in the final analysis be efforts to ask whether our brief lives have any significance or meaning that abides irrevocably, but if so that point is not always stated. And finally, the charge that theology is irrelevant may be rooted in self-deceit. Theology that grows from a yearning to be free, for example, is said to be hopelessly unrealistic by many of those whose social and economic hegemony is challenged in such yearning, but this kind of theology may be more relevant than its privileged critics care to admit.

Theology, however, is sometimes accused of being removed from empirical realities because it is. The ignored or distorted realities, and the particular theologies that so mistreat them, are varied. Contemporary creationist theologies purport to speak of the physical universe, but they exhibit only the most tortured connections with the best available evidence regarding the earth's age and origin. The historic Christian understanding of sin as pride, although it was said to relate to all human experience, is painfully disconnected from and insensitive to the experience of that vast majority of persons and groups who, because of systemic oppression, have had too little pride. Classic doctrines of revelation, to give a third example, make claims about a knowledge of God possessed by people everywhere, but these claims are not easily squared with the evident pluralism and relativism of human cultures. Something can be said in defense of even these theological constructs. Creationist theories may express a resistance to the ascendancy of scientism in our culture. The doctrine of sin as pride may effectively unmask the hubris of power. Revelation talk might be a way of asserting the pervasiveness of grace in human experience. Still, whatever their possible insight, theological claims are severely weakened if they sharply contradict, or are hopelessly removed from, the reflective experience of, and the disciplined conclusions about, the concrete lived realities about which they supposedly speak.

If they are to be credible, as I argued in the Introduction, Christian theological claims must be defended in relation to the CL. varied arenas of contemporary knowledge and experience.

The social sciences, especially those that reflect an openness to the influence of humanistic studies, offer particularly valuable resources and testing grounds for theology. To be sure, their conclusions are as faulty, selective, biased, and therefore subject to criticism as are those of any other form of disciplined human knowledge, including theological knowledge. That, however, only underscores the importance of interdisciplinary conversation, for the best guard against the fallibility of any field is its broadest possible exposure to others. The disciplines of cultural anthropology and history of religions, for example, offer information about concrete expressions of religion, Christian and otherwise, that can both challenge and contribute to the formulation of theological claims. Their data may on occasion provide models of interpretation that will prove suggestive for theological construction. But, certainly, their findings will establish restraints that discipline theological claims and, sometimes, effectively (even if never finally) accredit or discredit them. Theology that seeks to be defensible in our contemporary arenas of evaluative discourse cannot ignore these kinds of data.[1]

A theology's obligation to attend to empirical studies is especially apparent when its topic is tradition; here, in particular, theology will require and benefit from interaction with social scientific inquiry (broadly conceived) into the nature of concrete traditions. Theological interpretations of a religious tradition that identify it in terms of some "essence" will, at a minimum, be pressed to further reflection if that essence is shown historically to be seldom present in the tradition supposedly being interpreted. Similarly, theologies that dismiss talk of essence altogether may avoid a good deal of vacuity if they confront the pervasive attention to questions of continuing identity that the social scientist in fact finds in religious traditions. Theological considerations of continuity and change, limitation and creativity, the character of authority, the formative force of tradition, and so forth will also profit from exposure to the data of social and historical studies. This exposure will never enable us to pronounce a particular theory or theology of tradition to be absolutely adequate, but without it we cannot justifiably assume such constructs to be adequate at all.

The present examination of the nature of tradition, accordingly, begins with three case studies. These are not the only empirical resources to be employed in the discussion of this book, nor do they raise all of the "descriptive" issues that must be considered about the behavior of religious traditions, nor are they unchallenged.[2] They do, however, bring up a number of possibilities that deserve reflection at the outset of our examination, possibilities frequently neglected in theological discussions. In the concluding section of this chapter these will be identified as tentative conclusions and hypotheses, preparatory to the more theoretical discussion of subsequent chapters.

TECUMSEH'S REPOSE

On the afternoon of August 14, 1810, Tecumseh, the great Shawnee leader, arrived with his warriors to meet General William Henry Harrison at Grouseland, the governor's new mansion at Vincennes in what is now the state of Indiana. The meeting was prompted by a treaty Harrison had managed to conclude one year earlier with representatives of a number of other tribes in the area. The treaty gave 3 million acres of land along the river to the U.S. Government in exchange for $10,000. Tecumseh denounced the treaty when he heard of it, threatening to kill the Indian signatories and vowing to fight until the treaty was revoked. Harrison, wanting to avoid war if possible, requested the meeting at Grouseland; and Tecumseh agreed to attend. As one of Harrison's own men informed the general in advance of the meeting, Tecumseh was coming to say that "the Great Spirit intended [this land] as the common property of all the tribes, [and, therefore, it cannot] be sold without the consent of all."

When Tecumseh arrived he was ushered to an arbor adjoining a veranda at the side of the mansion. The general had covered the arbor with a canopy, and he had placed at its center a number of chairs for the principal negotiators and invited observers. According to an account published in 1825, at one point in the meeting General Harrison offered Tecumseh a chair, to which Tecumseh replied ". . . the *Earth* is my mother, and on *her* bosom I will repose" and then he "sat down suddenly" on the ground. These words of Tecumseh have become for many the classic statement of the American Indian belief in Mother Earth—in the earth as divinity, as goddess.

In his book *Mother Earth*, Sam D. Gill challenges what he says is the virtually universal assumption that American Indians have held a unitary belief in the earth as goddess.[3] Instead, Gill says, belief in Mother Earth emerged in the late nineteenth and twentieth centuries. An evaluation of Gill's thesis, which is widely acclaimed and denounced, is beyond the competence of this inquirer and unnecessary for the purposes of this study.[4] Gill's work is important in this context because his hypothesis about the emergence of belief in Mother Earth illustrates a more general claim about the behavior of vital religious traditions.

One strand of Gill's analysis has to do with the Tecumseh tradition. The first reports on the 1810 meeting were an extensive series of letters written by Harrison himself; they contain no mention of the Tecumseh statement. In fact, the earliest written mention of either the statement or Tecumseh's action (his sudden sitting upon the ground) did not appear until 1921, after which both the statement and the action were reported with rapidly increasing frequency and expansiveness. Two different traditions seem to have emerged, one following the 1825 account mentioned already and the other following the first published account, appearing in 1821, according to which

Tecumseh also referred to the earth as nourisher—"the earth is my mother; she gives me nourishment, and I repose upon her bosom." Gill also notes the quite varied interpretations of the intent of Tecumseh's statement in these reports. Some view Tecumseh's words as evidence of recalcitrance, some as a comment on the arrangements of the meeting, some as proof of Tecumseh's eloquence. Only in an account of the Tecumseh-Harrison meeting published in 1844 is Tecumseh's statement interpreted, for the first time, as a religious claim that the earth is a goddess. In sum, the meeting occurred in 1810; the statement was first attributed to Tecumseh in 1821; a religious interpretation of the statement was first offered in 1844.

Gill examines three other alleged examples of the American Indian beliefs in Mother Earth—those of Smohalla, the Zuni, and the Luiseno. In each case, he concludes, there is no basis for saying that the Indians in question held "a belief in a creator-goddess named Mother Earth or anything that might translate closely to this."[5] How, then, did the belief arise?

Gill's analysis focuses on two creative subjects in the emergence of belief in Mother Earth, the scholars and the Indians. The context for understanding the process of scholarly interpretation is the radically changed perception of the Indian after the beginning of the nineteenth century. Once the futility of the Indian cause had become apparent to Euro-Americans, the Indian, seen in the previous century as the savage hunter, was now said to be noble, brave, and eloquent. For example, after his death in 1813 Tecumseh himself, whom Harrison had called "insolent" and "arrogant," quickly became a Euro-American folk hero. The form of this adulation of the Indian, Gill claims, derived from a pre-1776, European myth of America and the Indian as a feminine benevolence, a kind of Pocahontas, closely associated with the primordial land. This earlier myth, recovered in the nineteenth century, provided a convenient framework for the self-definition and legitimation of the Euro-American project in the northern new world. Scholars of the late nineteenth and twentieth centuries (Tylor, Frazer, Eliade, Hultkranz, and others) extracted from the earlier myth their own myth about Indian belief in Mother Earth, despite a paucity of evidence for it.

The other creative subject in the emergence of Mother Earth, according to Gill, is the dynamic of Indian self-understanding in the nineteenth and early twentieth centuries.[6] The context of this dynamic is the white robbery of Indian land and the destruction of the Indian way of living with the land. The elevation of the earth to the status of deity in the Indian worldview would give the hundreds of Indian tribes a unified ideology on the basis of which to oppose White aggression. It would do so, moreover, in a manner that raised the stakes to the highest level and in terms that Euro-Americans—predisposed to value deity and already inclined to think of Indians as believers in the earth as deity—could not readily dismiss.[7]

The source of the Indian dynamic is the native traditions themselves. Gill's analysis is clear that the creation of Mother Earth, of the earth as deity, is a faithful extension of historic Indian sensibilities. There is ample evidence that many tribes had long considered the earth to be feminine, though in quite varied ways, and a few had in fact considered "the earth to be the personification of a female [figure] variously understood as mother or as goddess."[8] Perhaps more important is the well-documented Indian attitude toward the land, expressed in the widespread Native American practice of referring to the earth metaphorically in "personal and kinship terms."[9] Thus Mother Earth had long been implicit in Indian experience far more powerfully and pervasively than she was in the explicit myths of the Europeans. If, as Gill contends, she was invented as a "reasoned, sophisticated, and well-articulated" response to White conquest and destruction,[10] his analysis shows, too, that belief in Mother Earth was an innovation "continuous with" the metaphor, ritual, and experience of the Indian past.[11] If Mother Earth was a conjoint creation of Whites and Indians within the past century or so, she was also, in a sense, an Indian given. She was already powerfully if diffusely present as nourisher of the Indian soul. But still, according to Gill, a belief in Mother Earth as deity is something new in the traditions of the American Indians.

TORAH'S CONCLUSION

From sunrise until high noon during the Festival of Booths in either 458 or 398 BCE (the date is not certain), Ezra stood in the Water Gate Square in Jerusalem reading the Torah aloud to all who passed by.[12] The immediate response among those who heard was open weeping. The eventual response was the creation of Judaism as a single community scattered though it was across the world. The significant thing, for our study, is the shape of the Torah Ezra read, especially its terminus.

Torah means authoritative tradition and, though we are accustomed to thinking of it as a code of laws, Torah refers fundamentally to the narrative of the origins of ancient Israel. To speak of the Torah as "canon," or as the center of the Hebrew canon, is to refer to its character as authority.

Until the sixth century BCE, in all of its tellings, the Torah story included God's call to Abraham to move from Mesopotamia to Canaan, God's promise there that Abraham would become the patriarch of a mighty people, the eventual exile of the family into Egypt due to famine, the escape of the clan from Egypt over four centuries later led by Moses, the wanderings of these people in the Sinai Desert where they established a covenant with the God of Moses, and following Joshua their return to and gradual conquest of the land of Canaan, an achievement cemented in a military conference at Shechem, the place where Abraham received God's promise in the first place centuries before. Actually, that is the short version of the story; the ending of a longer version extends the conquest account through David's capture of Jerusalem. But in all of its recitals the original Torah always included the conquest of the land.

According to James Sanders's book, *Torah and Canon*, the Torah story that Ezra read aloud, that caused those who heard to weep and those who followed to become a single people throughout the world, had a strikingly different ending![13] What was the change, and why did it occur?

Until 722 the heirs of those who had conquered Canaan following Joshua lived and ruled throughout Palestine. In that fateful year, however, Sennacherib, king of Assyria, captured the northern region and carried the ten tribes of Israel who lived there into historical obscurity, except for a remnant that escaped south. Next Sennacherib's armies moved south, occupying more and more of the land until finally only Jerusalem was left, surrounded and without reasonable hope. The inhabitants of the city of David, site of the Solomonic Temple, believed, however, that God would preserve the land for them. Thus in the year 701 when Sennacherib's army suddenly withdrew (to deal with difficulties at home), those who had believed God would save them, their land, and their Temple felt joyously vindicated. In the relatively long time of freedom that followed this miracle they purged themselves of the cultural and religious vestiges of Assyrian hegemony and infiltrations of Canaanitic cult practices, guided in particular by a legal code discovered in 621 during the reign of Josiah.

But the miracle of 701, celebrated for over a century, only made it all the more incredible that in 587 BCE Jerusalem was again threatened and this time subdued. Nebuchadrezzar, king of Babylon, the new regional power, conquered Jerusalem, destroyed the Temple, and took all but the weakest of the inhabitants of the land into Babylon. Those whose Torah story culminated in the conquest of Canaan were now conquered and, worse yet, made to live far from their divinely promised land. Eventually they were scattered in communities across the Mediterranean world. How could they live as the children of

Abraham and David apart from their land? How could they take
their identity from a Torah that ended in, and thus presupposed,
the possession of their land? That was the question with which
the heirs of Israel struggled in their Babylonian exile.

Then, a century and a half or perhaps nearly two centuries
later, Cyrus, king of Persia, offered to let the exiles return.
Among the few who did eventually straggle back to Jerusalem
was Ezra. What Ezra brought with him was the Torah, but,
according to Sanders, this Torah story had a new ending. It had
been refashioned by the Jews in exile so that it could provide
them with an identity for living, if necessary, away from the
land. The Torah that Ezra read, Sanders says, was approximately
what we now call the Pentateuch. In this version of the formative story of Israel the conquest of the land was deleted! In its
place was a new ending, Deuteronomy, the legal code discovered in 621. The original Torah story had been split; the
account of the conquest and monarchy at Jerusalem had been
moved and made secondary. The Torah story now culminated
not in David and the land, but in the Mosaic law. The new ending would henceforth define the people of Israel, the Jews. The
authoritative tradition had been changed.

The legal material that concluded the revised Torah, though
never part of the original, was undoubtedly rooted in a long history. Elements of it were likely a part of the oral tradition for
hundreds of years, remaining unwritten for the most part in
accord with the common treatment of this kind of material in
the ancient Near Eastern world. It may have been recorded
finally by a priestly group who wished to exorcise vestiges of
alien practice from Hebraic life, the reform that finally was
accomplished under Josiah. But during the exile in Babylon,
this material came to play another role; now it became the conclusion of Torah.

The elevation of this legal material to the point of culmination, and thus centrality, in the Torah story was reasonable, for,
as we have said, the material was old and honored. More impor-

tant, its new placement was astute because the law, unlike the land, could be carried into the diaspora. But excluding the conquest from the Torah, and giving the story a new ending, had one other undeniable consequence: It made the Torah story something different. The authoritative tradition was new, and human choice had made it so.

CHRISTS AND CHRISTIANITIES

If one were to divide European history into four approximate quincentenaries, and divide the last again into two, one would find five quite different cultural periods each confronting a distinctive problematic, according to William A. Clebsch in his book *Christianity in European History*.[14] More than that, Clebsch says, the same periodization would present at least ten distinct types of Christianity, for, generally speaking, at the beginning of each epoch Christianity related to the cultural problematic in one way and toward the end it related in another. Obviously, throughout all five periods (or ten, if earlier and later in each is separated) Christians held something in common—Jesus Christ as savior and model of righteousness. But the Jesus who endured throughout appeared in such varied roles amidst such diverse experiences that Clebsch says one should really speak of different "Christs" and different "Christianities."[15]

In the first period of European history (to 476), the cultural situation was a struggle between unity and particularity, dictated by the Roman desire to create one world out of disparate cultures. In this period the Christian task was to determine and maintain properly a double citizenship, to Christ and to Rome.

Until 313 in this first period the problem for Christians was their suspicioned status due to their overriding allegiance to Christ. The Christian strategy in this setting was to declare "true" allegiance to the established earthly order without compromising the higher allegiance appropriate alone to Christ. The earthly exemplar of this was the martyr who was loyal to the empire, who never sought death, but who accepted it if necessary to keep the boundaries clear. The ideal was courage. The spiritual exemplar, the canonical model, for the Christian was the Christ who died sacrificially and in whose death all, not simply the actual martyrs, participated through the eucharist.

After 313 the problem became the confused status of Christianity now that it had been endorsed by the emperor. What now was the boundary, the mark of Christian distinctiveness? The Christian answer was represented in the vocation of the monk who withdrew from the established order, that is, who experienced martyrdom without bloodshed, a dying daily. That to which the Christian died was the demonic passions of the flesh. The human ideal, thus, was discipline, so the canonical ideal was Christ victorious over temptation.

In the second period of about 500 years (476–962) the cultural situation was the calamity and chaos accompanying the demise of Roman rule in the West. Tribalism replaced ecumenism, agrarian culture supplanted urban culture, and Germanic values succeeded the values of Greece and Rome. The problem—both Christian and imperial, for now they were one—was accounting for this catastrophe and replacing the lost earthly order, if necessary with one in heaven.

In the first half of this period (until Gregory the Great, in about 590) the problem of social and cultural chaos was addressed by theodicy, as, for example, in the work of Boethius. The answer Boethius provided was an assertion of a divine providence that somehow remains compatible with human responsibility. The ground of his confidence was "Lady Philosophy," at once a combination of classical wisdom and the third person of the trinity, now merged with the universal logos. In this way the Christian canon became Christ the logos, who "was the simultaneous, perfect embodiment in one person of divine reason and human reason, divine order and human order."[16]

During the time from Gregory through Charlemagne, Christians addressed the problem of cultural chaos through ecclesiastical organization, i.e., through development of the papacy as the vehicle of order after the end of imperial rule. The source of this solution was Pope Gregory's idea that the ruler must be divinely called, authorized through Peter, and bound by religiously grounded (Benedictine) rules for ruling. The ideal was a Christian ruler whose governance was based on conformity to Christ's standards. The canonical image, then, was Christ the King, the Ruler.

In the third of the five periods of European history (962–1556) the cultural context was the growing distinction of temporal and spiritual rulers, a problem appearing for the first time since the "maturation" of Christianity into the established religion during the fourth century. This distinction was addressed theologically in the assertion that "grace perfects nature." The two realms are neither equal nor opposite; the religious realm is superior to, yet continuous with and brings to perfection, the secular realm. This solution took two forms, that of the mystic and that of the theologian.

The mystic's approach, rooted in the practice of penance, sought to demonstrate the unity of the temporal and the spiritual in the soul's disciplined ascent to Christ, the culmination of which was a mystical union commonly described in sensual, even erotic terms. The canonical image was that of Christ the lover. The theologian's approach, grounded in the recovery of ancient philosophy, tried to show the unity of the temporal and spiritual in terms of reason's disciplined ascent to God. The culmination of this ascent was universal knowledge of God and all things in relation to God, a knowledge available independent of revelation and faith. The canonical image was Christ the teacher. The fact that both Christ the lover and Christ the teacher were deemed to be at one with the very human crucified Christ was itself a representation of the union of temporal and spiritual that the mystics and the theologians believed they had achieved.

In the fourth period of Western Christian history (1556–1806) the cultural problem was the breakup of Christendom. The general solution was to reestablish the unity of Christians through the cultivation of the religious faculties. The two forms of this effort were those of the moralists and the pietists.

The moralists said the religious faculty or capacity is expressed fundamentally through moral behavior. Thus their aim was to draw from Christ's life on earth the precepts that would ground a moral mode of living that transcended other Christian differences. The Christian ideal was the imitation of Jesus, so the canonical image was Jesus as model of moral behavior.

The pietists believed the religious faculty to be expressed fundamentally through pious feelings. Their aim was attainment of an affective mode that transcended other Christian differences. The Christian ideal was the achievement of a warm heart. Hence the canonical image was that of Jesus the friend, the human, crucified Christ with whom a transforming oneness could be realized

The cultural context, and for Christians the problem, of the fifth cultural period in European history (1806–1945) was the emergence of autonomous humanity. It was a time, as Clebsch put it, when "Europeans singly and collectively became their own do-it-yourself deities."[17] Clebsch continues:

> Moderns have employed their personal and cultural autonomy in a wide variety of responses to their Christian heritage. Some challenged the tradition at its roots. Others erected new schemes of religious authority to replace crumbling ones. Still others adapted the religion to the modern spirit. The adaptations made by activists and apologists involved a religious invention whose bold-

ness becomes clear only when it is set against the other options.[18]

Those whom Clebsch calls the activists and the apologists chose to bring "Christianity to terms with modernity" by transforming modernity in a christianly fashion.

The activists, responding to modernity as it was manifest concretely in the Industrial Revolution, sought to transform modernity socially and politically by serving the advance of justice and human well-being. The apologists, confronting modernity as it was expressed conceptually in scientific materialism, sought to transform it intellectually by demonstrating that the modern spirit harbored conundrums that only Christianity could resolve. Clebsch gives Lamennais and Bonhoeffer as examples of European Catholic and Protestant activists, and Newman, Kierkegaard, and Ritschl as varied examples of the apologists' strategy. The Christ of the former group is expressed by Bonhoeffer's phrase, *the man for others.* The Christ of the apologists is not so easily stated, given the variety of their approaches, but for them all Christ was somehow the autonomous unity of deity and humanity, what Kierkegaard called the *god-man.*

This schematic account does little justice to Clebsch's complex analysis and even less to the history that is his subject. Alternatives examples in each age and alternative schema for the whole can be offered.[19] This, however, only confirms the point to be made about Clebsch's book insofar as it is germane to this discussion. When we look at the actual history of that stream known as Christianity, as distinct from what our theologies may say that we ought to see, we are astonished that Christianities and their Christs appear in such an apparently irreducible diversity.

TWO CONCLUSIONS, TEN HYPOTHESES

The two obvious conclusions to be drawn from the above cases are commonly accepted among students of religious traditions. The first is that religions change quite significantly as they course through time with the result that their histories exhibit enormous variety. Clebsch's particular "Christs" and "Christianities" may be debatable, but the claim that Christianity and all other religions exhibit this kind of radical diversity is not disputed in the disciplines of religious studies and the history of religions. Yet Clebsch's own way of portraying the changing character of Christianity introduces, as well, the second fundamental conclusion: traditions also exhibit apparent constancies. It would seem, after all, that the Christianities Clebsch identifies are precisely that, "Christianities"; that is, pluralizations that are somehow related. Moreover, the ways they display their differences, that is, in terms of "Christs" who function as a "canon" of righteousness, appear to share something in common.

Continuity and change, then, are the primary categories to emerge in the case studies we have considered and the primary categories somehow to be accommodated by an adequate theory of tradition. The difficult question is how they are to be accommodated, and that, really, is a series of questions. Among them are these: What is relatively continuous, and what, if anything, is constant? How is identity over time (constancy or continuity or both) accomplished? What social and personal functions are served by preserving the identities of traditions? What changes? What motivates change, what are its most effective resources, how is it accomplished, and what, if anything, validates it? Finally, there is the broader question: What are the dynamics of traditions, whether in continuation or in change? In other words, where is the power of religious traditions located, and how do traditions exercise their power?

The ten hypotheses that follow all relate to the phenomena of change, or continuity, or both, and therefore to the questions raised by our two broad conclusions. Although these hypotheses are systematized only minimally, appearing instead for the most part as they seem to arise from the case studies, they are not, of course, represented as straightforward "readings" of the data. They are offered as propositions that the data, the case studies considered previously, may plausibly be said to suggest. The hypotheses are these:

1. Novelty or change emerges in religious traditions intentionally as well as unintentionally. Like Mother Earth, novelty grows quite naturally out of inherited resources as a reasonable response to new challenges. But we should not exclude the possibility that change also comes with a measure of conscious intentionality. Is it likely that the oral traditions of Indian peoples were so poorly remembered in the nineteenth century that those who birthed Mother Earth did so ignorant of their own creative contribution to the change? Is it conceivable that those who revised their written Torah never knew or simply forgot its earlier scope? In sum, novelty arises in tradition, and it is at least possible that this novelty, though often as unintended as a development in nature, is also sometimes as conscious as a human choice.

2. Novelty appears to be largely incremental and variegated. The developing version of the Harrison-Tecumseh meeting in the tradition about Tecumseh parallels on a smaller scale the incremental development of new ways of thinking about Jesus in the New Testament. Change builds in small steps with the presumable result that at each point continuity greatly outweighs what is new. But the small steps of change are also variegated at each point and the variety is not necessarily consistent, as the diverse interpretations of Tecumseh's intent demonstrate. The claims that Tecumseh was expressing his arrogance, commenting on the protocols of the meeting, and

articulating a religious conviction are not easily synthesized into a single account of Tecumseh's response to
Harrison. The emergence of novelty, therefore, seems
largely to be incremental but unstable in the sense that the
contrasts internal to novelty may threaten one another.

3. Change is generally produced by the interaction,
usually conflictual, between a religious tradition and its
socio-political environment. Mother Earth was a response
to the theft of Indian territory. The revision of Torah was a
response to the Babylonian exile. Each of the new
Christian emergents that Clebsch describes arose as a
response to, and in interaction with, a broader cultural circumstance. An important inference to be drawn from this
interaction is that the borders separating a religious tradition from its milieu are usually, perhaps always, exceedingly porous. The achievement and preservation of
identity and continuity in a tradition apparently do not
require the effective exclusion of determinative influences
from the environment.

4. Change, though often provoked from outside, is
accomplished primarily by the recovery and re-formation
of elements internal to the tradition. In Gills's account, the
scholars responded to the Indians and the broader socio-
political situation by drawing upon elements of European
mythology that appeared to shadow comparable elements
in Native American sensibilities. More important, the
Indians drew out indigenous motifs that countered the
challenges of their intellectual and political interlocutors.
It is true that the emergence of Mother Earth may have
involved the introduction of an alien element, that is, the
conception of deity, but this element was a formal framework into which ancient internal sensibilities and their
verbal expression were cast. The point is that even when
changes are provoked externally, they seem to be most
effectively accomplished by recovering and emphasizing

previously subordinated elements within the tradition rather than appropriating material elements from the outside.

5. Apparently traditions are efficacious, whether in continuation or transformation, throughout the continuum of human responsiveness, from abstract analysis to the affective dimensions that we commonly refer to as "feeling," but traditions appear to operate more powerfully through the more affective side of this continuum. Indeed, beliefs themselves seem to be most powerful as they are expressed through myth and action rather than through abstract analysis alone. In the story of Tecumseh, both his statement, "the earth is my mother," and his repose effectively communicated the relevant past to his present situation, and neither was a disquisition. Myth (of Mother Earth, for example), not genealogy or theology, offers unity to Indians today, and the complex of nurturing sensibilities, stories, and rituals drew Native Americans together in the nineteenth century. The legend of Pocahontas contributed far more to change Euro-American attitudes than did abstract theories. The Sinai narrative, and the ritual actions to which this narrative gives rise, define Jews today. Theory, we may assume, influences and helps to focus and legitimate or challenge the processes of a tradition, but theory may be efficacious only to the degree that it is integrated into cultic practice and mythic representation. The power of a tradition, in sum, is more in affection than analysis.

6. The behavior of traditions is pragmatic and has to do with survival, power, and legitimation. The survival potential of traditions is abundantly evident in Gill's interpretation of Mother Earth and Sanders's interpretation of the revision of Torah. Both developments occurred as efforts to sustain relatively powerless people in the face of external threats of extinction. The Euro-American story

described in Gill's work, however, suggests that the exploits of the powerful are also tied to mythic transformations of traditions. In this case the "savage warrior" image was replaced with a symbolic complex that integrated the Indian into a "feminized" understanding of the land. Clebsch's account represents this pragmatic function of change on a much broader, larger scale.

7. The pragmatic behavior of traditions takes the form of creating, sustaining, and recreating viable communal and individual identities. In Clebsch's work, the successive images of Christ are always the baseline for understanding successive forms of life, ways Christians are to be in the world. Each Christ is a model of individual and collective identity. If Gill is correct, the emergence of Mother Earth parallels the development of pan-Indian self-consciousness. According to Sanders, a Torah that ends in the conquest of the land is no longer a feasible guide to the identity of a people perhaps forever separated from that land. The end of Torah is changed from the land to the law to provide a new, viable communal identity.

8. The vehicle for authoring identity is frequently a canon, an authoritative locus. Torah, we have seen, is the canon whereby Jewish identity after the exile is re-created and sustained. In Clebsch's view, the Christian canon throughout history is the model of Christ in its successive manifestations. The Native American case, however, makes it evident that a canon, an authoritative locus, is not necessarily textual or theological in character. Canons can be complexes of ritual, mythic, or narratival frameworks. The body of coyote stories, for example, may arguably function as the canon of certain tribal traditions. Whether the Mother Earth mythos is or will become a canon for a pan-Indian identity today is an open question.

9. The creation and re-creation of identity in a tradition occurs both as a rearrangement within its canon, and

as a rearrangement of its canon. As Gill's account of Mother Earth suggests, change seems to occur primarily as the process of recovery and reconstruction within a canon (see hypothesis 4). The changes cited by Clebsch, too, may be viewed as reconstructive. It is as if the many Christs of Christianity were, as abstract possibilities, always present but usually subordinate within the Christian mythos. Their successive creation as dominant models of righteousness was by virtue of their elevation and recombination in unprecedented ways with other elements of the tradition. The new Torah was also a rearrangement of inherited materials. But the case of Torah suggests that canonical reconstruction is not always simply a rearrangement within an accepted authoritative locus; novelty may also be achieved by revising the locus itself. The new Torah was more than a novel arrangement of the canon; it was a new definition of the canon, partly continuous and partly discontinuous with the old. In sum, if we think of canon as a boundary, change may occur either as a change within the boundary or as a change of the boundary.

10. The relationship of a canon, that is, an authoritative locus, and a tradition is dialectical. The Torah defined the Hebraic tradition before the exile, the tradition redefined the canon in the exile, and the revised canon defined the renewed tradition after the exile. Moreover, the tradition's practice of commentary continues to affect the meaning of Torah in Judaism today. Tradition derives from canon and canon derives from tradition. Tradition creates canon and canon creates tradition. A corollary is that each is fluid. In some sense, canon and tradition are each open to change, and the change in either affects the definition of the other.[20]

These ten proposals are manifestly provisional. Presumably, the testing of them must be similarly tentative, and per gradus, and will involve the following questions: (1) Do the hypotheses in fact seem amenable to the three case studies discussed? (2) Do they appear to be consistent with, and do they illuminate, other data, other instances of the behavior of religious traditions? (3) Is there a persuasive systematic framework for understanding traditions—a theory of tradition—that plausibly integrates these and compatible proposals?

Although the second question will be addressed tangentially throughout the discussion to follow, questions 1 and 2 can be dealt with most adequately by historians of religions and others who have a broad, disciplined knowledge of the behavior of religious traditions. This study will be more useful if it addresses directly the third question. Developing a theory of tradition, therefore, is the task of the next three chapters.

⋘ 2 ⋙

MEDIATING THE PAST AND PRESENT

GADAMER AND TRADITION

The rehabilitation of tradition in contemporary philosophy and theology is the result primarily of the work of Hans-Georg Gadamer. To restore tradition to importance was not Gadamer's fundamental goal; his goal was to serve, like Martin Heidegger before him, as "critic of the modern surrender to technological thinking."[1] His concern was, and is, the philosophy of culture. Gadamer's elevation of tradition to significance in scholarly discourse has therefore been a consequence of his comprehensive analysis of culture, its dynamics, and the requirements for its viability, as this analysis emerged principally in *Truth and Method*.[2]

Since any serious effort to understand tradition today must take account of Gadamer's work, the fulfillment of that task is the purpose of this chapter. The first section provides an interpretation of Gadamer, placing his view of tradition within the larger context of his culture analysis. In the second and third sections Gadamer's view is analyzed critically. The criticism of Gadamer and the two basic revisions of his view proposed in these sections are substantive, but they are also compatible with his general position and hence are offered as extensions of

Gadamer's hermeneutical understanding of tradition. This analysis, revision, and extension of Gadamer is itself preparatory to the theory of tradition to be developed in Chapter 3.

INTERPRETING GADAMER

Gadamer's analysis begins with the facts that the methodology of the physical sciences has in the modern period become the paradigmatic path to reliable knowledge and that all other disciplines—especially the arts and humanities, the *Geisteswissenschaften*—have been diminished to the extent that they are unable to mimic the measurement and control of these "hard" sciences. The aesthetic theories proffered in the attempt to restore the *Geisteswissenschaften* to a place of cultural importance, especially during the nineteenth century, sought to base them on "the subjective universality of aesthetic taste."[3] In Gadamer's view, these attempts to ground the human sciences solely in the subjective activity of the mind were not only futile, they were disastrous because they led to an insuperable question: How can the gap between the subjective and the objective, between the perceptions of the appreciative subject and the qualities of the appreciated object, be bridged with any assurance of reliability? In fact, the gap so conceived cannot be bridged. The price of this defense of the *Geisteswissenschaften*, then, has been to deny them "any significance as knowledge."[4] Lacking the connection with truth that they had long enjoyed, the humanities and arts became reliquaries and their products cultural decorations.[5]

In *Truth and Method* Gadamer defends the *Geisteswissenschaften* as disciplines connected to the world and communicating claims to truth about it. He does this by analyzing and clarifying the relationship between the *Geisteswissenschaften* and the physical sciences, isolating what he takes to be their distinctive but equally valid claims to truth.[6] If previous efforts to describe this relationship had sought to assimilate the procedures and objectives of the *Geisteswissenschaften* to those of the physical sciences, Gadamer rejects this strategy altogether. He does not, however, intend thereby to give "objectivity" over to the hard sciences. Instead he seeks to uncover the particular kind of objectivity or connectedness with the world that is characteristic of the *Geisteswissenschaften* and to do so in the area where that objectivity would seem to be least evident, namely in the "aesthetic consciousness." Indeed, Gadamer sets out to show that the objectivity evident in aesthetic experience is not present only here; in fact it is the most fundamental kind of objectivity there is, for it is characteristic of human existence as such and thus of all forms of knowledge, humanistic and scientific.[7]

Gadamer traces the marginalization of the aesthetic as a consequence of its subjectivization in nineteenth century analysis. He then argues that this subjectivization violates our own experience of art.[8] A work of art quite clearly does far more than give pleasure; it presents us with a world. Since the world of art is continuous with, yet other than, our own world, it calls our world into question. "In and through [the work of art] . . . we learn to understand ourselves. . . ."[9] Thus the aesthetic object breaks the grip of our subjective interpretation; it communicates a world to us in spite of ourselves. It confronts us, interpreting us, calling us into question. In this sense, art "reveals being." But how is this possible? How can the aesthetic have such autonomy, such agency?

To show how the subject–object split is transcended in aesthetic experience, Gadamer turns to a discussion of play, for play, he says, is "the clue to ontological explanation."[10] A game is not primarily to be construed as the activity of the players; the players become enmeshed in the objective dynamics, the to-and-fro movement, of the game.[11] The game, thus, is the master—the game plays and it is the players who are played.[12] The overriding agency of play becomes even more apparent when our consideration moves from the playing of a game to play as performance.[13] Here the prior reality of "the play" becomes even more obvious. The play itself, the play's reality and claim to truth, overpowers and subsumes both actors and audience.[14] To be an actor or a spectator is to be already integrated into the reality of the play as such. The dichotomy between subject and object is overcome.

Gadamer then relates this analysis of play back to the case of aesthetic experience. The artist captures our world in an image or form. This structure is separable from the artist's intention and the viewers' interpretations, even as the structure of the game or the play is separable from the players, actors, and spectators. Relative to them the game or play has "an absolute autonomy."[15] Similarly, the aesthetic object is autonomous in relation to the artist and to ourselves. Its structure is the structure of our world transformed into ideality. We are taken up into its structure. But the power of the work over us lies in part in the fact that, so taken up, we are also taken up into our own structure, for the world the artist has transformed into ideality is, though also partly different from, continuous with our own world. In its repetitions (performances or displays) the work of art not only unfolds its own multiple inner possibilities,[16] it also unfolds the multiple possibilities inherent in the world it idealizes, that is, our world. We are called to ourselves, both to a recognition of what we know and to what we still can learn.[17] Who we are is called into question by the portrayal of who we might be; a claim is made on us.[18] The subject-object distinction, thus, is inapplicable; we do not find ourselves to be independent agents external to the game, the play, or the work of art. We find ourselves already immersed in a world where the separation of subject and object is overcome. In this world we are called into question and called to answer. Our answer is response, not methodological analysis, dialogue with the art work, not dissection.

Gadamer next applies this view of aesthetic experience, aesthetic understanding, to understanding in general.[19] "To be" at all as a human is already to bridge subjectivity and objectivity, because the hermeneutical situation is the primary and universal characteristic of the human existence.[20] Play, thus, is the clue to understanding in general. Hence Gadamer assimilates human understanding to the aesthetic experience of being played, of being immersed in the game.

We now arrive at Gadamer's specific analysis of "historical consciousness."[21] To understand as humans do is already to be immersed in an ongoing drama, one in which we quite literally are "played" by tradition. Tradition is the drama or the game of which we are a part. This is evident in the fact that we always approach the past with preunderstandings that themselves have been created by the past. Hence, against what he calls the Enlightenment's fundamental "prejudice against prejudice,"[22] Gadamer defends the prejudgments or prejudices provided by tradition, pointing out that they are the necessary preconditions of human understanding.[23] The Enlightenment overlooked this and supposed that criteria for good reasoning could be extracted out of a history of inheritance and placed above it as judge.[24] This disjunction of "mythos" (tradition) and "logos" (reason) was perpetuated by Romanticism insofar as it sought merely to turn the Enlightenment on its head, making logos subservient to mythos.[25] Both views overlook the fact that reasoning is always embedded in an inherited tradition, and tradition always extends itself through reasoning.[26] Mythos and logos constitute a unity, what Gadamer describes as "a texture of reciprocal effects."[27] Because this is the case, history is a "history of effect" (*Wirkungsgeschichte*)[28] and human understanding, being necessarily embedded in history, is "historically effected consciousness" (*wirkungsgeschichtliche Bewusstsein*).[29] "Historical consciousness," Gadamer says, "is . . . situated in the web of historical effects."[30] Whether we are aware of it or not, the "efficacy of history is at work . . . in all understanding."[31] "It determines in advance both what seems to be worth inquiring about and what will appear as an object of investigation."[32]

If history is a succession of effects, it follows that understanding has to do with the past as it effects and affects us. Understanding is not the reconstruction of an event as it was for itself.[33] Gadamer does assume that the past event or text is real, that is, something in its own right.[34] But understanding is not and cannot be somehow grasping that reality as it was. The past is not like a building, to be rediscovered or reconstructed in idea or experience; it is more like the crest of a sweeping wave, gentle but definite in its direction. It was something before it envelopes us in the present, but what it was now resides in its present power, actual and potential. To take account of tradition, then, cannot be to return to a point before the present; it is to immerse ourselves in the past as it has an impact on the present

The image of the wave is misleading, however, insofar as it suggests a continuous smooth movement from past into present. Discontinuity is as real as continuity in the sweep of tradition. That is why Gadamer characterizes "participating in an event of tradition" as "a process of transmission in which past and present are constantly mediated."[35] That which is transmitted is different as well as similar, strange as well as familiar.[36] The past is an "other" that calls us into question.[37] Hence the past challenges us. Understanding is accepting and responding to the challenge that the past presents.[38] For this reason the process of understanding takes the logical form of questioning, and because this questioning is carried on at the level of language,[39] Gadamer can say that understanding is dialogue.[40] His description of questioning, of dialogue, is remarkable, even moving:

> To conduct a conversation means to allow oneself to be conducted by the subject matter to which the partners in the dialogue are oriented. It requires that one does not try to argue the other person down but that one really considers the weight of the other's opinion. Hence it is an art of testing. But the art of testing is the art of questioning. For we have seen that to question means to lay open, to place in the open. . . . Dialectic consists not in trying to discover

the weakness of what is said, but in bringing out its real strength."[41]

Dialogue is questioning and questioning is being opened by, opening, and keeping open the possibilities that the past presents.[42]

Gadamer notes, though, that openness is also limitation. The questioning created by and in relation to the other is necessarily particular—it represents a specific horizon with its own inherent presuppositions.[43] Hence the continuous dynamism of understanding is rooted not only by the unsettling openness that the other engenders, but also by the limitedness, the incompleteness, that the other necessarily represents. The aim of understanding, Gadamer concludes, cannot be "the chimera of perfect enlightenment,"[44] whether in the other or of ourselves; it must be a "fusion of horizons."

Perhaps the image of a "fusion of horizons" suggests, more adequately than any other, Gadamer's view of tradition. A "horizon is the range of vision that includes everything that can be seen from a particular vantage point."[45] In understanding, horizons meet and alter one another. A horizon includes more than what is near and clear; it includes that which is farther away, and it includes, too, what might be called a *visionary vector* that draws the viewer away from the immediate toward the distant and less distinct. This characteristic of a horizon means that our awareness of what is near is enhanced by virtue of its contrast with what is far, but it also means that we are always being drawn to the vaguer limits, to the range of outer possibilities. Thus horizons are open and changing. Gadamer writes:

> In fact the horizon of the present is continually in the process of being formed because we are continually having to test all our prejudices. An important part of this testing occurs in encountering the past and in understanding the tradition from which we come. Hence the horizon of the present is never formed without the past. There is no . . .

isolated horizon. . . . Rather, understanding is always the fusion of these horizons supposedly existing by themselves. . . . In a tradition this process of fusion is continually going on, for there old and new are always combining into something of living value. . . .[46]

Gadamer's analysis of history and historical consciousness seems to have a paradoxical implication for our understanding of tradition that deserves special attention. As Richard Bernstein observes: "On the one hand, Gadamer tells us that hermeneutic understanding is always tempered by the 'thing itself' that we are trying to understand. We seek nothing less than to understand the *same* text or the same piece of tradition."[47] On the other hand, a tradition is not always the same thing, for if a tradition is realized in its effects, and if its effects are diverse, then in some sense the tradition itself is inherently diverse. Given the diversity of meanings evident in the history of the interpretation of a text, an event, or a tradition, one can ask, as Bernstein himself does, in "what sense, if any, we can speak of the *same* text," event, or tradition.[48]

Apparently Gadamer's reply would be something like Paul Ricoeur's view of the inherent plurivocity of a text.[49] A tradition *is* something, but it is a complex structure of related possibilities such that, on the one hand, it is capable of richly different realizations throughout the course of history, yet, on the other, it is not amenable to any and every adaptation. Christianity, for example, is capable of an extraordinary variety of manifestations—such as those identified by William Clebsch and, no doubt, many more—but it is not capable of any and every formation that might be conceived. Each tradition is a "thing in itself" if, but only if, that means it is a particular complex of interrelated potentialities. The possibilities inherent in the structure of a tradition are played out concretely in the ever-renewed interaction of past and present.[50] Questioning or dialogue, Gadamer writes, "opens up [these] possibilities of meaning," it brings out "the undetermined possibilities of a thing."[51] Speaking of the "dialogue between tradition and its interpreter,"[52] Gadamer says: "This occurrence means the coming into play, the playing out, of the content of tradition in its constantly widening possibilities of significance and resonance. . . . Something comes into being that had not existed before and that exists from now on."[53]

The meaning of a tradition changes as it makes its way through history. For this reason, no single interpretation of a tradition is "correct 'in itself'."[54] A tradition is many things, some of them good and others bad, some to be judged true and others false.[55] The variety of things that a tradition is, that is, the multitude of possibilities that it harbors, become known as these potentials are actualized in history. "Every actualization in understanding can be regarded as a historical potential of what is understood. . . . We are aware that others after us will understand in a different way. And yet . . . it [is] the same work whose fullness of meaning is realized in the changing process of understanding, just as it is the same history whose meaning is constantly in the process of being defined"[56]

We have examined the understanding of tradition that emerged from Gadamer's analysis of culture, specifically from his effort to clarify the role of the *Geisteswissenschaften* as mediators of knowledge in the cultural process. As important and insightful as Gadamer's view of tradition may be, it contains at least two areas of inadequacy that, if not corrected, become particularly misleading when his view is applied to religious traditions, their behaviors, and the loci of their efficacy. These two areas, and the revisions they require, are the subjects, respectively, of the next two sections.

PLAYING AND BEING-PLAYED

Gadamer's analysis implies the constitutive necessity of tradition. This is perhaps the most important, and valid, consequence of the view he develops. His is more than the claim that we are all historical creatures and therefore that the past is the inescapable ground *upon which* our future will be made. He shows that the past is the material *with which* the future is made. Tradition is not simply formative, it is in-formative or constitutive of the creation of the future. To be is to be traditioned—to be the recipient, transformer, and transmitter of a past. In Gadamer's view, Cicero was right: Tradition is like a second nature. Or as Gadamer says: "In fact history does not belong to us; we belong to it. Long before we understand ourselves through the process of self-examination, we understand ourselves in a self-evident way in the family, society, and state in which we live. . . . The self-awareness of the individual is only a flickering in the closed circuits of historical life."[57] But if this passage states clearly the constitutive character of the past, which Gadamer rightly insists upon, it does something else, too. It suggests that the past is the pervasive predeterminant of the present. The circuits of historical life are almost entirely closed. The past, Gadamer's language suggests, is a prison.

The brooding overtone of determination in Gadamer's account of tradition, illustrated by the preceding passage, is resisted by Gadamer's analysis in several important ways. First, Gadamer argues that prejudices, the foreunderstandings given by tradition, are the conditions of understanding;[58] thus because understanding is itself creative it would seem to follow that the prejudice derived from tradition is a condition of creativity, not necessarily a restraint upon it. Second, Gadamer conceives of tradition as a conflictual variety of voices that exists "only in the multifariousness of such voices."[59] Because traditions *are* manifold possibilities most of which will always be as yet unrealized, the natural progression of a tradition is the playing out of its novel possibilities in changing environments. This brings up a third argument in favor of the freedom of tradition: Traditions are never hermetically sealed, insulated from encounters with and transformations by other traditions.[60] What Gadamer says about the perpetual journey of the human spirit—the movement into the alien and the return home of a changed self[61]—applies no less to the movements of traditions. The flow of life is never a confrontation of self-contained subject and fixed object. Understanding is always a mutual interaction in which two or more subjects, be they individual or collective subjects, persons or particular histories, are each transformed by the other—a "fusion of horizons."[62] Hence, against both the Enlightenment and Romanticism, Gadamer consistently claims that tradition does not constrain freedom, creativity.[63] Tradition is its ground.

Still, as much as Gadamer accents tradition as the context and vehicle of creativity, many readers find in his work a persistent conservatism.[64] As much as he attempts in *Truth and Method* and in subsequent responses to his critics to affirm the freedom of life in tradition, the mood that lingers throughout his work is nicely captured in his statement: "history does not belong to us; we belong to it," and history is closed.

Gadamer does not dispel this mood, in my judgment, because his own systematic analysis, though not his system itself, prevents him from doing so.[65] The primary impediment, I believe, is Gadamer's place of departure—the "question of truth as it emerges *in the experience of art*" (emphasis added). The point to be noticed is that *experience* here refers fundamentally to the experience of the observer of art, not the creator. This emphasis on the observer's orientation can fairly easily be missed because Gadamer's discussion of play—which is actor oriented, for the most part, not spectator oriented—is a prominent part of his larger investigation of the experience of art; and Gadamer even tells us that play is "the mode of being of the work of art."[66]

The important thing, however, is what Gadamer does not say. He does not tell us that play is the mode of being of the *creation* of art; it is a clue to the appreciation of art. And, in fact, the play that turns out to be a clue to the being of art is play that has acquired, and is thus transformed by, the appearance of an audience—play, as Gadamer says, that has been "transformed into structure."[67] In point of fact, the topic of play appears rather abruptly in Gadamer's analysis and after thirty pages or so it disappears almost completely from the discussion. What Gadamer says thereafter about the nature of understanding, aesthetic understanding and understanding in general, is determined by Gadamer's opening account of the *observer's* experience of art. In sum, play clarifies but does not alter a discussion whose parameters have already been set by Gadamer's initial interpretation of the observation of art.

How might Gadamer's analysis of tradition have been different if he had begun with an analysis of play, not with the observation of art? To speculate on that we need to examine, and develop in ways he could have but did not, what Gadamer says about play.

Gadamer looks to the phenomenon of play for "an alternative to the Cartesian model that rivets our attention on 'subjective attitudes' [*Vorstellung*] toward what is presumably 'objective'."[68] In this regard he notes that those who enter the game are taken up into and become one with its activity. The game "absorbs the player into itself."[69] We cannot think of the playing of the player as a subjective activity that is distinct from and stands over against the game as an object. The game cannot be reduced to the activity of the player or players, of course, but the game's reality is not instantiated except as it is instantiated in the activity of the player. In play, the specter of subjectivism disappears; subject and object presuppose one another.

Gadamer views play as a natural phenomenon whose "to-and-fro" activity is self-extending and self-renewing.[70] It is also freeing. Indeed, the "peculiar freedom and buoyancy" of play, Gadamer says, "determines the consciousness of the player."[71] So much so that "the players are not the subjects of [the] play."[72] The play plays the players. "All playing is being-played."[73]

The game has its own distinctive space or place, denoted not only by boundaries or a playing field, but also by the boundaries of appropriate activities usually called *rules*. Indeed, the rules or patterns of propriety are the most prominent features of the reality of the game apart from its instantiation in the play itself. The rules constitute the canon of the game.

What Gadamer fails to explore adequately, in my view, is the creativity of the player. That is understandable if, as I claim, Gadamer's effective model of analysis is not play or artistic creation but the observer's experience of art. In any case, although Gadamer does talk about the player's creativity, it is primarily his or her creativity in instantiating the game, which for Gadamer is already about as "fixed" as a sculpture or a painting. My contention is that if we focus on play*ing*, that is, if we escape the confines of Gadamer's restrictive starting point, we will see that all playing is indeed being-played, as he says, but, equally, all being-played is playing, creating, constructing, transforming.[74] How is this so?

There is, first, the obvious point that rules or canons for play are simply the outer limits that, precisely as limits, also direct the player's attention to the task of multiplying the possibilities within. The stipulation of what is not permitted is also an invitation to explore and expand from within what is permitted. Limitation, as Jonathan Z. Smith has said in his discussion of canon, calls forth ingenuity.[75] Hence as much as it is true to say that the game plays the players, the players also develop and alter the game by exploring and expanding the game from within, both with respect to what is possible (strategy) and how it is possible (tactics). Players play the game, change the game from within.

The changes that occur in play do not simply succeed what went before, they inherit what went before. Prior play is constitutive of succeeding play even when what follows moves far beyond it. In games, the past is not necessarily inhibitory, but it is obligatory at least in the sense that what follows must somehow take it into account. If it does not, it is another game. The past is taken up into what follows and makes a difference to what follows. The change within games displays constitutive, not merely successive, continuity.

But rules also change. Especially in free play—for example, children playing house, adults engrossed in conversation, couples making love—the canons of play are fluid. Their fluidity varies, of course. There is more than a little evidence that in modern Western culture this variation relates partly to gender roles. According to the research of Janet Lever as reported by Carol Gilligan,[76] boys tend to view the rules of games as inviolable and thus they make rules applicable to new situations by the addition of rules of arbitration. (In religions this process is called *commentary*.) For girls the rules of games per se are usually subservient to the more important rules of relationships, so that a conflict within a game may simply end the game in order to continue the relationship. Variations in the fluidity of rules also relates to cultural differences. But the basic point is this: In play, there is a changing of the rules as well as a changing within the rules.

Gadamer's acknowledgment of the creativity of the player, therefore, is much too timid. Play is play*ing*, as well as being-played. The game plays the players, and the players play, *and* play with, the game.

If we take as our model for understanding tradition the activity of playing and its appropriate corollary, the creation rather than the observation of art, Gadamer's basic view of tradition remains intact, but the consequence of this subtle shift in starting point is profound. What remains, first, is the basic claim that we belong to history, that to be at all is to be traditioned, that tradition is constitutive of the present. Second, traditions, like games and plays, are not reducible to the activities of individuals and groups within them, but neither do they have reality except as they are instantiated in these varied, concrete activities. Third, traditions are natural phenomena whose very "to-and-fro" movements are the ground, so to speak, of their being extended and renewed. They live precisely in the dialectic of continuity *and* change. Fourth, traditions, like games and artistic activities, have their own distinctive spaces and places, which we usually call *canons*. They serve as the font of creativity, and perhaps also as the principle of identity,[77] within a tradition.

The change that follows from grounding a Gadamerian analysis in playing or artistic creation is the radicalization of creativity in Gadamer's view of tradition. The "freedom and buoyancy" of traditions is far greater than Gadamer seems to recognize. Our ingenuity inhabits and lives from tradition, to be sure. In this Gadamer is quite right. But tradition inhabits and lives from our ingenuity. From this it follows, first, that the varied social locations of the players of a tradition are fundamental to understanding the way a tradition is played, individually and collectively, at any given time and place; and, second, that playing a tradition can and may include resistance to patterns of inheritance no less than their repetition.[78] It also follows, more generally, that creativity is as "natural" to a tradition as is continuity and that no domain of a tradition is in principle immune from it. The vocation of creativity applies not only to an expansion of the alternatives *within* a tradition's canon but also to an expansion of the alternatives *for* its canon. If we belong to tradition, tradition belongs to us.

But we do belong to tradition, too, as Gadamer says. The past is constitutive of creativity. Ingenuity, whether it operates within a canon or upon a canon, is still traditioned ingenuity, not simply in the sense that it has a history but also in the sense that its alteration of tradition lives from that which it changes. The past is taken up into the present as an agent of its own re-formation.

If, as we have argued, creativity in a Gadamerian view of tradition must be radicalized, it must also be "somaticized," even naturalized. That is the claim of the next section.

GROUNDING THE LIFE OF LANGUAGE

Enlarging the role of creativity in Gadamer's view of tradition is helpful, but it is not yet enough. Gadamer's view, so emended, still lacks an adequate account of *how* a tradition is efficacious. His analysis of the power of the past is limited almost exclusively to an examination of language, for, in his view, "the essence of tradition is to exist in the medium of language."[79] In this respect, Gadamer, like many other so-called postmodern thinkers, perpetuates the purview of modernism; he carries on the Enlightenment's reductionistic preoccupation with the human, limited now not simply to the dictates of human reason or the structures of the human mind but to the patterns and functionings of human linguisticality. Yet Gadamer's own discussion occasionally betrays the insufficiency of this modernist "linguicentrism." In this final section I shall examine the telling "slips" in Gadamer's discussion and say why they should be taken seriously, and how.

Gadamer persuasively argues that all understanding is interpretive, and that all conscious interpretation is linguistic. He fails, however, to address an additional possibility: that there might be a prelinguistic, largely nonconscious mode of apprehending whatever is given, out of which our conscious, interpretive linguistic understandings emerge. In other words, he does not consider the hypothesis that, within the range of interpretive understanding generally, our human conscious interpretive understanding derives from and continuously interacts with a vague, largely inchoate mode of human interpretive inheritance that occurs at the level of bodily feeling and that, as such, is embedded in the larger sphere of the efficacies of the natural process.

Gadamer's own account of the power of language in the final pages of *Truth and Method* suggests, and perhaps even presupposes, the hypothesis of a nonlinguistic mode of apprehending the immediate past. At one point, for example, Gadamer writes: "Language often seems ill suited to express what we feel. In the face of the overwhelming presence of works of art, the task of expressing in words what they say to us seems like an infinite and hopeless undertaking. The fact that our desire and capacity to understand always go beyond any statement that we can make seems like a critique of language." [80]

Two pages later, reflecting on the process of conceptual interpretation, he says: "We have seen that conceptual interpretation is the realization of the hermeneutical experience itself. That is why our problem is so difficult. The interpreter does not know that he is bringing himself and his own concepts into the interpretation. The verbal formulation is so much part of the interpreter's mind that he never becomes aware of it as an object." [81] As we have noted, Gadamer says that all understanding is interpretation and, usually, that all interpretation is linguistic. Here, however, he postulates an element of the process of understanding and interpretation that is not conscious. What he seems to mean is that we are conscious of the outcome of the process of thinking and speaking, but not of the process itself. At the very least what follows is the reality of a preconscious element that is powerfully efficacious in the understanding process. If Gadamer wants still to insist that this process—"bringing one's own concepts into the interpretation"—is linguistic, he must now conclude, however, that some linguisticality is not conscious.

In fact, much earlier in *Truth and Method* Gadamer had already toyed with the idea that, as we might put it, knowing exceeds being conscious. He says: "We do not understand what recognition is in its profoundest nature if we only regard it as knowing something again that we know already. . . . The joy of recognition is rather the joy of knowing *more* than is already familiar" [or, in the translation of an earlier edition, "The joy of recognition is rather that more is known than only the known"].[82]

A passage in *Philosophical Hermeneutics* contains the same suggestion: "Reflection on a given preunderstanding brings before me something that otherwise happens *behind my back*. . . . For what I have called *wirkungsgeschichtliches* [effective historical consciousness] is inescapably more *being* than consciousness, and being is never fully manifest."[83]

Finally, a section toward the end of *Truth and Method* suggests that the verbal world is the outcome of a preverbal and perhaps preconscious process rooted in something beyond itself:

> the inner mental word is not formed by a reflective act. . . .
> In fact there is no reflection when the word is formed, for
> the word is not expressing the mind but the thing
> intended. The starting point for the formation of the word
> is the substantive content (the species) that fills the mind.
> The thought seeking expression refers not to the mind but
> to the thing. Thus the word is not the expression of the
> mind but is concerned with the similitudo rei. . . . [T]he
> word is that in which knowledge is consummated.[84]

One can dismiss such statements as slips that a more careful writer should and would avoid. I prefer, for reasons to be mentioned later, to explore the possibility that these references—to a level of nonconceptual. albeit interpretive, experience where subject and object are presumably intertwined—are insightful. Their insight can be expressed in an adaptation of one of Gadamer's own statements, quoted previously: Even as we understand through the process of conscious examination, we also apprehend at the prelinguistic and largely non-conscious level where we most fundamentally live. The focus on language and thus consciousness, taken alone, is a distorting mirror. The consciousness of the individual is only a flickering in the closed circuits of our bodily and historical life.[85]

This statement, in effect, is the hypothesis developed within the American philosophical tradition of "radical empiricism." Radical empiricism—anticipated by Jonathan Edwards, formulated by William James, John Dewey, and Alfred North Whitehead, and applied to the interpretation of religion by Henry Nelson Wieman, Bernard Meland, Bernard Loomer, and more recently by William Dean and Nancy Frankenberry[86]—may be summarized in four points.

The first and basic point is the proposal that our primary connectedness with things is at the level of largely nonconscious feeling.[87] It is an activity of the body, or at least of the self as an embodied organism, rooted in and interacting with the rest of nature. Whitehead, for example, acknowledges the central importance of sensory experience that is "handy, and definite in our consciousness."[88] But he insists that there is another, more fundamental, dimension of experience that is "vague, unmanageable . . . , heavy with the contact of things gone by. . . ."[89] This is our bodily commerce with the world—intuitive, felt, tacit. Whitehead writes:

The more primitive types of experience are concerned with sense-reception, and not with sense-perception.[90]

[T]he most primitive perception is "feeling the body as functioning." This is a feeling of the world in the past; it is the inheritance of the world as a complex of . . . derived feelings.[91]

What is inherited is feeling-tone with evidence of its origin: in other words, vector feeling-tone. . . . Thus perception, in this primary sense, is perception of the settled world in the past as constituted by its feeling-tones, and as efficacious by reason of those feeling-tones. Perception, in this sense of the term, will be called "perception in the mode of causal efficacy."[92]

[Perception in the mode of causal efficacy] produces percepta which are vague, not to be controlled, heavy with emotion; it produces the sense of derivation from an immediate past, and of passage to an immediate future; a sense of emotional feeling, belonging to oneself in the past, passing into oneself in the present, and passing from oneself in the present towards oneself in the future; a sense of influx of influence from other vaguer presences in the past, localized and yet evading local definition, such influence modifying, enhancing, inhibiting, diverting, the stream of feeling which we are receiving, unifying, enjoying, and transmitting. This is our general sense of . . . an efficacious actual world."[93]

In Whitehead's view, we do not first experience the world through one or more of the five senses. Our primary awareness, largely unconscious and unanalyzed, is of an interrelated matrix of giveness within which we ourselves are imbedded, to which we are inextricably related. Conscious sense experience and intellection are fashioned out of this more basic sense of the world given in dim, imprecise feeling.[94] "In the higher grades of perception vague feeling-tone differentiates itself into various types of sensa—those of touch, sight, smell, etc.—each transmuted into a definite prehension . . . by the final percipient."[95]

A second element of radical empiricism is the judgment that feelings at the preconceptual and largely unconscious level are always weighted, patterned, or directional. They are always "vectors."

The primitive form of physical experience is emotional—blind emotion—received as felt elsewhere in another occasion and conformally appropriated as a subjective passion. . . . Thus the primitive experience is emotional feeling, felt in its relevance to a world beyond. . . . In the phraseology of physics, this primitive experience is "vector feeling," that is to say, feeling from a beyond which is determinate and pointing to a beyond which is to be determined.[96]

What is inherited are not innocent, indifferent buzzes; they are forces, values that incline us, influence us, move us. Like strong winds they bend us in particular directions. They are "meanings." This must be said, however, with some hesitation because we are predisposed to associate "meaning" with language, and thus to ask about these vector feelings, "what do they mean?" The most adequate answer is that they mean themselves. They are causative, they are powers. They are the basic realm of causal connectedness in which we dwell. Hence, their meaning is what they *do* to us, including what they enable us to do, to see, to think, to imagine, to create.

A third supposition is that the relationship of the human subject and her or his given environment is, in either case, neither simply "causing" (creating, imagining, constructing) nor "being caused" (receiving, picturing, corresponding). Each is to some degree creative subject and to some degree created object, plastic or malleable coparticipants in an interconnected process. Hence the relationship of "self" and "world" (both social and natural) is best described as interactive, codeterminant, or reciprocal.

This leads into a fourth aspect of the radical empiricist hypothesis, concerning the interactivity within the self. In human experience, the more primitive level of feeling is intertwined with sensation and reflection. Our conscious sensory awareness of the world, and then our imaginative reflection on this conscious awareness, are abstractions constructed out of the raw material of inchoate, largely preconscious feeling. Feeling, in other words, permeates sensation and thought. But the opposite is true, too. "It must be remembered . . . that emotion in human experience, or even in animal experience, is not bare emotion. It is emotion interpreted, integrated, and transformed into higher categories of feeling."[97] The worlds of sensation and ideas have an impact on the more basic level of feeling. Formed feelings at the level of our most primitive awareness of the world both influence and are influenced by what we experience in the five senses and what we think about. This interaction means that there is no such thing as "pure experience" if that term suggests that a subject can take account of a datum "as it is." All experience is perspectival. *Interpretation* refers to perspectival appropriation insofar as it is cognitive.[98]

Radical empiricism, in sum, is the hypothesis that we are bodies more than we are minds, even though minds are absolutely essential, and that the dimension of largely preconscious feeling, which our bodies receive and enact, should be, no less than language, a part of any theory about how it is that we relate to our environments, "know" our world, and inherit and transform our particular traditions. "It is evident," as Whitehead notes, "that [this mode] of perception . . . has [not] received chief attention in the philosophical tradition. Philosophers have disdained the information about the universe obtained through their visceral feelings, and have concentrated on visual feelings."[99] There are, however, a number of reasons for taking this hypothesis seriously.

First, the hypothesis of a preconceptual and largely unconscious mode of awareness provides a plausible interpretation of the way "lower" forms of life take account of their environments. Because humans evolved from and remain rooted in nature, it would be odd if through evolution humans had managed to abandon this mode of awareness entirely. (Indeed, some such way of taking account of the world appears to be an appropriate description of the relatedness of the newborn humans and their environments. Again, it would be odd if this kind of awareness were simply to cease as human beings mature.) Second, this hypothesis, implying as it does a continuity between humans and nonhumans, is one way of overcoming the deleterious dualisms of mind and body, and humanity and the rest of the natural order.[100] Third, there is some reason for

supposing that such a mode of awareness actually manifests itself
at the edges of consciousness, in so-called personal knowledge
and in more intuitive senses of our connectedness to things.[101]

For our purposes, however, there is a fourth consideration, to
be addressed in Chapter 4. The radical empiricist hypothesis—
which holds that the fundamental connectedness of humans and
their worlds, including their pasts, occurs at a level of preconceptual awareness and inheritance—helps us understand the
locus of a tradition's power. It suggests that our cultural and religious traditions are transmitted fundamentally at the level of
bodily feeling where the human immersion in nature is most
intense. The efficacy of traditions is located very significantly—
perhaps mainly—in rites of bodily enactment, in the felt dimensions of community, and in the largely precritical play of symbol
and myth.[102] Radical empiricism makes sense of this.[103]

Gadamer's analysis of tradition, I have argued, is inadequate
in two respects. First, it gives insufficient scope to the creative
play that is proper to religious traditions. Second, it neglects the
prelinguistic processes of inheritance in which all other experience, including our conscious and conceptual participation in
religious tradition, is grounded. I do not claim that one failure is
causally related to the other. I do observe, however, that correc-
tions of these inadequacies are mutually supportive. The preconceptual dimensions of traditions are fonts of creativity no less
than of continuity, for if, as Gadamer and Ricoeur have
claimed, the inherited past is multifarious or plurivocal, then
the tensive richness of the past communicated at the level of
bodily feeling would in fact serve to undermine repetition for
its own sake. In other words—and contrary to our deeply
ingrained modernist assumptions—the valuing of conformity
over creativity is not a tendency intrinsic to tradition as such;
the preference for sameness and the suspicion of novelty may
more properly be understood as a product of specific conceptual
strategies—theologies, for example—intentionally cultivated to
protect the status quo by those whom it benefits. When

grounded in the richness of feeling, truly conserving traditions, it would appear, are traditions at play.

With Nicholas of Cusa, Gadamer speaks of creativity as the life of language.[104] But Gadamer himself neglects the effusive, precognitive ground from which vitality springs. To quote Gadamer speaking about another matter, "what originally constituted the basis of the life of language . . . is . . . marginalized" in Gadamer's own analysis.[105] Unwittingly, Gadamer marginalizes the basis of the life of language. Fortunately, however, Gadamer's intuition is more adequate than his systematic analysis. If, indeed, language is often "ill suited to express what we feel," if the role of the past is "inescapably more being than consciousness," and if in human experience "more is known than only the known"—then we may be well advised to root the play of tradition in concrete natural processes, especially the actions of the body. The development of a theory of tradition that extends Gadamer's analysis, more adequately grounding the creativity of tradition in the concrete vitalities of our lives, is the task of the next two chapters.

❈ 3 ❈

CULTURE AND CANON

TOWARD A THEORY OF TRADITION.

"Theory's day is dying;" Stanley Fish wrote not long ago, "the hour is late; and the only thing left for a theorist to do is to say so."[1] Fish's view is the verdict of a number of recent critiques of theorizing.[2] Some of these critiques conclude that theory inevitably distorts its data, by abstracting from its richness, for example, or by trying to fix its endless play of difference. Others see theory as a strategy for displacing and absorbing those who inhabit the political and cultural margins of society, by systematically ruling out of consideration their alternative realities and modes of knowing. The first set of critiques view theory as illusion and the second as oppression, but all of these critiques object in one way or another to the "totalization" that theory is said inevitably to impose.[3] Briefly, at least, these judgments require consideration.

WHAT THEORIES ARE AND DO

The question to be asked of theory's critics is whether the dismissal of theories may not be more dangerous than their employment. The answer depends in part on what theory is

55

thought to be and do. If a theory is a scheme that pretends to place once and for all everything within its purview, one answer is required. But if theorizing is a hypothesizing moment in the interrogative process, essential but always tentative, another answer may be justified. As Cornel West has observed, "uncritical allegiance to grand theories" may indeed prevent us from recognizing, for example, certain types of human oppression, but opposition to "theory *per se*" may keep us from finding the "causes of . . . [these] forms of human misery and human suffering."[4] From this standpoint, opposition to theory may be more oppressing and deluding than the disease for which it allegedly is the cure.[5]

As understood here, a theory is a complex hypothesis. Theory, so conceived, is a phase within the constantly repeated interrogative process through which humans interact in and with their worlds. Theory can be useful, however, at different levels of the interrogative process. It could be an hypothesis that, so to speak, frames a discipline of inquiry, postulating its subject matter and proposing, at least by implication, a method for its examination. Or a theory could be a complex hypothesis within a particular discipline that offers a specific construal of the subject matter in question for further investigation.[6] Either way, whether as constitutive of a field or as "contributive" to its progress, theory begins in what C. S. Peirce called *vagueness*, that region between what is so confused it cannot yet be hypothetically negotiated and what is so clear, for the time being, that it need not be.[7] Theory is a hypothetical ordering, a construal of data, a postulate about how data might fruitfully be related.[8] As such, theory is simply an invitation to investigation by plotting a possible course that the inquiry might take.

Theorizing is expansive; it posits relationships between varied kinds of data. The expansiveness of theory making might very well carry forward to the pursuit of absolute generality, as is illustrated by the construction of theories in the physical sciences. But useful theorizing can also be limited, or at least indefinite, in its anticipated applicability. It can suggest a way of ordering a particular set of data within a particular sphere, leaving open the question of the applicability of this hypothetical rendering to somewhat similar data in other spheres. The theory of tradition developed in this study has limited applicability. For one thing, the conception of tradition to be proposed will not cover all of the processes that might meaningfully be called a *tradition* even within, say, Western cultural history. The theory might apply to aspects of the history of Euro-American art or politics, for example, but there are other streams of artistic style and political belief to which this conception of tradition will not apply. Although these other streams would not be "traditions" in the strict sense employed here, certainly there are looser senses of the term *tradition*, or different specific senses, that still apply quite reasonably to these strands of art or political history. Although the theory of tradition to be developed in this work likely will have useful applicability elsewhere, "religions" (using that term generally) will be its central focus. The theory, in short, is to be a hypothetical rendering of the nature and functioning of religious traditions. But there is a second way in which the theory to be proposed has limited or at least indefinite applicability: It will not necessarily illuminate the character and behavior of all religions. Because the data with which it deals primarily are drawn from scholarly interpretations of oral cultures and Western textual cultures and religions, the theory will be proposed with less certainty about its value for analyzing, say, the religions of the East. Whatever utility it may prove to have elsewhere, the theory of this book is intended to illuminate the character of Western "textual" religions generally, and Christianity in particular. If successful, the theory of tradition offered here will clarify the patterns of inheritance characteristic of these religions, especially Christianity, including the interactions of their complex legacies and their current forms of theological inquiry.

If theory—whether general or limited in intent—is defensible, indeed essential, it is nevertheless important to acknowledge that theorizing always falsifies in a sense, for even the best theories fail to capture the depth and complexity of the data they address. Some falsifications, however, are relatively more fortunate than others. Good theories are fortunate falsifications; they construe the data so that we can see connections we had not seen before or had not seen before as fruitfully. Whether theories are true is important (whatever meaning *truth* is given in a particular community of discourse), but elevating particular hypotheses to the status of "truth" is not the most important aim of theory making. Theories seek what might be—whether or not what might be, might also be (in some sense) what is. That is why Whitehead said it is more important for a theory to be interesting than true.[9] Theories outline conceptual adventures; their primary purpose is to attract the mind to possible terrains, with the alluring hint that the exploration of these potentials could tell us something of value we had not thought about before. And even theories judged to be true are so only for a time; they are not true, or even interesting, for eternity. But eternity is not where we live. A theory useful for a while is as useful as a theory can be.

Recent discussions of theory that focus on the nature of "praxis" have convincingly delineated the interactive character of theoretical reflection and action.[10] But it is no less necessary to think of theories as interacting with other theories, with other hypothetical construals adjacent to, overlapping with, or encompassing the theory in question. Assuming that the elements of life about which theories hypothesize are overlapping and interactive, it follows that good theories will be similarly related. In this chapter our task is to seek to give some order to the diverse observations about the behaviors of religious traditions as these have emerged in the previous discussion. Our task, in other words, is to begin to develop a theory of religious tradition and thus, first, of tradition. But as we have looked at them in this study, the behaviors of traditions, religious and otherwise, seem curiously intermingled with, if never quite reducible to, the behaviors of cultures. Hence it may be fruitful to begin our attempt to make sense of traditions by first examining similar efforts to develop a theory of cultures.

CULTURE: NEGOTIATING CHAOS AND ORDER

Recent theorizing about culture has generally followed Clifford Geertz in thinking of cultures as "socially established structures of meaning in terms of which" human actions, understood broadly, gain their meanings.[11] But what has been of particular interest in the recent studies, and especially important to the present task, is the nature of the relationships that Geertz compresses into the small phrase, *in terms of which*, for the crucial question, it seems, is how symbol systems relate to human actions. What, in other words, is the character of that inter-action wherein humans use and are used by their cultural constructs? To clarify this, a brief history of the Western understanding of culture is in order.

Before the Enlightenment, *culture* simply meant "cultivation"—the care of crops, animals, and human minds.[12] During the eighteenth century, however, cultivation in the last sense, as applied specifically to human development, emerged as the dominant meaning of culture and became associated with another concept, "civilization." To *civilize* was to bring humans into a social organization, and to be *civil* was to behave in a way appropriate to that organization, to be orderly, educated, polite. To be civil, in sum, was to be cultured—the two terms were joined. But during the eighteenth century an additional conjunction of ideas also took place. Conceptions of culture and of civilization, now more or less one, coalesced with Enlightenment notions of progressive historical development. *Culture* and *civilization* took on historical proportions, referring both to an achieved state of affairs within history—civilization in contrast to "barbarism"—and to the historical development toward that state of affairs. The Enlightenment's penchant for a universalization of history then placed all historical developments within this framework, with the achieved civilization of England and France, especially, at the center. Thus, by the end of the eighteenth century, civilization and culture were "interchangeable terms,"[13] now referring to a single, universal, historical evolution that culminated in the European ideal of the human.

Soon thereafter, however, civilization and culture were to be separated. First, a line of thought from Rousseau to Romanticism attacked civilization as a superficial external form, to be distinguished, respectively, from what is natural and from what is inner or spiritual. Then, the moral ambiguity of the industrial revolution rendered no less ambiguous the process of civilization which industry was said to represent. Hence "culture" came to be distinguished from civilization, suddenly in disrepute, and allied instead with art and religion and their supporting institutions. But that was temporary, too. Eventually the progressive critique of religion eliminated religion from the alliance, leaving culture associated almost solely with "the arts." Even today this association gives *culture* one of its two basic meanings.[14]

The other meaning of *culture*, more recently acquired, is actually akin to the larger, "historical" connotation of *culture* and *civilization* when these terms were still in tandem. For our purposes the history of this second meaning is the most important one. The Enlightenment had assumed that the driving force of the cultivating or civilizing process in history is reason, the enlightened comprehension of the self and the world. Moreover, *almost* every intellectual of the eighteenth century took the new physical sciences to be the model of this force. The scientific investigation of the physical world was taken to be, or at least to consummate, the cultivating process that alone represents a truly civilized understanding. But not everyone in the eighteenth century was content with this elevation of the physical sciences. The most conspicuous dissenter, perhaps, was Vico who, in 1725, marvelled that "the philosophers should have bent all their energies to the study of . . . nature, which, since God made it, He alone knows; and that they should have neglected the study of . . . nations or [the] civil world, which, since men made it, men could hope to know."[15] In fact, Vico held not simply that we can know the human world because we make it; he also held, according to Raymond Williams, the still more radical notion that we are able to know our world in and by our making it. Williams writes: "[Vico's] description of a mode of development which was at once, and interactively, the shaping of societies and the shaping of human minds is probably the effective origin of the *general* social [scientific] sense of 'culture' [today]."[16]

If Vico began this second way of viewing culture, one that somehow associates culture with the social process rather than primarily with artistic expression, his concept was advanced still further by J. G. Herder, who maintained that the "historical self-development of humanity" is too variable and complex to be reduced to a single process (that culminating in Europe) guided by single principle (reason). Therefore Herder proposed instead the idea of multiple organic processes differentiating people and nations. According to Williams, this conception of varying streams of social development shaping humanity into "specific and distinct 'ways of life' is the effective origin of the *comparative* social [scientific] sense of 'culture' and its . . . plural 'cultures'."[17] Culture is cultures—multiple, developing social processes or milieux of meaning.

It was this idea to which E. B. Tylor gave expression in the late nineteenth century when he designated cultures as complex, organic wholes.[18] Until very recently, anthropology, founded by Tylor, has continued to understand cultures in organic terms. The diversity within each particular form of human life has been readily acknowledged, but the term *culture* has functioned precisely to highlight those elements within each variegated form of collective existence that give to it "continuity and depth."[19] A *culture*, then, has been viewed as a "coherent *body* that lives and dies. . . . Culture is a process of ordering, not disruption. It changes and develops like a living organism."[20] James Clifford summarizes the development of this modern, social scientific understanding of culture as follows:

> The concept of culture used by anthropologies was . . . invented by European theorists to account for the collective articulations of human diversity. Rejecting both evolutionism and the overly broad entities of race and civilization, the idea of culture posited the existence of local, functionally integrated units. For all its supposed relativism, though, the concept's model of totality, basically organic in structure, was not different from the nineteenth-century concepts it replaced. Only its plurality was new. . . . Despite many subsequent redefinitions the notion's organicist assumptions have persisted. Cultural systems hold together. . . .[21]

Current theories, however, question precisely the assumption that cultures are like living organisms, that they grow and change as a plant or an animal, and, especially, that cultures rather easily "hold together." Metaphors centering on growth, continuity, and identity fail to do justice to the sharp mutations, persisting contradictions, radical displacements, and stark breaks in the behaviors of cultures.[22] In fact, the analogies for understanding cultures, in current theory, are hermeneutical rather than organic ones. The assumption of modern hermeneutics is the apparent infinitude of meanings into which a text can dissolve; whether a text is held together by something even remotely like an inherent structure or meaning, however complex, is debatable at best. "It is high time," says James Clifford, "that cultural and social totalities are subjected to the same kind of radical questioning that textual ensembles have undergone in recent critical practice."[23]

Clifford states the implications of multitudes of contemporary anthropological studies when he characterizes culture as negotiation.[24] A culture is not organically unified, cumulative and continuous; it is always being bartered and bargained for.[25] Cultural identities are never givens; they are constantly negotiated in open-ended dialogue.[26] Indeed, a culture is the struggle to create, maintain, and re-create individual and collective identities.[27] Hence although stable orders do come into being, they are in the nature of the case contested orders to be subverted and transgressed.[28] To the extent that stabilities do endure, they do so, Clifford thinks, by repeatedly being put at risk in novel situations.[29]

The "essence" of culture is negotiation, or as Roy Wagner puts it, culture is invention.[30] Wagner, much like Clifford, argues that the concept of culture is itself an invention but that this conceptual invention takes place, as Wagner says, "objectively, along the lines of observing and learning, and not as a kind of free fantasy."[31] The concept of culture, in other words, is invented in interaction with given data. In Wagner's view, the same kind of conceptual interactivity that gives rise to "culture" as a concept also characterizes cultures themselves.

> Invention and convention stand in a *dialectical* relationship to one another, a relationship of simultaneous interdependence and contradiction. This dialectic is the core of all human (and very likely all animal) cultures. . . . My [concept of *dialectic*] is that of a tension or dialogue-like alternation between conceptions or viewpoints that are simultaneously contradictory and supportive of each other.[32]

If Clifford and Wagner differ, it is primarily in the fact that Clifford places greater emphasis on the role of the contextual, particularly the socio-political, factors in the interactive process that we call *culture*. Clifford's term *negotiation*, as compared to Wagner's *invention*, already indicates as much.

In the work of Marshall Sahlins, the emphasis on the "objective" factors in the negotiated process is still stronger. Sahlins seeks the revival of a kind of structuralism, not like that of Saussure for whom structure abrogates the role of history in cultural processes, but a dynamic structuralism. For Sahlins, structures (or "cultural schemes") are historically ordered and history is structurally ordered in the "creative action of the historic subjects, the people concerned."[33] Although Sahlins insists that different structures make for different histories,[34] he also holds that historical actions alter structures.

The inseparability of the reproduction and the transformation of cultural structures, or, more generally, of cultural continuity and change, is one of Sahlin's central insights. Behind this insight are two premises, one about cultural structures and the other about their "worldly circumstance." Sahlins understands cultural schemes, taken in the abstract, to be complexes of "logical possibilities" successively "presented" in historical processes.[35] Sahlins should have said *elicited* or *provoked* rather than *presented*, however, because, more than Wagner or even Clifford, he assumes (and this is his second premise) that "empirical realities" can and do defy inherited structures, thereby forcing their transformation.[36] "As Durkheim said, the universe does not exist for people except as it is thought. On the other hand, it need not exist in the way they think. . . . The worldly circumstances of human action are under no inevitable obligation to conform to the categories by which . . . people conceive them."[37] Hence, although every transformation of structure is also to some extent a reproduction, the resistance of "worldly circumstance" means that every reproduction of cultural schemes is also to some extent their transformation. This resistance is most apparent in the differentiation amid which cultures move. The differences between cultures are only the most obvious of these. More pervasive, and perhaps more important most of the time, are the differences within cultures.[38] Things never stay the same and what is new never blends fully into familiar modes of thought.[39] Thus, even when "the old names . . . are still on everyone's lips [they] acquire connotations . . . far removed from their original meaning."[40] But change is never total. "Always," Sahlins says, "functional revaluations appear as logical extensions of traditional conceptions."[41] There must be some continuity with the past "or else the world is a madhouse."[42] Hence, the more things change, the more they stay the same; the more things stay the same, the more they change.[43] Even though their particular relationships are always the product of the specific conditions in which they occur, continuity and change go together.[44]

Sahlins's view means, first, that customary interpretive antitheses must now be rejected. History and structure, stability and change, static and dynamic, past and present, and so on are always synthesized in the cultural process.[45] More important for our present purposes, Sahlins's analysis implies that the cultural process, inevitably and always, is a risk, a gamble. The resistance of "empirical reality" to inherited categories, mentioned earlier, is the objective dimension of this risk.[46] The subjective dimension is the fact that the individual "interest" of human actors changes, "makes a difference" to, the inherited structures.[47] "In their practical projects and social arrangements, . . . people submit [their] cultural categories to empirical risks. . . . Culture is therefore a gamble played with nature. . . ."[48]

Despite their differences, Clifford, Wagner, and Sahlins alike abandon the nineteenth century notion that cultures are organic wholes that move rather naturally through processes of integrated maturation and development. They agree instead that the tendency of human collectives is constantly to flirt with fragmentation. Yet that is not the whole story. As Clifford says, metaphors of unity and development are not simply to be replaced with those of conflict and dissolution; human collectives are more ambiguous.[49] Although patterns of similarity and difference seem to have no secure ground, the assumption of forms of human connectedness cannot be entirely abandoned.[50] Thus, as compromised it as it may be, the idea of culture cannot be dismissed.[51] It is retained, however, not as a way of referring to settled identities, but as an indication of those processes wherein identities—collective and individual in interaction— are constantly sought, achieved, threatened, subverted, revised, and (as if the difference could be clear) replaced.

Therefore, if we adopt a Geertzian approach to cultures we can continue to speak of cultures as our most comprehensive social symbol systems in terms of which our actions, understood broadly, have their meanings, or better, their places.[52] But we must now be clear that these symbol systems behave in ways quite unlike the orderly development of an organism or the functioning of a computer program.[53] For while their control is often experienced personally to be as inevitable as an animal's growth and as irresistible as a computer's commands, the records of cultures require a somewhat different reading. Symbol systems are so tensive within themselves, so malleable before the resistant worlds they traverse, and so vulnerable to our innovative interests, that always they risk dissolution. Clifford writes: "Groups negotiating their identity . . . patch themselves together in ways different from a living organism. . . . [Culture] is a long, relational struggle to maintain and recreate identities. . . ."[54]

Hence, it may be true, as Geertz says, that without culture human behavior would be "mere chaos,"[55] but it is also true that the advent of culture removes only the *mere*, not the *chaos*. More than that, if culture precludes mere chaos it also precludes mere order. Culture is the play of conflicting symbols, conflicting interests, and conflicting symbols and interests, in a world only partly hospitable to our symbolic expectations. With these as its players, the game of culture is as much process as structure, stability as change, dissolution as construction, past as present, action as giveness, the collective as the individual. Culture is a struggle—the negotiation of identity amid chaos and order.

With this understanding of culture as a background, we shall now begin to explore the idea that tradition is one type of cultural strategy, one way of negotiating chaos and order. Tradition, we will propose in the next chapter, is the cultural negotiation of identity that takes place within, and with, a canon.[56] This proposal, however, assumes the defensibility of the concept of canon. In the next section of this chapter we will evaluate arguments against the notion of "canon." Then in Chapter 4 we will examine the nature and function of canon, and the role of canon in tradition.

IN DEFENSE OF CANON

Though it has long been central to the self-understanding of many traditions, the value of "canon" is now sharply challenged. There are good reasons for these challenges to canon, whether in its traditional religious form or its traditional secular form.

Religiously, canon has often been viewed as a privileged locus of thought or action, to which relevant thinking and acting must conform because it is somehow derived from deity. In Judaism and Christianity, for example, canon has been viewed as the authoritative deposit of divine revelation. Thus construed, canon has a distinctive character as unique truth, and a distinctive function as unique norm.

As a secular concept, canon has been conceived of as distinctive in character and function because of the universal applicability of its content. In the West, the secular canon has been thought of as the "classics," those texts that, though emergent from particular times and places, are applicable to all times and places as the norm of what it means to be human. The privilege granted to the canon on the secular view, therefore, has less to do with claims about a distinctive source, that is, deity (explicitly, at any rate[57]), than with claims about the timeless quality of its wisdom or form. But both views, the secular and the religious, attribute to canon a special character from which follows its unique function as norm.[58]

The contemporary critique of canon is partly devoted to an attack upon the claim of its special character. This attack is remarkably straightforward and, I think, incontestable. It is the observation that with any reasonable scrutiny of any canon, its distinctive quality, however construed, disappears—at least (since everything is distinctive in some senses), it has no unique distinction without parallel in other canons. Whatever qualities the elements of any canon are said to have, other canons may arguably be said to have similar qualities or different qualities that are nonetheless comparable in value. The customary view of canon, then, is an act of faith at odds with the evidence.[59] On this the current critique of canon is entirely right.

A more ambiguous aspect of the critique of canon, however, relates to customary claims about canon's special function. This critique has both a political form, deriving more recently from Michel Foucault, and a philosophical dimension, deriving generally from Jacques Derrida. In its political form it is a judgment that the function of canon is a wrongful, not a rightful, norm of thought and action, because in fact the function of canon is and always has been to legitimate the prevailing social order. This is so because the content of canon is always largely the world-view of the dominant classes. The social purpose of canon, then, is "ideological conditioning,"[60] the production of a consciousness acquiescent to one's place in society, usually a place of subordination. As Frank Kermode contends, canons are constructs by which the dominant forces of society maintain their interests both by controlling which texts are to be taken seriously and by determining what it means to take a text seriously.[61]

The philosophical criticism holds that canon is always an illicit attempt to fix meaning. This charge is most often associated with what is called variously the *deconstructionist, poststructuralist, Derridaean*, or *new rhetorical* point of view. Its assumption is "an infinity of signification: just as there is no decidable meaning to a text, so . . . would there be no central or major texts, no ground on which a canon might stand, only the free intertextual play of books taught and read."[62] In this view, canon is an illusion because "reality" (though the term is eschewed) is in fact an endless play of difference admitting no privileged or continuing construals of the sort that canon is usually taken to imply.

As important and informative as they are, these criticisms of canon are not easy to sustain, at least as stated. To take them in reverse order, it is difficult to see how the Derridaean construal of reality can avoid being either a commonplace or an act of faith. If the claim is that every interpretation is in principle, and apparently in fact, defeasible at some point by some alternative critique, the claim is valuable, but seldom if ever denied; it is simply the observation that no interpretation is privileged and none is impervious to critique and reversal or substantive revision. From this claim would only follow the very common judgment that conclusions, whether collective (like canons) or more individual (like theories), must always be viewed as incomplete, open to criticism, and subject to change. It would not follow that theories, canons, and the like cannot be developed and defended at a given time, or over a length of time, as more adequate than alternatives.

Taken in a stronger, more substantive sense, the Derridaean construal of reality would seem finally to rest on an act of faith without compelling pragmatic warrant. As a claim about discourse, its typical assertion that texts have no single, demonstrable intrinsic meanings, which is hard to deny, is taken to imply that texts mean only what readers say.[63] Texts are open to an infinitude of interpretation; in fact they demand it, for Derrida's notion of "*differance*" means that meaning is always "differential" and always "deferred," a "restless play . . . that cannot be fixed or pinned down. . . ."[64] The plays of Shakespeare, to illustrate, mean what their successive communal interpretations say they mean, and apart from these interpretations Shakespeare's plays have no meaning.[65] What must be said about individual texts must be said, too, about collective texts or any of the other composites (stories, rituals) of which canons are made. It is not simply that they are plurivocal, having multiple interrelated meanings; they have no intrinsic meanings except those we give them. In this view, the concept of canon, insofar as it assumes intrinsic textual meaning (however fluid and complex) and thus textual agency, presumes what cannot be sustained.

But why? Why can we not equally well say, for example, that a play by Shakespeare or any text is to be viewed as a grouping of multiple but interrelated meanings that successively come into view in varying interpretive relationships, and thus, that the meaning of *Hamlet* in a particular interpretive situation is always the product of the interaction of the interpreter (taken in the broadest sense to include the whole interpretive environment) and the play, and, therefore, that the play itself, like the interpreter, can be seen to have some measure of relative autonomy and some level of efficacy and restraint in the interpretive process?[66] Why must we deny that a work has any "purposive activity . . . independent of the reader" to avoid, as surely we should, "positing fixed, abstract intentions, stable subjects, or determinate meanings"?[67] The answer to this question—whether the text has some intrinsic complex of meanings and efficacy not reducible to interpretation—is clearly not something we can determine by direct inspection. The answer, however, can be approached pragmatically

If pragmatic considerations are to be determinative, Cornel West has made what seems to me to be a decisive point.[68] The fixation on difference, he observes, will always result in resistance but never in revolution.[69] Every achievement, that is to say, must in the nature of the case be challenged in the endless struggle of difference, the perpetual play of alternatives. No newly established discursive meaning or no social order, however tentative and fallible, could rightly claim superiority, even for a time. The possibility of justified stabilities is given up. What is given up with it, Elizabeth Fox-Genovese argues, is the notion of obligations beyond the narrowly immediate and particular.[70] The consequence is a "social vision of pure atomized fragmentation,"[71] the corollary of which is an equally dubious anthropology—an ironic reincarnation of the individualism that postmodernism seeks to overcome. To quote Allon White: "[An espousal of] pure difference which refuses to theorize the unity-in-difference of humanity ends by replicating the individualism of the self-sufficient bourgeois ego—a dangerous fiction if ever there was one."[72]

Whether a social vision that valorizes the endless struggle of difference is a fiction is perhaps not so easy to determine finally, but that it has difficult political implications is at least a plausible contention. The problem is this: In a world where there is only the unending play of difference nothing can rightly be elevated to a place of continuing validity, not even the equal entitlement of the conflicting differentia—their right to be heard, their right to equal participation in the field of discourse, and so forth. Nothing can claim permanent entitlement, nothing superiority, not even justice. The allowable result is what Fox-Genovese calls the "worst forms of political domination,"[73] namely, the rule of power. Krupat writes:

> At least in its extreme version, [this view] tends to see the canon as formed *exclusively* by power relations: the canonical texts are the surviving victors on the battlefield calling for due praise. If they are an obnoxious group, we . . . must . . . beat them. But this is to adopt a Thrasymachean per-

spective, the world view of primitive capitalism, a crude form of social Darwinism, or indeed an equally crude version of Marxist class struggle. It is to adopt Foucault's bleak vision (somewhat modified in the last work) of discourse as power and power as everywhere, so that even to fight and win is only to become oppressor in one's turn—to force people to read *our* books now, not theirs. . . . And this sort of Hobbesian war of all against all forever is very far from what most . . . pragmatists desire.[74]

In the end, then, the Derridaean stance implies that of Foucault. The Thrasymacheanism they entail is pragmatically unwarranted, if, at least, the values in terms of which it is to be judged are egalitarian ones.[75] Finally, however, it is also unwarranted empirically. The claim that canon is used to legitimate the prevailing social order is (or may be[76]) true enough, so far as it goes, but it overlooks the fact that canon also can be, and often is, the tool for subverting regnant dominations.[77] What a canon gives it usually can take away, for canons, voluminous contemporary studies now agree, are inherently polyphonic and plurivocal. Although, for the reasons we have examined, a canon might not best be described as an *infinitude* of meanings, an *endless* play of difference, its meanings are too multiple and too fluid to furnish univocal legitimations of any one order or ideology.

Perhaps the most available illustration of the ideological diversity of canon is the Christian Bible, a canon proclaimed by its caretakers throughout the centuries to be essentially singular in doctrine, ethic, and historical fact. One might think that the multitude of Christian churches, denominations, sects and, especially, ideologies would be evidence enough of the irreducible multiplicity of voices and visions within its canon.[78] This evidence has been suppressed, however, by an overriding theological commitment to canonical unity in league with the sword of "heresy" on which all Christian "otherness" has been

impaled. But contemporary studies of the Christian canon will
not so easily be dismissed. Studies of Christian parables during
the past two decades have shown them overall to be agents of
differentiation, less designed to teach a single point about this or
that issue than to validate many sometimes incompatible points
or to advocate no point at all—in short, to communicate a sense
of life's plurality and fluidity.[79] Recent studies of the development of traditions in the Christian Old Testament unveil the
dynamism and diversity of the Hebraic heritages of story. What
is told about, learned from, and represented in the traditions of
Moses, the prophets, the exodus, the exile, and so on, is stun-
ningly playful in its variety.[80] As for the overall unity of the
Christian canon (ignoring the diversity of the theologies that
flow from it), Walter Brueggemann demonstrates that the
Hebrew Bible contains two opposing ideological trajectories, a
Mosaic heritage that is revolutionary in its thrust, and a Davidic
heritage that supports consolidation, and that these same alternatives reappear in the New Testament.[81] Elisabeth Schussler
Fiorenza, Dennis MacDonald, and others establish the sharply
divided mind within the New Testament about the status and
role of women.[82] Several scholarly studies describe the frankly
antithetical world-views of the gospels.[83] Others demonstrate
the various ways these diverse scriptures, taken as canon, can be
used.[84] The evidence goes on and on. So conclusive is it, indeed,
that even conservative Christian scholars are now compelled to
speak of the "polyphony of Scripture."[85]

One is tempted to say simply that this diversity should be
expected in view of the many periods, peoples, experiences—
and stories emanating from each—included in the Christian
canon. That observation is well-taken, but probably there is
more. It has to do with the nature of stories. The diversity of
Christian canon, or of any canon in which story predominates,
may have as much to do with the character of stories as the
diversity within the materials the stories are about. It is easy to
see how in telling and retelling stories people can again and

again renegotiate their identity through the pluralities of rush-
ing time. But, as Dennis Tedlock has argued with respect to the
Zuni and Arnold Krupat with respect to Pueblo cultures generally, storytelling is itself often polyphonic. Not simply are there
different stories representing different characters or values; the
same story is often constructed so as to place and maintain a
number of viewpoints in tension, with the teller's voice being
only one among many.[86] Tedlock shows that Zuni stories are
"fashioned in such a way as to include in their telling not just
the story itself but a critique or commentary on those stories."[87]
Given the dominance of stories in most if not all traditions, and
the fact that the written stories of traditions arose in oral recita-
tion, it seems likely that story, when the central agent of a tradition's memory, is itself an agent of canonical pluralization. If the
multiplicity of the material compressed into canon predeter-
mines its diversity, the story form in which that material is often
cast is that diversity's double guarantee.

A canon is a contest of varied visions and voices. Its diversity
may not be infinite, but it is expansive and substantial. The
canonical treatment of its internal diversity, moreover, is a negotiated or playful one. Thus, like the cultures it inhabits, and the
stories and theories that form it, a canon is a "debating ground,
. . . a fertile . . . jungle of sources" rather than a "monolith."[88] It
is therefore implausible to argue that a particular canon as such,
or canons in general, function in any straightforward or distinctive way to legitimate particular world-views. The argument
that the concept of canon should be dismissed because canons
are inherently oppressive therefore fails.

But what is the argument for canon? That depends on what
we take canons to be and to do. To that discussion, and the concept of tradition that develops from it, we now turn.

⪻ 4 ⪼

CANON, CHAOS AND ORDER

A THEORY OF TRADITION

The discussion that concluded the preceding chapter opposed two exclusionary positions regarding canon. In one view, canon has so little unity as to be illusory; in the other, canon has so much unity as to be oppressive. The first pushes canon over the precipice of infinitude, leaving it entirely to its varying interpreters to pick up the pieces and assemble them as they choose. The second presses canon into a rock-hard oneness—making it, at best, an inflexible deposit impervious to interpretive variation and, at worst, a rolling stone that crushes human creativity beneath its irresistible advance. These arguments against canon fail. But, as was noted at the end of the preceding chapter, we still are left with the question: What is the argument *for* canon? What is canon's importance? That depends on how we understand the nature and function of canon.

WHAT CANONS ARE AND DO

To theorize canon between the extremes we have found wanting it may be useful to propose at the outset a crude analogy. The proposal is to think of canon as a kind of galaxy, in this case

a "galaxy" of meanings.[1] Viewed in lay terms, galaxies stand
somewhere between planets and constellations. Planets are precisely circumscribed heavenly bodies with fixed movements.
They are something close to the epitome of blunt givenness.
Constellations, by contrast, are clusters of stars arbitrarily delineated by human observers and named, usually, for familiar
objects or mythological figures. Constellations are human
inventions; they exist in the eyes of beholders.

In terms of organization, as I have said, a galaxy falls somewhere between a planet and a constellation. A galaxy, like a
constellation, is a group of heavenly bodies. But it is less arbitrary than a constellation. It is massively there, a given, reasonably unitary and rather easily distinguishable from other objects
in the night sky. Functionally, it exerts its own gravitational pull,
a kind of inner drive that affects external bodies and also contributes to its own development. But the unity of a galaxy is
more arbitrary, more interpretive, than a planet. A galaxy is
rough and fluid in its unity; it lacks the brute givenness, the self-
based definition, of a planet. In fact, the more closely it is examined, the more obvious its ragged edges, its internal swirl, and
the multiple ways it could be construed from differing places in
space and time within the galaxy and beyond it.

Canons, I suggest, should be thought of as galaxies. Just as a
galaxy is composed of a vast and varying multiplicity of elements, a canon is dynamic, richly plural, and pluriform. As a
galaxy is nevertheless something of a unity, so a canon has
enough unity and structure to be one thing rather than another.
At any given time, and from any given perspective, canon has a
coarse and practical unity, though that unity is always differently
construed from different perspectives.

Like a galaxy, a canon's rough unity translates at the broadest
level of analysis into an identifiable "gravitational pull."[2] Like
that of a galaxy, the gravitational force of a canon, though real, is
interactive. What a canon means, its "pull," is a product of its
own internal structure—that vast and ever-changing complex

of possible meanings—only as this structure relates to and is construed in the always plural history of its interpretive relations.

To think of canon as a galaxy of meanings—as something between the greater givenness of the planet and the greater arbitrariness of the constellation—enables us to clarify certain features of canon.

The first is its boundedness. Tradition is cultural negotiation   1.
circumscribed by a canon, a more or less explicit field of play formed in history. The field, the canon, may be defined as a list of documents, a set of stories, a complex of myths, a body of doctrine or concepts, a cluster of symbols, a group of rituals, a pattern of cultivated sensibilities, and so forth, or combinations of these. (Obviously, whatever element or elements define the canonical field, all of these are usually aspects of life within canon.) But in some way a limitation is set. The limitation, as we shall see, does not establish the unity of canon. Limitation, instead, establishes identity. The boundedness of canon creates the tentative and proximate identity of a negotiating process, the   —
identity of a tradition. To negotiate or play within, and with, these boundaries is what it means to be a participant in the tradition.

Canonical boundaries are probably the cultural correlate of the material marks of identity that attach to smaller human units, allowing us to say what it means to be a member of a particular nation, family, club, political movement, and so on. If so, the function of canonical boundaries for the individual is primarily ritualistic, not immediately practical—although, as we shall contend later, ritual does have an indispensable, though indirect, personal utility. But the drawing of boundaries may in fact have direct social utility. Jonathan Smith has suggested that in the life of traditions, limitation begets ingenuity.[3] If so, the   —
genius of canon may be precisely in the fact that it imposes a material integration upon what is incorrigibly diverse. The friction of that imposition transmutes diversity into dynamic con-

flict—forced together, dry sticks make fire. The audacity of that imposition invites a similar boldness: the transformation of canonical multiplicity into a particular construal adequate to the needs of a particular time. But the patent selectivity of that imposition assures that no one construal of canon can long endure, for just as any circumscription that creates canon is partially arbitrary, so every circumscription that construes canon in this way or that is patently partial.

Whatever the social function of boundaries, however, the history of canons demonstrates that their boundaries are not only what we negotiate within, but also what we sometimes negotiate with and about. When an argument breaks down, the premises originally shared may themselves have become the point of contention. In such circumstances it is time to go back to basics, to what counts as good evidence and good argument. So, too, with canon. [We negotiate within canon, but when canon seems inadequate we negotiate with canon.⁴] It could hardly be otherwise; canons invite this kind of challenge. The fallibility of the parts of canon—the fact that each distinct construal of canon could, at most, be adequate only for a while— inevitably allows questions about the adequacy of the whole. Thus when a canon seems to falter, it is rightly put to the test. It is successfully defended, or it is abandoned, or it is renegotiated, thereby creating a somewhat different field of play.⁵

2. The second feature of canon is what Charles Altieri calls its [curatorial character.] A canon is a unity and a diversity in interdependence, for every canon is *a* preservation, *a* collection . . . of "rich, complex contrastive frameworks" of meaning.⁶ The unity of canon, therefore, is that of a multilith, not a monolith. Its possible meanings are multiple and conflictual. So, too, are the canonically grounded or canonically consistent ways of appropriating those meanings.⁷ Not only is there multiplicity and conflict in the content of canon, but the form of canon—particularly if we consider the self-critical character of story—tends constantly to question assumptions, unsettle conventions, create

oppositions, and pluralize meanings. Canon is irreducibly diverse.[8]

But canon is also unity, nonetheless. However ragged its edges, fluid its internal movement, and multiple its ways of being interpreted, canon is always some particular collection forged amid diversity for some practical purpose and fraught with some historical consequence.[9] Canon is not simply a collection; it is a force. It is not the same force throughout its history (i.e., canon has no abiding essence) and its many successive expressions are not homogeneous (i.e., canon is never univocal). Yet, though ragged and fractious, canon in each historical circumstance is a force that in varying degrees resists some interpretations and supports others, inhibits some ideals and promotes others, counts for some tendencies and opposes others.

This objective unity has a subjective correlate. The fact that a canon is experienced as some kind of distinctive pull contrasts so sharply with the observable diversity within canon as virtually to demand that those who experience a canon's directionality either dismiss it as a chimera or try to make some particular sense of it, i.e., to construe it somehow as one.[10] What is experienced as a *unified* diversity requires a comparable construal, that is, as a diversity unified in this way or that. Canon's unity, then, is also the unitary interpretations that it provokes, as tentative and partial as these construals must be.

3.
The third feature of canon is its normative character. To speak of the normativeness of canon is to speak of canon's gravitational pull.[11] Canons are claims. This is the case, first, because canons project ideals[12] and, second, because these multiple ideals, so presented, are thought to have demonstrated their worth as an evolving community of guides, interlocutors, and adversaries. Canons are agents, alleging their adequacy, indeed their indispensability, for accomplishing something essential to human well-being.

The normative claim of a canon as such, however, must be distinguished from the manifold claims implicit in its many component parts and thus, also, from the assertions adherents may make about various of these particular meanings. To assert the normativeness of a canon is not to make a claim about any particular construal of it. Given the diversity of canon, this must be the case. A canon is not an answer, a point of view, a truth, a way of life. It is many answers, points of view, claims to truth, ways of life. The normativeness of a canon, therefore, can apply to this diversity only taken as a whole.[13] The claim can be only that in this field of many voices viable answers may continuously be found and made. To assert the normativeness of a canon is to make a claim for the adequacy of these voices in their interplay. Thus if, as we have seen, the form of canon is multilithic, not monolithic, the normativeness of canon is heterodox, not orthodox.[14] The normative character of a canon is the depth of its fecundity.

The fourth feature of canon is its contestable character. Canon is a field of negotiation or play.[15] This is so both because of the diversity of canon and its environmental histories. The diversity of canon demands an interpretation, as we have emphasized, including an interpretation of interpretative propriety—negotiation, in other words, as to what kind of negotiation within canon is itself canonical. But every construal of canon, whether of its meaning or its mode of appropriating that meaning, is necessarily partial and to that extent arbitrary in relation to the whole of canon's diversity.[16] Every decision about canon, then, is a violation of canon's richness and thus an incipient challenge that some of this richness be recovered. For if a canon in its broadest reaches has a changing but real gravitational pull, so do its varied components. They, too, have agency, purposive voices. Hence every establishment is at the same time an invitation to disestablishment; the affirmation of one set of canonical voices, of whatever sort on whatever issue, harbors the echoes of other, relatively neglected, voices making their claims.

If the structure of canon requires contest, so does its procession through history. The value of each construal of canon is, at best, temporary. What saves one age, unchanged, betrays the next; the solution for one setting is later a threat. At worst, a construal of canon that benefits some simultaneously disadvantages, even destroys, others. Endurance unchallenged is a danger. Therefore the value of a canon is not the permanence of its solutions but the "size" of its resources. Size means the multiplicity of visions it harbors, but it also means the fluidity with which it adapts meaningfully to changing circumstance.[17] The possibilities within a vital canon are presented, elicited, and provoked in its intercourse with historical circumstance. The parties to this historical contest are the historical subjects who dwell within a canon, vying for its resources and claiming its sanction—but not they alone. The canon that is the field of contest is also a participant in the contest, for, as we have seen, canonical voices speak. The adaptability of canon does not mean canon's feeble submission to those who inhabit it.[18]

The fifth feature of canon is its contemporaneity. Canons present the diverse resources with which people live their lives. They employ these resources, elevating some to preeminence, subordinating others, dismissing others, and remaining oblivious to most. They presume the adequacy of this broad resource, and in this sense privilege it, not because it has come down from the past, but because through the ages it has seemed to prove its wisdom and, especially, its generativity.[19] However, it is repeatedly necessary to test canonical resources, sometimes as a whole, to be sure, but also and more frequently as they are construed in particular ways.

The necessity of evaluation most often becomes apparent because the canonical resources begin to appear inadequate to the adherent or because they are severely challenged from other perspectives. In fact, however, the need for evaluation always exists and is always urgent. Canons, we have seen, allow for change—monumental change—as well as for continuity. But

neither should be romanticized. Nothing guarantees that continuity is better than change or that change is better than continuity, whatever the criteria of evaluation! And because some
measure of continuity and change is inescapable, it is perhaps
more pertinent to note that the combinations of continuity and
change actually made are by no means necessarily better than
those that might have been made. Canon is threat as well as
hope, the possibility of destruction as well as healing. Living
with canon is risk.

Thus those who inhabit a canon are inevitably driven to evaluate and justify their particular construals in relation to other
visions, both inside and outside their canonical home. Canon
cannot provide the measure in terms of which adherents justify
their commitments or choices from within the diversity of a
canon, however, because it is the canon that presents the diversity. The evaluation of canonical commitments as ways of life,
thus, must in the nature of the case take place outside the canon,
in the arenas of contemporary discourse. Of course, canonical
voices, too, are to be full participants in this evaluative discourse.
They are as entitled as any other to make their cases and proffer
their challenges to rival visions. But here, in the evaluation of
what is adequate and inadequate, true and false, redemptive and
destructive, canon has no privilege. Canon is a contemporary,
one alternative among others, one inquirer among others, in
the tasks of assessment and validation.

The sixth feature of canon is its existential character. Canons
are negotiating spaces or fields of play within which, and in relation to which, personal and corporate identity is both given and
won.[20] In conversing within and with canons, people work out
who they are. To quote Altieri:

> As . . . Pound and Eliot insisted, a vital canon provides the
> richest imperatives to make ourselves new: in the works it
> preserves, we find alternatives to what the dominant cul-
> ture imposes on us: and in the modes of questioning and

comparing that we develop for adapting canon, we find ways of organizing psychic energies capable of engaging and even extending our own age's most radical thinking.[21]

But to speak of canon in this sense—not only in terms of its *character* as bounded, curatorial, normative, contestable, and contemporary, but also in terms of its *function* as the locus of human identity making—is to turn to the topic of tradition proper. For tradition, we are proposing, may be viewed as one type of cultural process, namely, as the negotiation of identity that takes place within, and with, a canon.

TRADITION: NEGOTIATING IDENTITY WITH/IN CANON

Human historicity assures that inheritance is inevitable, and human finitude assures that inheritance is selective. Neither, however, guarantees that inheritance is effective. To be effective, inherited social forms must be, as Raymond Williams says, "lived, actively, in real relationships."[22] This means that selective inheritance, if effective, must somehow be the stuff of personal and, because humans are social, collective identity. History is efficacious when it is one's own, when there is "self-identification" with it.[23] If, as in this discussion, the selective inheritance in question is canon, then to be effective a canon must be the material of collective and personal identity. Canon must be existential.

In considering the connection between canon, or any social form, and human identity, we ought at the outset to acknowledge its enormous danger. Significantly, Williams's apparently innocent term *self-identification*, mentioned previously, was taken from the following statement: "The true condition of hegemony is effective self-identification with the hegemonic forms."[24] Williams's statement reflects the fact that the existential power of canonical forms is closely related to their potential

for oppression. But the nuance ("*true* condition") and circular-
ity ("*hegemony* is . . . identification with the *hegemonic*") in
Williams's statement suggests that what is destructive, that is,
hegemonic, about a social order is not its pervasiveness or
power. What is destructive is the disappearance of the fissures
within the social order and the loss of the gap between that
order and the self that inhabits it. In fact every order, canonical
or otherwise, is, as Williams says, "full of contradictions and . . .
unresolved conflicts."[25] For that reason no self can correctly
identify itself with or be identified with an encompassing social
order. A canon, thus, can become hegemonic only by way of
two illusions. One illusion collapses the diversity of canon into a
monolith; the other dissolves the distance between the canon
and the self. The canon's pretended unity becomes the self's
pretended identity. Thus distorted, canon closes off the existential quest.

Properly understood, however, canon is space for the existential quest. Indeed, properly understood a canon is necessarily
antihegemonic, for insofar as and in the sense that the space of a
canon is itself normative, so, too, the diversity within that space
is privileged. In this sense canon guarantees the right (though
not the truth) of all that falls within it to speak and be heard. In
short, canon secures alternative voices; it resists hegemony. It
provides a diverse and dynamic space within which, through
which, and sometimes against which, the identity of the self is
both given and made.

But how? How does canon become existential? How is
identity negotiated with/in canon?

Alasdair MacIntyre has recently argued that humans are
essentially storytelling animals.[26]

I can only answer the question "What am I to do?" if I can
answer the prior question "Of what story or stories do I
find myself a part?" We enter human society, that is, with
one or more imputed characters—roles into which we

have been drafted—and we have to learn what they are in order to be able to understand how others respond to us and how our responses to them are apt to be construed. It is through hearing stories . . . that children learn or mis-learn . . . what the cast of characters may be in the drama into which they have been born and what the ways of the world are. Deprive children of stories and you leave them unscripted. . . . Hence there is no way to give us an under-standing of any society, including our own, except through the stock of stories which constitute its initial dramatic resources. Mythology, in its original sense, is at the heart of things.[27]

MacIntyre's discussion applies as well to the question "Who am I?" as it does to his query as an ethicist, "What am I to do?" And his analysis is largely correct when it suggests that we come to know who we are as we place ourselves in a narrative; that is, as we tell a story within which we are placed. That is how we "live" our selective inheritance, how we inhabit canon "actively, in real relationships."[28] Canon becomes existential as we learn to tell of ourselves in its terms.

But MacIntyre's account of self-identification is, or can be, misleading. No viable context for self-identification is likely to be *a* narrative, not only in the obvious sense that every tradition is a multiplicity of narratives, but also in the sense that virtually every canon, and thus every tradition, is story, counterstory, and nonstory. A canonical framework is better described as space than story. To be sure, a canon requires integration, however tentative and partial, in order to be inhabited, and perhaps more often than not that integration is achieved through a narratival rendering of it. But narrative is not usually the whole of the canon; the line of story is not the space of identity. In addition, the concept of narrative, unless carefully elucidated, can prompt an exaggeration of canonical order. It can conjure up the idea of a single story under which all diversity is subsumed and all contingency is overwhelmed by a conclusion already determined.[29] Traditions are not that neat; neither are the processes of collective and personal identity making—nor should they be.

A tradition is a space—many feelings, many rituals, many images, many stories, many concepts, many casuistries, in concert and conflict. To say who one is in the terms of a tradition is to "take on" its manifold stories, to be sure, but also its feelings, rituals, images, arguments, and so forth, as one's own. It is to place oneself—or, often more likely, to be placed—within its dynamic, plural, and pluriform swirl. The inhabitants of a tradition enter its stories, enact its rituals, play its roles, explore its visions, try its arguments, feel its sensibilities. There they continuously ask who and where they are, negotiating the identity of this space in relation to themselves, and themselves in relation to the space. For the inhabitants of the tradition, only one thing is absolutely constant: They are the ones who negotiate there. Tradition is the space in which they stand, or better, work—work out their own identity.

To say that one "takes on" the resources of a tradition is ambiguous and properly so, for the range of assuming these resources is broad and dynamic. At one end of this range the inhabitant is a recipient, experiencing the tradition's resources as a gift. At the other end the inhabitant is a challenger, experiencing these resources as adversary. Each posture, however, is an abstraction. There is no pure receptivity because every inheritance within canon is perspectival, every experience of canon is a particular construal of it. Nor is there pure challenge because each confrontation with a tradition requires some acceptance of its terms in order to communicate the challenge at all.[30] The only pure departure from a tradition, the only complete rejection of its canon, is indifference to it. Thus to indwell a tradition is always to relate to it in some degree both as gift and as task. Its canon is received and cherished, and challenged and changed.

There is probably no one prescription for the effective combination of continuity and change. The provocation for change seems most frequently to come from outside a tradition,[31] whereas the material for change is most likely to be drawn from a tradition's past.[32] In effective change, explicit syncretism seems rare. More commonly a challenge, external or internal, prompts the reformulation of a central indigenous element or the recovery and elevation of an element of the tradition previously neglected or subordinated. Old stories, beliefs, practices, sensibilities, or combinations of these, are rearranged or recontextualized.[33] The change thus accomplished is then represented as the rediscovery of something ancient, as, in a sense, it is. Because of this a tradition will always appear to be fundamentally conservative. That is misleading, for two reasons. First, it is the tradition itself that opens itself to provocation; indeed, there could be no acceptance of an external reality as a provocation if there were no internal sense of actual or potential inadequacy. Second, inherited elements, once reformulated and reconfigured, introduce novelty. Old symbols, newly related, always mean something somewhat new.[34] Moreover, as Caroline Walker Bynum concludes, these "traditional symbols can have revolutionary consequences. . . . Symbols can invert as well as reinforce social values. . . . Old symbols can acquire new meanings, and these new meanings might suggest a new society."[35] The dominance of conservatism in tradition is more appearance than reality. In fact tradition is both conservation and liberation.

That is why tradition must be understood as the negotiation of chaos *and* order, order *and* chaos. The dynamic of tradition requires both. Either alone is impossible, and either in excess is dangerous. Order alone threatens the creativity that transforms old values and engenders new ones. Chaos alone threatens the continuity that transmits values, ancient or recent, as resources for the next circumstance. Together, each is vital—chaos enriches and order preserves. Hence, to take on the resources of a tradition should not be viewed simply or even primarily as the task of creating order from canonical diversity, though it is partly that. The task is no less to rescue tradition from stifling uniformity by "trying to knock the conventional off balance."[36] To take on the resources of a tradition is to play within and contribute to its perpetual doing and undoing—to receive and give, honor and challenge, accept and create, continue and change.

This includes, as has been said repeatedly, a willingness to challenge the canon itself. The creation of every canon, after all, is the payment of a price. Whatever may and must be said about its rich diversity and perpetual contestability, a canon is always a "selective memory"[37] and selection is always sacrifice. A canon is this or that, something concrete and valuable, but it is also something not chosen and thus something lost. True, the alternative to a selective memory and the sacrifice it entails is doubtlessly illusion, either the illusion of a universal memory or the illusion of none.[38] Thus, whether or not to remember selectively is no real choice. But there is a decision to be made within the space of a tradition and that choice is whether to attempt to be self-conscious of, and self-critical about, the selectivity of its canon. The responsible habitation of a canon, it seems clear, cannot be viewed solely as the making of corporate and personal identity. It must also address the integrity of the space wherein identity making takes place. This means that the critical pursuit of corporate and personal identity with/in canon requires a willingness to ask about the canon's identity. That is why canon must be negotiated *with* as well as within. In this negotiation, as we noted earlier, canon becomes a contemporary—(one alternative among others) one inquirer among others, one advocate among others, in the continuing, public task of assessment and validation.

That tradition is an advocate, as well as a gift and task, should be clear from the preceding discussion. Like that of a cultural scheme, the efficacy of a tradition's canon does not simply dissolve before the succession of worldly circumstance.[39] Like those of a text, the meanings of a canon do not reduce to the multiple interpretations it is given.[40] Like a galaxy, a canon, and thus a tradition, exerts gravitational pull.[41] In this discussion that "pull" has been conceived as a dynamic set of complex, interrelated possibilities whose options are elicited and provoked in the varied advance of history. The crucial point, however, is that traditions, like canons, are powers. We must note once again the oppressive and destructive as well as the liberating and redemptive potential of such power. Neither should be obscured by concentration on the other. But neither—a tradition's potential for good and evil—will be fully attended to except in light of a still more basic reality: like a game, the traditioned life is playing *and* being played.[42]

In the previous section several characteristics of canon were noted—canon as bounded, curatorial, normative, contestable, and contemporary. The nature of tradition may be seen to parallel these. The creativity of a tradition is the tensive character of the life lived within, and sometimes against, its boundaries. The viability of a tradition is the vastness of its collected resources, unified enough to sustain needed continuity and diverse enough to create something new for new times. The power of a tradition is the worth of its space, the productivity of its complementary and competing voices, as it progresses through the novelties of history. The dynamism of a tradition is its contestability and therefore its perpetual contest. The relevance of a tradition is its contemporaneity, what it brings to and receives from the discourse of truth in every age. But the life of a tradition, its vitality as a real way of being in the world, is the assumption of its resources as one's own. Tradition is canon lived—the negotiation of corporate and personal identities with/in canonical space.

The constructive argument of this and the previous chapter is, in sum, as follows. Cultures may be interpreted as comprehensive symbol systems in terms of which human actions, in the broadest sense, gain their meanings, but the "terms" of this interaction between interpretive frameworks and action are tenuous. Cultural processes, far from being integrated and naturally developing wholes, are processes of bartering and bargaining, sustaining and creating, establishing and subverting. Put succinctly, cultures are negotiations. In these negotiations, moreover, continuity and change are inescapably present and interrelated. Finally, what is negotiated in a cultural process is corporate and individual identity.

Traditions, in the strict sense used here, are processes of cultural negotiation that take place in relationship to canons. Canons are reasonably defined "spaces," bodies of material—texts, doctrines, symbols, rituals, and so on, or combinations of these—within which and with which the negotiation is conducted. Canons are bounded, curatorial, normative, contestable, and subject to examination in contemporary arenas of discourse and adjudication. Canons are also existential; they are the spaces with/in which adherents continuously and repeatedly negotiate who they are. Thus, tradition, as understood here, is canon made existential, canon lived. Negotiating identity in relationship to a canon is a process of employing the materials of canon—which necessarily means construing the canon in this way or that—as a framework in terms of which one understands oneself, one's social and natural world, and one's place in it. But canonical negotiation can also be a process of advocating the revision of canon in the name of expanding or diminishing its potentialities. (The two processes are intertwined inasmuch as the question of what is possible within canon is also necessarily involved with the question about the domain of the canon itself, and vice versa.) If, however, the progressive determination of who one is takes place with/in the selective and thus privileged space of canon, the adequacy of the identities a canon creates and sustains is tested in the unprotected space of contemporary public discourse. There a canon's particular alternatives, and by implication the canon as a whole, is exposed to evaluation. If cultures are porous, so are traditions. Hence, the negotiation of identity within canon and with canon also inescapably involves negotiation beyond canon.

Discussions of what we have called canonical negotiation will rather naturally be conducted with special attention to the role of the cognitive, the intellectual, in the development of traditions. Even studies that focus on story, myth, symbol, and ritual are usually governed by the assumption that what "counts" is the cognitive meaning of these elements of tradition. This intellectualist bias then drives the analysis still further toward the supposition that what really matters about a tradition is its beliefs, perhaps as they are dispersed throughout and expressed in partially hidden, disguised, or undeveloped forms. The outcome of this analytical drift is that the more affective elements of tradition—what they are and what they do—are reduced to what they can become as exemplars or vehicles of belief. The affective is marginalized in the analysis of tradition's functioning; beliefs, doctrines triumph.

One of the most obvious implications of our discussion of tradition to this point, however, is that in actual traditions the affective is not marginalized and the cognitive is not triumphant (except, perhaps, in the imagination of its specialized practitioners who in some traditions are called *theologians*). If the cognitive plays an important role in traditioned life, as it does and should, its role is by no means of sole importance. Traditions "behave," in fact, as if their more affective dimensions are also crucial, even to their intellectual undertakings to say nothing of their functioning as a whole. Why might this be so? How might the affective contribute to negotiation with/in canon? In view of the continuing dominance of what I have called the intellectualist bias, addressing these questions is of particular importance today for an understanding of tradition.

Ritual, perhaps the most obviously affective dimension of traditions, will be the primary datum in terms of which we seek to understand the place of affectivity in the dynamic of tradition. Why is ritual important? How does it contribute to canonical negotiation? What does it do? How does it accomplish what it does? And why is what ritual accomplishes not pursued instead in a more fully cognitive fashion? In short, how and why does ritual—and, mutatis mutandis, other affective elements of tradition—contribute to the life of a tradition?

IN DEFENSE OF RITUAL

In "The Bare Facts of Ritual," Jonathan Z. Smith examines "bear-hunting rituals as reported especially from paleo-Siberian peoples."[43] Smith details four stages of the hunt ritual, three of which occur within the human-social sphere: the preparation for the hunt, the departure from camp, and the return to camp. The other stage, third in the sequence, is the kill, which provides the principal material for Smith's analysis.

> The third moment in the hunt [is] governed by strict rules of etiquette. Most of the regulations seem designed to insure that the animal is killed in hand-to-hand, face-to-face combat. For example, in some groups, the animal may be killed only while . . . standing on its hind legs facing the hunter. . . . In addition, it may only be wounded in certain spots . . . and the wound is to be bloodless. The controlling idea is that the . . . animal freely offers itself. . . . Therefore, the animal is talked to before the kill.[44]

Sometimes, Smith says, the bear is addressed in "dithyrambic praise poems" and entreated: "You have to come to me, Lord Bear, you wish me to kill you. . . . Come here, come. Your death is at hand, but I will not chase after you."[45]

Smith's analysis of ritual is grounded in the rather safe observation that, in fact, hunts are not conducted as reported. "Can we believe that a group which depends on hunting for its food would kill an animal only if it is in a certain posture? [Or] that any animal, once spotted, would stand still while hunters recited

dithyrambs and ceremonial addresses [or,] according to one
report, love songs! Can we believe that, even if they wanted to,
they could kill an animal bloodlessly . . .?"[46] Smith concludes:
"The hunter does not hunt as he says he hunts, he does not
think about his hunting as he says he thinks; but . . . we must
presume that he is aware of this discrepancy, that he works with
it, that he has some means of overcoming this contradiction
between 'word and deed.' This, I believe, is one major function
of ritual."[47]

In "Bare Facts of Ritual" Smith says that ritual *resolves* or *over-
comes* the gap or incongruity between the ideal and the actual,[48]
and in *To Take Place*, a more recent work, Smith discusses without dissent (on this point) views that emphasize the stabilizing
function of ritual.[49] In both discussions he acknowledges ritual's
conserving function, its capacity to reduce possibility to, and
validate, some actual state of affairs. Yet also in *To Take Place*
Smith writes that "ritual precises ambiguities; it neither over-
comes nor relaxes them,"[50] and in *Map Is Not Territory* Smith
associates ritual with traditions of mapping the world that "neither deny nor flee from disjunction, but allow the incongruous
elements to stand. They suggest that symbolism, myth, [and]
ritual . . . are all incapable of overcoming disjunction. They
seek, rather, to play between the incongruities."[51]

The contrasting ways Smith speaks of ritual properly represent, in my judgment, the contrasting functions of ritual. As
Smith says, at a general level ritual can be understood as "a
means of performing the way things ought to be in conscious
tension to the way things are."[52] Sometimes that performance
accentuates the tension—the discrepancy between the real and
ideal—thus creating a felt contrast and, consequently, a threat to
the status quo or at least a heightened awareness of a novel
prospect. But sometimes ritual tends to resolve the gap, either
by performatively integrating the ideal with the real, or by subordinating that which is possible to the status quo, that is, by
putting possibility "in its place."[53]

It may be more adequate, however, to say that ritual performance is always, in some measure, both conserving and creative.
For just as what Smith terms the *locative*, the *utopian*, and the
unnamed third mapping of the world (referred to previously)
remain "coeval possibilities" never purely instantiated in "any
particular culture at any particular time,"[54] so, too, the ritual
potential corresponding to each such mapping is always present
in every ritual act. Every ritual, that is, every performance of the
contrast between the actual and the ideal, carries within it a
range of potentiality that may be demarcated in a threefold
way—as the power to promote ratification of the given (the
locative map), or to promote flight from the given to the ideal
(the utopian map), or to promote play between them (Smith's
third map). But because, as Smith says, none of these is ever
purely instantiated, it follows that ritual is always to some extent
the third; it is play between the poles of actuality and potentiality in a manner that tends to a greater or lesser degree toward
one end of the continuum or the other.[55]

Smith's work on ritual draws upon, and critically advances, a
body of reflection that began in the nineteenth century, in the
writings of Robertson Smith and J. G. Frazer, with the claim
that ritual is the most basic form of religious expression, from
which myth and other more cognitive phenomena emerge as
efforts to express or interpret ritual action.[56] Ritual, to use language from a contemporary theorist, was thus said to have
"ontological status,"[57] even if as a kind of poor science. Ritual
was also more or less consciously associated with "the primitive" which, under the impact of evolutionary modes of
thought, was more or less demeaned, at least by the mood sur-
rounding the theory if not explicitly by the theory itself.

Less as a rejection of these latter attitudes than as recognition
that the claim ran counter to the evidence,[58] subsequent studies
moved to the question, What do rituals do? Bronislaw
Malinowski and A. R. Radcliffe-Brown held in differing ways
that rituals facilitate and strengthen the stability of society and

life within it—"regulate, maintain, and transmit from one generation to another the sentiments on which the constitution of the society depends."[59] This "structural-functional" view, that ritual is primarily an instrument of order, dominated the discussion until very recently. The view was based on Emile Durkheim's assumption that society is best interpreted as an organism whose "natural" state is one of harmony and equilibrium. Thus, it seemed to follow that the elements of social life serve that end.[60]

When, in the 1960s and 1970s, Clifford Geertz challenged this "somewhat overconservative view of the role of ritual"[61] his complaint, however, was highly nuanced and hardly based on the supposition that ritual itself fosters social change. He argued, instead, that ritual, which is both a cultural form and a pattern of social interaction, fosters ambiguity and conflict whenever its cultural home is discontinuous from its social context. In such circumstances ritual is a vehicle of disorder and dislocation. But the change that occurs is a function of the incongruous location of the ritual, between incompatible cultural and social orders, not of ritual itself.

It remained for Victor Turner to reject outright the conservative view of ritual. Turner defined *ritual* as "prescribed formal behavior for occasions not given over to technological routine, having reference to beliefs in invisible beings or powers regarded as the first and final causes of all effects."[62] Turner undermined the view that ritual, so conceived, is primarily conservative by focusing on what he took to be "the *sine qua non* of ritual: liminality."[63] A liminal state is a transitional position "betwixt and between the positions" established by legal and social convention.[64] "Practically all rituals of any length and complexity," Turner held, "represent a passage from one position, constellation, or domain of structure to another."[65] Since a liminal state is always dialectically related to social structure, it is always "anti-structure" and, as such, always introduces a temporary suspension of structural relations—"communitas"[66]—that is carried back into social life as the impulse to experimentation, alteration, and even radical transformation.

Turner's theory that ritual is liberative, not conservative, has been the basis for numerous fruitful explorations of the transformative function of particular rituals.[67] In this respect, Turner has beneficially transformed attitudes toward ritual. But whether ritual *primarily* promotes change and counters continuity, as Turner suggested (usually, though perhaps not always[68]), is open to question.[69] Of course, Turner's claim cannot be refuted when he simply stipulates that *ritual* means "transformative celebrations" and insists that ratifying celebrations are to be called *ceremonies*.[70] That stipulation, however, is arbitrary. There is nothing in Turner's basic understanding of ritual—"prescribed formal behavior . . . having reference to . . . invisible . . . powers regarded as the first and final causes of all effects"—to indicate that ritual will always primarily transform and never primarily sustain. In fact, the emphasis on change in Turner's analysis hinges not on his understanding of ritual so much as his exclusive association of ritual and liminality. But that association is arbitrary, too.[71] It obscures or seriously misrepresents the function of other kinds of rituals, for example, etiquette—those "greetings and departures, gestures/manners, and 'social forms' [through which] social reality and social relationships are endlessly stated and restated."[72]

Etiquette, simply by virtue of being formalized behavior, stands in tension with the contingency of ordinary interaction. Thus, like liminal phenomena, etiquette conveys an "anti" quality that confronts the ordinary with an aura of "otherness" or altarity. The handshake that begins a meeting proposes an obligation of social relatedness as such (civility, let us say) that is indifferent to the vagaries of any particular meeting with its wide range of possible processes and outcomes—pleasant or unpleasant, harmonious or conflictual. Unlike liminality, however, etiquette is not "anti" its structure; it is part of structure, part of that internal dynamic of a social structure by which it perpetuates itself. On the other hand, the altarity inherent even in etiquette reminds us that perpetuation is never pure, never won without some measure of alteration; confirmation always carries the whiff, at least, of challenge.

Thus Turner's analysis of liminal ritual illuminates our understanding of other forms of ritual, such as etiquette, that remain integral to structures and their continuation. But the illumination carries both ways. The predominately confirming, continuing function of etiquette is never entirely lost in ritual, even in the most liminal of performances. To paraphrase Roy Wagner, the ritual innovator remains committed to the social structures he or she is precipitating and innovating against.[73] As our analysis of Jonathan Smith's work suggested, ritual is never purely locative or purely utopian. Ritual creates, shapes and changes, but it also conserves, enhances and sustains.[74]

Rituals *do* things—that is the judgment of all the theorists of ritual we have examined, whatever their other disagreements.[75] And we have argued specifically that rituals function both to continue and to transform. In this respect, they are like every other element of a tradition—myths, symbols, texts, and so on. But this similarity of function immediately presents us with two questions: Why? And, how? That is, *why* are rituals practiced when other elements of tradition seem to function similarly? Further, *how* do rituals do what they do?[76]

Answers to these questions quite possibly lie in the fact that humans have bodies.[77] The importance of the body is now increasingly acknowledged in (to use obviously overlapping categories) the social sciences and humanities[78] especially by linguists,[79] feminist thinkers,[80] philosophers,[81] and historians of religions.[82] And, in fact, the specific relationship of the body, body symbolism, and ritual has for some time been the subject of ethnographic inquiry.[83]

The aim of the present discussion, however, is to consider and critically extend two different philosophical hypotheses as to the connection between human embodiment and ritual, simply in order to indicate the *kind* of general perspective that would make sense of the fundamental role that ritualized behavior seems to play in the transmission and transformation of traditions. The first view to be examined is that of Maurice Merleau-Ponty, growing out of the European tradition of Heideggerian reflection. The second is that of Alfred North Whitehead, which stands in the American tradition of radical empiricism.

Merleau-Ponty's philosophical work was in part an attempt, initiated in *The Structure of Behavior*,[84] to understand the relationship of the meanings that the world has for human consciousness to the world thus viewed to be meaningful.[85] His strategy, beginning in *The Phenomenology of Perception*,[86] was to develop a "phenomenology of lived existence" that would overcome the opposition, characteristic of traditional metaphysics, between human subjects and their worldly objects.[87] Central to his approach was an analysis of the "body" as a relational mode of being—an analysis in which he sought to avoid the Scylla of empiricism, which reduces the subject to one causally related object among others, and the Charybdis of intellectualism or idealism, which posits the self as an autonomous subject.[88] Merleau-Ponty thus began with a concept of the subject as already embedded in the world of natural and cultural relationships.[89] To be is to be a body[90], and to be a body is to be "intervolved in a definite environment,"[91] to be "tied to a certain world."[92] From this Merleau-Ponty inferred that the gap or "abyss" between the bodied subject and the world is not a barrier to knowledge but is instead a lure to further interaction.[93] The interaction of the body-subject and the world, he also said, is a cobirthing of each.[94] The chief expression of this cocreation is speech, which is neither purely natural, as from the empiricist point of view, nor purely conventional, as from the viewpoint of the intellectualist.[95] Speech is a creation of meaning grounded in, though not reducible to, natural processes.[96] Thus, speech is a manifestation of the intimate link of the self and its world that, "like a wave, gathers and poises itself to hurtle beyond its own limits."[97]

Merleau-Ponty's earlier work, as he later acknowledged, tilted toward what he termed *intellectualism* because it focused on the "intentional threads [inherent in the self] which attach us to the world."[98] Primacy, in other words, was given to the body-subject rather than to the intersection of self and world wherein each comes into being. But in the somewhat fragmentary writings before his death Merleau-Ponty appeared to be relocating the fulcrum of his analysis by way of a phenomenology of vision. In one illustration, seeing the tiles on the bottom of a pool of water, he wrote: "When through the water's thickness I see the tiling at the bottom of a pool, I do not see it *despite* the water and the reflections there; I see it through them and because of them. If there were no distortions, no ripples of sunlight, if it were without this flesh . . . , then I would cease to see it *as* it is."[99] Attention to the medium of the interaction of body-subject and world—in this instance, the water—allowed Merleau-Ponty to attend to the milieu that is prior to both viewer and the viewed.

To understand the significance of Merleau-Ponty's shift we might recall another of his aquatic references, the one mentioned earlier in which he spoke of the force of a wave that "gathers and poises itself to hurtle beyond its own limits." What emerged in his later analysis, then, is a strong sense of the power of the milieu within which both the body-subject and its world are coformed. In his last work, Merleau-Ponty's fundamental image for this formative milieu was "flesh."[100] By this image he indicated a field of forces, "wild, brute Being," that throws forth both self and world—much as the sea, for example, tosses about both the struggling swimmer and the capsized raft with which she grapples, even though each to some degree also forms and forces the movements of the other.

For Merleau-Ponty, therefore, talk of embodiment is a way of examining the concrete relationality of the self and its world within which each coconstitutes itself and the other. But it is more. Especially in his later work, it is a way of talking about the formative character of that concrete matrix within which particular self-world relationships come into being, and the nature of being thus immersed, created, and cocreative within this matrix.

Speech, we have seen, is for Merleau-Ponty the primary form of the self-world cocreation. Speech is rooted in the power of the body (i.e., the body-subject) to create and express meaning. In this regard speech is like all bodily behavior. But Merleau-Ponty claims a distinctiveness for speech that action as such does not enjoy. "While the meaning of a gesture is strictly inseparable from the gesture itself and can only be repeated by a repetition of the gesture, the meaning of a sentence, once expressed, . . . does not need to be said to be thought."[101] Or as Merleau-Ponty says, "alone of all expressive processes, speech is able to settle into a sediment and constitute an acquisition for use in human relationships."[102] This sedimentation is a pattern— "a certain structural co-ordination of experience,[103] a certain modulation of existence," thus making speech alone of the expressive processes capable of indefinite reiteration.[104]

As insightful as it is, Merleau-Ponty's analysis of human expression exhibits a curious neglect of the "sedimented" character of another kind of human behavior, namely ritual action. For like speech, ritual represents "a certain structural co-ordination of experience, a certain modulation of existence." Like speech, the meaning of ritual is in the action, not anterior to it or a pale reflection of it.[105] Like speech (and for the same reasons), ritual is neither purely conventional nor purely natural.[106] Like speech, ritual seems able to catch up and grasp its own meaning, albeit (also like speech[107]) always within a particular interpretive context. Therefore Merleau-Ponty should have concluded that ritual, like speech, can be said "to recapitulate, retrieve, and contain"[108] what is past, and to do so creatively.[109]

So long as Merleau-Ponty continued to think, even if uncomfortably, within what he labeled the intellectualist frame-work, his neglect of the way that ritual seems to serve the "pri-mary [or primordial] process of signification"[110] is understandable. Within this framework, we have noted, the production and transmission of meaning devolves finally to the conceptual intentionality of the body-subject, however relational in charac-ter that self might be by virtue of its bodiedness. Thus it is understandable that he located the generation and perpetuation of meaning in speech. But Merleau-Ponty frequently exceeded this limit even before his later ruminations. It is "behavior [that] creates meanings" Merleau-Ponty recognized, not verbal behavior alone.[111] And in his discussions of myth,[112] appearance and reality,[113] and sensation,[114] Merleau-Ponty grounded mean-ing in what he termed a *preconscious possession of the world*.[115] In fact, the way that language itself expresses meaning, Merleau-Ponty argued, can scarcely be understood without attending to an obscure emotional milieu within which meaning is already expressed:

> If we consider only the conceptual and delimiting mean-ing of words, it is true that the verbal form . . . appears arbitrary. But it would no longer appear so if we took into account the emotional content of the word, what we have called its "gestural" sense. . . . It would then be found that the words, vowels and phonemes are so many ways of "singing" the world, and that their function is to represent things not . . . by reason of an objective resemblance, but because they extract, and literally express, their emotional essence. . . . The meaning of a sentence appears intelligible throughout, detachable from the sentence and finitely self-subsistent in an intelligible world, because we presuppose as given all those exchanges, owed to the history of the language, which contribute to determining its sense. . . .

> But in fact . . . the clearness of language stands out from an
> obscure background . . . in emotional gesticulation.[116]

If it is consistently carried through, Merleau-Ponty's shift
from a phenomenology of perception to a phenomenology of
"flesh" is particularly significant for our consideration of ritual.
It indicates that all structured behavior, not merely speech, is the
mark and carrier of meaning.[117] This is so because "flesh"—that
"wild Being" which like the sea continuously gathers, poises,
and hurtles itself forward—is the affective matrix that continuously tosses human being upward into expression and recedes,
leaving the sedimentation of ethos, language, and ritual. *All
such sedimentations, including ritual, may be regarded as the
"concrete emblems"*[118] *of the milieu in which we dwell.* The
patterns of ritual respond to, reflect, and extend the patterns of
being. Thus from Merleau-Ponty's later perspective one can say
that through its ritual enactments "the body [serves] as the carrier . . . of our tradition, passing on its culture, its history, its
life."[119]

An alternative account of ritual action as a carrier of tradition
is suggested by, though not developed in, the work of Alfred
North Whitehead.[120] Whitehead's process-relational ontology is
similar in certain respects to the ontology of "wild being"
toward which Merleau-Ponty moved in his later years, but
Whitehead's view emerged out of an Anglo-American tradition
of philosophical reflection especially influenced by modern science.[121] Whitehead wrote: "The [modern scientific] point of
view is expressed in terms of energy, activity, and the vibratory
differentiations of space-time. Any local agitation shakes the
whole universe. The distant effects are minute, but they are
there. . . . There is no possibility of detached, self-contained
local existence. The environment enters into the nature of each
thing.[122]

Whitehead found this general orientation germane to an
understanding of human nature, society, religion, and culture

because he took seriously the supposition that the human realm is grounded in nature. The tendency of those who tie human reality closely to the natural order is to reduce the social and personal experience of humans to the quantifiable processes examined in biology and physics. Whitehead held, on the contrary, that the distinctively human features of experience—for example, our political, ethical, religious, and aesthetic sensibilities—belong as much to "the nature of things" as do the phenomena investigated by the quantitative sciences, and that an adequate account of things has no more license to explain away these qualitative aspects of human reality than it has to dismiss the relativity of space–time or the evolution of the species. Nor did he find such reductionism to be required. Human experience and physical phenomena, according to Whitehead, represent something more like two poles of a continuum than wholly distinct realities.

The world as portrayed in Whitehead's technical philosophy is a fantastically complex matrix of events. Its range of complexity is astonishing, from the occasions of "empty" space to the richness of human experience. But the variations are not absolute; indeed, the similarities throughout are striking. The varied realms of what in Newtonian language have been termed *mind* and *matter* are both composed of small atomic unities "webbed" into "societies," with spatial and temporal expanse; and these societies are themselves interrelated. Each atomic unity, or "actual entity" to use Whitehead's technical term, emerges within the processive flow and under its influence. Each is a synthesis, at least marginally creative, of the diverse influences inherited from the past. And each such synthesis projects itself into the subsequent processive flow, into the future as a factor in and influence on all future becomings.

Three features of Whitehead's philosophic vision are especially pertinent to an interpretation of ritual. One is that the past is formed power. Each present moment inherits and thus inhabits energetic forces, structured in particular ways. These forces are specific powers that incline, promote, challenge, provoke, predispose, or lure the present becoming in certain directions rather than others. If, as Merleau-Ponty says, being is wild, that is so because of the sheer power of the forces wherein we dwell, the particularity of these vectors, their diversity, and the constant flux of their dynamic interaction. But if these forces are like many competing currents of winds above and waters below us, still they combine at any one point as a general, effective power over us. Thus, in each circumstance wild being is particular being, making its impress in particular patterns oriented toward particular purposes embodying particular values—with varying degrees of efficacy and duration.

At the level of human being the impress of the past contributes to the rise of particular patterns of feeling, speaking, and bodily action. To the extent that this impress remains more or less constant, the patterns to which it gives rise may become more or less formalized as ethos, language, and ritual. These formalized patterns are indeed the mark—the "sedimentation," to use Merleau-Ponty's term—of the forces wherein we dwell. But they are more. They are also the manifestation of these forces, the mode of their active expression. Their instantiation *is* the presence of these forces in our lives. Thus, like ethos and language, the rituals of the body ex-press the powers wherein we dwell and thereby recite the body's knowledge of things.

A second feature of Whitehead's view particularly relevant to an understanding of ritual is his claim that the present is the creative appropriation of the past, of inherited power. The Whiteheadian cosmos is composed of atomic unities or atoms of energy, existing momentarily, synthesizing the patterns inherited from the past, then giving themselves as potencies for succeeding actual entities. Each occasion is something for itself, so to speak, for it is always this particular synthesis of forces and not some other. Nevertheless, each actual entity is overwhelmingly dominated by repetition. But Whitehead argues that every becoming actual occasion has at least an abstract possibility of novelty and, further, that at increasingly more complex levels of cosmic organization the degree of effective novelty itself increases.

At the human level novelty significantly qualifies inherited patterns of feeling, speaking, and acting. To be sure, even here novelty is secondary; the formalized enactment of inherited powers is still basically the repetition of pattern. The customary emotion, gesture, or phrase plays its customary function, transmitting to the future more or less precisely what has been given by the past.

Sometimes, however, novelty intrudes quite significantly from the background of mere abstraction. The contrast between what is and how "what is" might be different both alters, and intensifies, human experience. Alteration occurs even if the novelty introduced remains unrealized potentiality, for "what is" now continues in the shadow of some genuine alternative. And whether or not significant actual change occurs, the contrast between actuality and potentiality intensifies experience. It does so in part because the pattern inherited is now rendered more complex by the lamination of actuality and possibility, thus evoking greater complexity of feeling. But contrast also intensifies experience because the introduction of possibility is at the same time the introduction of uncertainty, for to some extent possibility is always both the promise of salvation and the threat of destruction. Thus, whether or not significant change results, the intrusion of potentiality is itself creative. It enriches the patterns we inherit and strengthens our experiential ownership of them. Ritual, like ethos and language, is altered and enlivened by novelty. As such, ritual, too, is the adaptation and intensification of the powers wherein we dwell.

The third pertinent point in Whitehead's analysis is his contention that just as the past makes a difference to the presently becoming actual entity, and just as the present entity makes a difference to itself, so also the present makes a difference to the future. If, per Merleau-Ponty, "wild, brute being" makes its mark on us, Whitehead adds that we make our mark on it, for we are a part of its flow. The cosmic process is not predetermined; to some extent it is always open, always contingent. And what becomes in the future is affected, though not determined, by what creatively becomes in the present. Thus Whitehead, far more than Merleau-Ponty, is clear that what "being" brings into being alters future being. The present changes the nature of things. For this reason, patterned actions of the body, like patterned feeling and speaking, do more than "contain, retrieve, and recapitulate" (to use, in reverse, Merleau-Ponty's words) what is past. They do more than vivify. Ritual, like patterned speaking and feeling, is always to some extent a creative act that transforms the powers wherein we dwell.

This Whiteheadian interpretation of ritual's power, of how ritual action serves as a carrier of tradition, must, in conclusion, be augmented by Whitehead's doctrine of radical empiricism. As indicated earlier,[123] radical empiricism is the hypothesis that (1) our primary connectedness with the world is at the level of largely nonconscious feeling; (2) this feeling is always weighted, patterned, or directional, (3) the relationship of the self and the world within this felt milieu is interactive or reciprocal; and (4) within the self the relationship of nonconscious feeling with sensation and reflection is also interactive. The second and third elements of this hypothesis obviously cohere with the first and third points made previously about ritual. The other two claims of radical empiricism, however, require additional discussion.

The first claim asserts the massively *physical* character of our commerce with the world—what Merleau-Ponty calls our *preconscious possession of the world* and what Whitehead develops technically as the doctrine of *perception in the mode of causal efficacy*. It implies that our habitation of religious traditions, too, is largely a nonconscious, bodily habitation. In the actions and feelings of the flesh we primordially live and move and have our being. Ritual is not the only mode of fleshly indwelling, for we feel and act in ways not ritualized. But ritual is basic to our bodily commerce with things. In fact, ritual may be peculiarly apt in that role because ritual is bodily action, and such action seems to be the most inclusive form of the human way of being. Action, in other words, involves feeling, willing, and intellection in a way each does not so fully require the others or action itself. Be that as it may, ritual action can be understood as at least one way we effectively ex-press, alter and enliven, and transmit the dynamic structures of our particular traditions. The patterns of ritual reflect and transform the patterns of being, the "invisible powers" within which we live.[124]

The fourth element of the radical empiricist hypothesis warns against "separatist" analyses of the various forms of human functioning. However we divide up the self in analysis, our distinctions are abstractions. Feeling, willing, thinking, acting, and so forth always intermingle and interact. Thus, in some sense "language" may indeed run "all the way down," as many postmodern thinkers today contend. But not only language, probably all the dimensions of human being, at least in some embryonic form, pervade all the levels of human reality from the most abstract and conceptual to the most concrete and affective. Thus, too, talk about a *"pre*conscious" or *"pre*cognitive" grasp of the powers in which we live should be taken to mean only that such modes of grasping are somehow more fundamental than consciousness or cognition, not that they enjoy chronological priority.

The more important point, however, is that feeling, thinking, acting, and so on interact and enhance one another in varying ways. Analysis, for example, is already implicit in the complex of potentials inherent in religious ritual. Quite naturally, then, ritual can issue into a fully developed analytical dimension of being religious that in turn interacts with and alters other dimensions, including ritual action. Similarly formalized action qualifies religious feeling, on the one hand, and religious believing, on the other. That ritual alters feeling is clear. Indeed, even when an intellectualist bias led to the dismissal of ritual's importance in almost every other respect, ritual's capacity to affect emotion remained undisputed. But it is now becoming equally clear that the affective context, including ritual, profoundly affects the character and conclusions of reflection. The same stories, ideas, doctrines and texts take on quite novel complexions as they are transported from primarily oral to chirographic cultures, and from chirographic to typographic cultures.[125] These changes result in part from the varying ritual circumstance that each such transition entails.

The point of this section is not that ritual is the primary carrier of tradition. Human feeling, action, and speaking are so tightly intertwined that claims to primacy, except perhaps for quite specialized considerations, are unwarranted. Nor does the discussion imply that particular rituals are pervasive or universal in human experience. That, finally, is an empirical question (though it would be an exceedingly difficult one to resolve). If, as Levin believes, the "round-dance" is a universal ritual practice, that might indeed indicate a single, pervasive "geology of being."[126] But it is also conceivable that at least the most prominent features of our habitations are those of regional streams of being, particular legacies of felt inheritance. If so, our rituals, too, would fall into more localized patterns. Finally, the foregoing discussion does not imply that ritual is uniquely the guarantor of a tradition's health. Ritual, like the more explicitly cognitive elements of tradition, is subject to dissipation, and probably for the same reasons. Belief, we have argued, diminishes in effectiveness when its rootage in the past is too shallow or its use of the past is too rigid. So, too, with ritual; formalized action that does not play with/in a canonical space is likely to prove impotent. To summarize, rituals are neither the primary nor the privileged vehicles of tradition, nor are particular ritual practices indisputably universal.

The foregoing does contend, however, that ritual is indispensable to tradition. Ritual action is a way that embodied beings register bodily the patterns of their habitations, alter and enliven these patterns, and thus make a difference to their tradition's future and their own. If tradition is the negotiation of identity with/in the dynamic space of canon, then ritual no less than conceptual analysis is a means of that negotiation. And the heavily noncognitive element in ritual negotiation renders the word *play* a particularly apt characterization of it. In the play of ritual enactment we engage our canonical space: encountering and obscuring, elevating and diminishing, affirming and opposing—in sum, continuing and changing the resources to be found there. Without ritual, traditions perish.

≪ 5 ≫

IMAGINATION AND CHARACTER

TRADITION IN
THEOLOGICAL CONSTRUCTION

In North America, academic and mainline theologies languish at the margins of religious and cultural influence.[1] Their marginality is due in part to the constitutional separation of church and state as well as to the pluralism of the American experiment.[2] The foregoing study, however, suggests an additional reason for the limited impact of theology today, one having to do with the current practice of theology, for there appears to be a stark contrast between the way cultures and traditions are actually affected and influenced and the way "professional" American theologians for the past half century have attempted to speak and make a difference. Cultures move and are moved through the creative reconstruction of their inherited symbols, a reconstruction that takes place within the context of full-orbed communal existence. But since the end of neo-orthodoxy, and perhaps since the end of early twentieth century American liberalism, the dominant theologies in America, as we shall see, have treated our religious and theological pasts with indifference, or without imagination, or as material for reflection that can be utilized in abstraction from the concrete affective/intellectual dynamics of practicing communities. This, I believe, is a fundamental reason for the cultural and religious impotence of theology today.

To clarify so sweeping a judgment, it will be helpful first to rehearse the argument to this point, indicating how it implies the need for what I shall call *constructive historicism* in theology.

IN DEFENSE OF CONSTRUCTIVE HISTORICISM

If the goal of this study has been to make a claim about the character of an effective theology, the locus of the study has been frankly extratheological.[3] The inquiry has focused on data drawn from philosophy, certain of the social sciences, religious studies and the history of religions, on the assumptions that the nature of an effective theology will be significantly clarified by an examination of the functioning of religious traditions more broadly and that the functioning of traditions will be illuminated by the data of these extratheological fields. The outcome of the inquiry has been a theory of tradition, proposed as a means of clarifying the nature of a theology that can hope to make a difference religiously and culturally.

Among the claims that have grounded this discussion are two basically uncontroversial judgments and ten hypotheses.[4] The uncontroversial claims are that religious traditions, at any given time, are continuing in some respects and changing in others. The hypotheses are these:

1. Novelty or change emerges in religious traditions both intentionally and unintentionally.

2. Novelty appears to be largely incremental and variegated.

3. Change is generally provoked by the interaction, usually conflictual, between a religious tradition and its socio-political environment.

4. Lasting change is accomplished primarily by the recovery and reconfiguration of elements internal to the tradition.

5. The efficacy of traditions, whether in continuity or change, ranges throughout the continuum of human functioning and responsiveness, from abstract analysis to the dimensions of action and feeling.

6. The behavior of traditions is pragmatic and has to do with survival, power, and legitimation.

7. The pragmatic behavior of traditions takes the form of creating, sustaining, and re-creating viable communal and individual identities.

8. The vehicle for authoring identity within a tradition, using the term broadly, is frequently a canon, an authoritative locus.[5]

9. The re-creation of identity in a tradition occurs both as a rearrangement within its canon and a rearrangement of its canon.

10. The relationship between a canon, that is, an authoritative locus, and "tradition" as the response to canon is dialectical.

A version of Hans-Georg Gadamer's hermeneutical philosophy both accommodates and complements these hypotheses.[6] Gadamer demonstrates that in the process of tradition the past is more than the ground upon which the future is made—more than the land upon which the new house of the future is to be constructed. The past is the material of the future; the future is made from the past, constituted by what has gone before. And if "play" is taken to be central to a Gadamerian analysis, the making of the future is always a remaking, a reconstruction, of what has been inherited. Repetition is never a privileged goal; indeed, repetition, in any substantive sense, is never possible. The goal is to reorder the elements of the past, sometimes accenting continuity and sometimes difference, and thus to reconstruct the meaning of the past in and for the contemporary situation. Gadamer may be too silent about the destructive potential of inherited tradition and thus the need to critique its possible reconstructions. Moreover, he may be inadequate regarding the power of human play and the function of human feeling in the dynamic of tradition. Even so, Gadamer's insistence on the constitutive character of the past in the present for the effective construction of a viable future is a compelling one. Focusing on and extending Gadamer's own account of play, and making systematically explicit and coherent (by appeal to radical empiricism) Gadamer's own intuitive sense of the importance of feeling, markedly enhance the Gadamerian claim that the past is the material, and not simply the background, of playful construction in the present.

This constitutive understanding of the role of the past, drawn from Gadamer, can be set in the context of an interpretation of culture. A culture is a comprehensive structure of potential meanings in terms of which individual and collective identities are continuously negotiated. Abstractly, a culture may be viewed as a vast complex of alternative possible identities. In the negotiating process these identities are elicited, clarified, evaluated, adapted, and assumed or rejected. The acquisition of any identity is tenuous, for each will at some point, to some degree, be defied by novel circumstance. Hence the cultural process is a risk, a gamble, whose outcomes are never assured and whose achievements are never abiding.

A tradition, as defined here, is one type of cultural process—it is the negotiation of identity that takes place within, and with, a canon.[8] A religious tradition, by extension, is the negotiation of identity that takes place within a religious canon.[9] Canons are complexes of myths, stories, rituals, doctrines, texts, or institutions; and usually they are combinations of these. Canons are inherently polyphonic, too diverse in their meanings and too fluid in their internal relationships to legitimate univocally any one order or ideology. Yet, though without precise definition, they are, rather like galaxies, quite specific enough to exercise power, to exert some broad and general but distinctive "gravitational pull." Six features of canon have been identified:

1. A canon is bounded, a limitation that establishes the identity of a tradition and creates the pressure that helps to foster negotiation—both negotiation within the boundaries and the renegotiation of the boundaries.

2. A canon is curatorial, a collection of multiple, diverse and conflictual meanings.

3. A canon is normative, a collection of diverse meanings alleged as a still unfolding whole to be adequate for the successive needs of those who live within its boundaries.[10]

4. A canon is contestable, a field of negotiation or play. This is so both because of the diversity of its content, which thus requires particular and competitive construals, and the challenges to it that emerge in historical experience. Thus the adequacy of a canon, as such, is the size and adaptability of its resources.

5. A canon is contemporaneous, an agent as well as an object of assessment in the varied arenas of our contemporary evaluative discourse; there to test and be tested, change and be changed, and accepted or rejected.

6. With respect to its function, a canon is existential. A canon is a field in which identity is both given and won, the space of pluriform stories, feelings, rituals, images, arguments, and doctrines with/in which individual and collective identity is constantly being negotiated.

Throughout the discussion, the destructive as well as the constructive potential of canon has been emphasized. The resources of a canon are not inherently good. Particular construals of those resources that save in one age, in another destroy; those that elevate some, oppress others. The existential character of canon intensifies canon's potential for destruction, for the identity that canon gives is necessarily an order of sorts, and an order can always become hegemonic. When the order of identity is granted monolithic finality and when the self is assimilated to it without remainder, the field of play becomes a tomb. Thus if cultural negotiation is a risk, so, too, especially is that form of cultural negotiation that takes place with/in the space of canon, namely, tradition. One reason, then, for seeking to clarify the nature of canon—to disclose its inherent plurivocity, essential dynamism, and inescapable contestability—is to unmask the illusion of canonical finality that seems to seduce most if not all traditions.

Another reason for clarifying the nature of canon and thus tradition, however, is to unmask an alternative illusion, that of canonical dispensability. Canons seem to be inescapable, but we must be careful here. Just as cultures are porous and fluid, so, too, are traditions. Their porous character means that traditions are frequently provoked to change from the outside. Moreover, their structural fluidity, not to say fragility, means that traditions are internally weighted toward change, as is made evident by their histories (in distinction from their rhetoric about their histories). But change, to be lasting and efficacious—for good or ill, we should remember—is effected more through the creative appropriation of canonical resources than through the explicit use of external symbols. The distinction between internal and external can never be drawn absolutely, of course, precisely because the boundaries of traditions are so permeable. But insofar as relative distinctions are possible, the constitutive character of the past for a viable future, disclosed in the analysis of cultures, holds as well for traditions. In this Gadamer and the culture theorists are compelling: Though frequently the provocation for change, and sometimes the material as well, comes from the outside, the material for effective, lasting change will most likely be drawn from a tradition's own inherited resources. The inherited rituals, practices, sensibilities, beliefs, doctrines, texts, argumentations, and so forth are rearranged and recontextualized, and debated and tested, in an effort to provide a more adequate habitation for the present and the anticipated future. The canonical past thus played is the power, the effective force, of a tradition.

Finally, playing the past, and being played by it, is far more than a merely conceptual activity. Inherited texts, beliefs, and doctrines are central to this process, but not exclusively so. The realm of the affective, of which ritual is a conspicuous example, is also fundamental to the negotiation of identity within a tradition. Ritual performance plays between the actual and the possible, with consequences that sometimes favor one and sometimes another. As a whole, however, ritual both creates and conserves, changes and sustains. It does so, we have speculatively suggested, by reflecting, intensifying, and transforming through its own behavioral patterns, the patterns or "sedimentations" of the regions of being in which we dwell. But whatever the explanation of the power of ritual, it seems quite clear that feelings and actions, no less than ideas and analyses, are carriers of tradition and thus are essential to its effective continuation.

The two principle implications of the preceding argument for an understanding of the theological task, to be developed further in the next two sections, can be summarized here. The first implication is this: To make a cultural and religious difference a theology must integrate inheritance and creativity, or, to use the terms of William Carlos Williams, *character* and *imagination*[11] To be sure, theologies that elevate imagination over inheritance, on the one hand, and inheritance over imagination, on the other, may also play useful roles in the process of theological construction. By their respective excesses they may serve as correctives to alternative exaggerations or as reminders of dimensions of the theological task being neglected altogether. Moreover, in their onesidedness they may establish claims and crystalize insights that greater rhetorical balance could not so forcefully achieve. Even so, theologies that fasten on either inheritance or creativity to the virtual exclusion of the other cannot be ends in themselves in the formulation of an effective theology. To make a difference to religious communities or to the culture of which they are a part, the process of theological reflection must culminate in the creative reconstruction of inherited symbols—imagination and character, character and imagination. To insist on inheritance alone is nostalgic anti-quarianism; to insist on creativity alone is faddish modernism. To affirm their combination is to understand that humans are historical.

If *historicism* is the current term for referring to those modes of thought that attempt to clarify the meaning and implications of human historicity, then the view of theology here defended is a historicist one. This particular version of historicism holds that cultures, traditions, and religious traditions move effectively by reconstructing their pasts, and theologies will contribute effectively to this process only through a similar reconstruction of inheritance. This view should be distinguished from traditionalist historicisms that give the past a normative role and urge conformity to it, from essentialist (Hegelian) historicisms that posit a fixed dialectical development from the origin of history to its telos, and from deconstructive types of historicism for which the past is important only, or primarily, as a limit to be overcome. To affirm the positive, constitutive role of the past for the creation of a viable future does not in the least imply a use of the past that is uncritical, on the one hand, or simply critical, on the other. Accordingly we should say that ours is a "constructive historicism." Its principle claim is that the past creatively appropriated, imaginatively reconstructed, is the material out of which the future is effectively made.

To this, however, must be added a second implication of the preceding study for an understanding of theology and thus a second claim of *constructive historicism*: The conceptual reconstruction of a tradition's past is inextricably tied to the affective life of that tradition. If history cannot live without creativity and creativity without history, neither can live long apart from the affections, for feeling and thought in interaction serve as the vehicle of a tradition's recovery and innovation. This does not necessarily mean that every effective theologian must be a believer; quite obviously the sensitive observer, too, can contribute to the reconstruction of a tradition's inherited symbols. But it does mean that the ongoing task of theological construction will falter unless it somehow has vital roots in practicing religious communities that allow it both to draw upon and contribute to the imaginative play within the tradition. Whether or not he or she is a believer, the theologian is an artist as well as a critic of tradition—seeking to discern the varied conceptual possibilities apparent within the lived realities of a tradition, formulating and elaborating these potentialities, evaluating them in terms of the needs of the community and the broader arenas of critical discourse, thus advocating some variants over others and, finally, serving in ways appropriate to the individual theologian's circumstance the integration of these reconstructions back into the felt practices of the community from which they originated. This insistence—that the effective reformulation of inherited symbols must be rooted in the affective dynamics of practicing communities—is also a part of what is meant here by *constructive historicism*.

CONTEMPORARY THEOLOGY: NEGOTIATING IMAGINATION AND CHARACTER

So common is the affectively grounded reconstruction of the canonical past in Christian history that one might suppose the claim here presented about the character of theology to be utterly mundane. After all, histories of Christian theology are precisely histories of the ways Christian thinkers have imaginatively re-formed their conceptual resources to meet the demands of new situations; histories of Christian piety are accounts of the transformations of sensibilities in successive times and varied places; histories of Christian worship are descriptions of the creative adaptations of inherited liturgy; and the story of Christian stories is a history of constantly revised, often radically transmuted, inherited narratives. As William Clebsch and numerous others have shown, even in the specifically European strand of Christianity there have been many Gods, many humanities, many Christs, and many salvations—and in this sense, many Christianities.

The novelty of the current proposal, thus, is not the claim that Christian history is a succession of communal reconstructions of the Christian past, but that this is as it should be, especially in theology. Theology ought to be the *community's* creative *reconstruction*, and it ought to be the creative construction of the community's *canonical symbols*. As obvious as this judgment might now seem in light of the preceding argument, taken as a whole it is not widely evident in theology today, whether in what we shall call its *conservative, liberal*, or *radical* forms.[12]

Conservative theologians will endorse vigorously the insistence that the resource of effective theological reflection is the canonical inheritance of the Christian past. For this reason theirs might be termed one-sided *theologies of character*, elevating as they do the specific inheritance that gives to Christian existence its particular identity. But with equal vigor conservatives will reject the claim that this canonical resource is to be played or negotiated (or, as they might prefer to say, manipulated). There are essential teachings of the past, they would say, that are not to be reconstructed creatively; they are to be reduplicated—with appropriate adjustments in external form in order to speak better to new times and places, of course, but reduplicated in essentials nonetheless. Works by Clark Pinnock and George Lindbeck—two different, important, and in certain respects, quite original thinkers—illustrate the failure of what here is called *conservative* theology to engage adequately and openly in the creative reconstruction of the canonical past.[13]

Initially Pinnock's *Scripture Principle* appears to be the straight-forward defense of conservative evangelicalism.[14] The scripture principle holds that

> the Bible is . . . God's own written Word, and that we can consult his Word, which reveals his mind, and seek to know his will in it. It means that God has communicated authoritatively to us on those subjects about which Scripture teaches . . . and that we believers willingly sub-ject ourselves to this rule of faith. . . . The [biblical] text is not reduced to an expression of human experience and tradition, as in liberalism, but is a contentful language deposit that addresses [us] . . . with the authority of God.[15]

As Pinnock proceeds, however, it becomes evident that his evangelicalism is hardly an obscurantist one. Pinnock readily acknowledges, indeed insists upon, the manifestly human and historical character of the Bible—its conflicting interpretations of God's promise to Abraham in the Old Testament; its varying portrayals of Jesus in the New; the liberties taken by the New Testament writers in adapting Old Testament texts and repre-senting sayings of Jesus; the apparently nongenuine character of some sayings attributed to Jesus; the presence of legend in the Bible; and so forth. Pinnock emphasizes these features of the biblical text because he believes that the Bible's form as well as its content should be determinative of the way Christians use it. In terms of content, the Bible reveals itself to be a teacher, but it is "the kind of teacher that draws us into the process of learning and helps us learn to think theologically and ethically ourselves in new situations."[16] This is made clear in part by *how* the Bible says what it says: "there is a rich diversity in biblical teaching, which adds to its profundity. . . . Tight consistency is not what we find when we read the Bible. It is like . . . an orchestra rather than a single solo instrument."[17] "God seems to . . . instruct us in this way," Pinnock adds, "in order to bring us to greater matu-rity."[18]

The key to Pinnock's hermeneutic is his claim that the New Testament, in its use of the Hebrew Bible, teaches us that "a text can . . . [possess] a surplus of meaning potential that transcends the meaning it originally had."[19] "Like a musical score or a painting," he says, "the biblical text is available for fresh interpretation without end. . . . A text can be seen to possess more significance later than was noticed or even intended at first."[20] Pinnock insists on attention to the original meaning of a text as the anchor for interpretation,[21] but the Bible, he concludes, is "a canon in which the truth unfolds gradually and dialectically."[22]

Nevertheless, according to Pinnock, "the Bible must rule."[23] The Bible's teachings are truths, whether in their original or their extended meanings, that are binding for Christians. Thus Pinnock insists: "if the Bible asserts as a fact or truth [something that is] controverted by some scientific theory, the believer would have no other choice than to side with the Scriptures against the scientist."[24] Apparently, a Christian is not necessarily bound to side with the original meaning of a Scripture against a scientific theory, but if in prayerful study within the community of faith a Christian concludes that either the original or extended meaning of Scripture contradicts a particular claim of science, then the Christian is bound to reject that claim in spite of its scientific warrants.

Despite the quite remarkable concession to the theological imagination implicit in Pinnock's principle of the "extended" or "surplus" meaning of Scripture, his position nevertheless differs from mine in two basic respects. The principle difference concerns Pinnock's claim that the canon is normative for the believer and thus is that to which the believer must conform. Once this is asserted his recognition of the Bible's diversity and his enrichment of the Bible's content through the concept of potential or extended meaning are placed within strict a priori limits. For if the Bible as a whole is to be normative, then the Bible as a whole must have some discernable, consistent meaning that no diversity of meanings, however real, and no extension of meanings, however promising, can be permitted to exceed. Thus Pinnock proclaims, "We surely have a right to expect coherence . . . [of the Bible]. The Scripture principle would be overthrown should the Bible turn out to be self-contradictory . . ."[25] Indeed it would! Thus Pinnock's assertion that there is a single, identifiable, over-arching biblical meaning—derivative from his insistence on the Bible's normativeness—is the second point where his view differs from mine.

In *The Scripture Principle* Pinnock does not explain how, in view of the Bible's manifest diversity and fecundity of meaning, one might nevertheless speak of the Bible's evident unity. In other works, however, Pinnock employs George Lindbeck's concept of a "basic grammar" of Christian faith.[26]

In *The Nature of Doctrine*,[27] Lindbeck offers not so much a theology as a metatheology, a theory of theology based on what he calls a *cultural-linguistic* interpretation of religion.[28] This interpretation is offered in contrast to two alternatives, the cognitivist interpretation of religion, which Lindbeck says is premodern in character, and the experiential-expressivist view, which he associates with liberal Christianity.[29] In the former alternative, theologies are understood to be "informative propositions or truth claims about objective realities."[30] In the latter, theological statements are historically relative and malleable attempts to express the universal "experience of the divine" that everywhere has a common character.[31] According to Lindbeck, the mistake of the first, traditional view is its assumption that objective, universally valid knowledge is possible; the error of the second, liberal view is its supposition that there is a common human religious experience.

In Lindbeck's cultural-linguistic approach, humans are thoroughly social and historical beings whose experiences always necessarily derive from their particular, historically formed linguistic traditions. These varying inheritances are primarily narratival, providing their inhabitants with an overarching story, an interpretive framework in terms of which experience is organized and identity is established and sustained. To be a participant in a tradition is not to have a particular experience or hold particular beliefs, but rather to interiorize and live its narratival portrayal of life. To participate in a religious tradition is to internalize its story and learn its way of life "by practice."[32]

According to Lindbeck, the interpretive framework of the Christian tradition is the biblical narrative. Christian doctrines are the "rules" or "communally authoritative teachings" that indicate the abiding claims of the Christian narrative.

> To be sure, adjustments . . . take place in the interpretive scheme. . . . Yet amid . . . shifts in [for example] Christological affirmations and in the corresponding experiences of Jesus Christ, the story of passion and resurrection and the basic rules for its use remain the same. . . . Theological and religious transformations . . . can be seen . . . as the fusion of a self-identical story with the new worlds within which it is told and retold.
>
> There is nothing uniquely Christian about this constancy; supernatural explanations are quite unnecessary. This is simply the kind of stability that languages and religions, and to a lesser extent cultures, observably have. They are the lenses through which human beings see and respond to their changing worlds. . . . The world and its descriptions may vary enormously even while the lenses . . . remain the same.[33]

Given the assumption of a self-identical story, the task of theology is to assist the formation of Christian identity, and "truth" for theology is its faithfulness to its fundamental narratival portrayal. Faithfulness, Lindbeck says, "does not necessarily mean repeating [inherited doctrine]; rather, it requires, in the making of any new formulations, adherence to the same directives that were involved in their first formulation."[34] As examples of such directives Lindbeck offers three "regulative principles . . . obviously at work" in the ancient trinitarian and christological affirmations, to which he attributes "unconditionality and permanence."[35] "First, there is the monotheistic principle: there is only one God, the God of Abraham, Isaac, Jacob, and Jesus. Second, there is the principle of historical specificity: the stories of Jesus refer to a genuine human being. . . . Third, there is the principle of . . . Christological maximalism: every possible importance is to be ascribed to Jesus that is not inconsistent with the first rules."[36] These rules are a part of what Lindbeck calls the grammar of the religion that church doctrines seek to reflect."[37]

Much of Lindbeck's analysis is right. He understands, as do Pinnock and conservatives generally, the constitutive importance of the past for the effective formation of the present. Moreover, at least in principle Lindbeck is committed to an inclusive canon, with all of its ("apparent," some more conservative theologians would say) variation, conflict, contradiction, goods, and ills. But despite these important moves in the direction of constructive historicism, Lindbeck's "pretheological" understanding of religion[38] and the theory of tradition advanced in this book contrast sharply, in two respects of particular relevance here.[39] First, Lindbeck posits for religions in general and for Christianity in particular a "self-same story," an abiding grammar or core. Second, Lindbeck attributes to the canon, thus construed as a particular unity, a normative character. The role of creativity in theological construction is thereby seriously curtailed. These, of course, are also the contrasts identified previously in the discussion of Pinnock.

Lindbeck and Pinnock assume that a canon is unitary in its fundamentals, that this unity is reasonably demonstrable, that it can be conformed to, and that such conformation is necessary to preserve the authentic identity of the tradition. The preceding study has challenged the claim to anything like this kind of canonical unity. That Lindbeck, as a theologian, might propose a particular construal of canon is not only understandable but also necessary, as we have seen. But the claim that any particular construal of canon has extratheological justification or, more important, that a canon is even capable of being so construed on a nontheological basis has been denied. Indeed, it has been argued that such a degree of canonical unity would fail to meet the needs that a viable canon must serve in the changing circumstance of history. Unitary canons die; plurivocal canons endure. And plurivocal canons, as such, cannot be conformed to. Negotiating *within* the boundaries of a vital canon is always creative; it is never simply conformation. Appropriate thinking and acting may—and, in important senses, always will—exceed the uses to which the same canonical resources have been put in the past. And often what is altered was once thought basic.[40] Thus, for example, theologies that arise out of the experience of abuse may find little of value in what Lindbeck calls the principle of christological maximalism; the Christ they recover in the canon, and in whom they profess to find recovery, is Jesus the gentle, vulnerable, and trustworthy friend.[41] Creativity also involves, sometimes, negotiation *with* the boundaries of canon. Hence, Black Christian theology, James H. Evans observes, must bring together two canons, the biblical canon as a narrative of hope and the African American folk stories that highlight the relentless realism of Black experience.[42] Such adjustments of canonical limits are rather common, especially in folk and popular (as distinguished from mainstream and "professional") expressions of Christianity. Whether or not, finally, they can be sustained in the fierce tests of practical as well as conceptual adjudication, both forms of negotiation—within, and with, the boundaries of canon—are "canonically" permissible, because canons are rich and diverse fields of affective and cognitive, and thus theological, play.

Conservative theologies do not account for this feature of canon. In fact they resist viewing canon in this way, claiming that it forfeits the constraints essential for the maintenance of Christian identity. But the canons that define traditions, and hence the traditions themselves, are not simply fields of play; they are also agents in the play. In Gadamer's terms, games are played but they are also players. Hence conservatism's fear that the identity of tradition might be lost, usually cast as a concern about "heresy," is misguided. Conservatism underestimates the power of the canon, its "gravitational pull," its capacity to define itself in each new circumstance. Therefore conservatism presumes to become the guardian of tradition, defining the boundaries of its resources and the possibilities of its permutations. Fortunately, the power of canon is always sufficient eventually to break the grip of such pious possessiveness, but theological conservatism, as described here, is still a terribly inhibiting mindset. It can be temporarily effective because it employs inherited symbols and because, in doing so, it draws upon the full breadth of canon. But finally conservatism is stultifying because it fears the imagination. And it fears the imagination because it underestimates the power of canon to take care of itself, to criticize as well as to be criticized, to change as well as be changed—in short, to play those who play it.[43]

An ironically similar neglect of canon's pluralism and power is evident in what I have called *radical theologies*, by which term I refer primarily to the work of the poststructuralists or deconstructionists. These theologies often embody in an impressive fashion the creative task of the theologian and thus might be called *theologies of imagination*. Indeed, they valorize novelty. According to Mark C. Taylor, the most influential of the poststructuralists in American religious thought, the vocation of the theologian (or, strictly speaking, the "a/theologian") is to deconstruct the inherited symbols of Western Christianity.[44] Christianity's God is dead, says Taylor, its conception of self has disappeared, its history has ended, and its canon is closed. Now the task of the a/theologian is to enter without restraint that carnivalesque space wherein reigns perpetual novelty, the endless play of difference.

Taylor's project may be viewed as the effort to complete a process begun in the Enlightenment's destabilization of classical Christian totalitarianism by, in turn, destabilizing the Enlightenment's imperialism, a colonizing thrust that reached its zenith in Hegel's vision of the absorption of all difference within the advance of Absolute Spirit.[45] Taylor pursues this project not only by continuing in a certain fashion the Kantian claim that all philosophical and theological judgments are finally human constructions rather than readings of extralinguistic givens,[46] but also by underscoring, following Derrida, the post-Kantian and poststructuralist claim that such constructions, properly understood (i.e., deconstructed), are always fraught with irresolvable tensions, disunities, disorders, and inevitably, the strategic repression of these elements. The assumptions underlying this project are twofold. First, it rejects the Enlightenment view that certain forms of language (science and scientific, or methodologically sound, philosophy) have direct access to a reality to which they refer and in which their claims can be securely grounded. Second, it proposes that language itself is an infinitely interwoven fabric of signifiers with no demonstrable representation of a reality beyond it. "The signifier," as Carl Raschke has said, is "void of all ontological gravity."[47] Language constitutes a world of its own within which each item refers only to other items in the same system.

It is this context that Taylor challenges the "network of notions that traditionally have grounded" Christian theology:[48] God, self, history, and the Book. God is the Primal Origin and Ultimate End whose Word "brings the world into being and providentially directs its course."[49] The self, made in the image of God, is the centered, freely active, and responsible individual.[50] History is the "purposeful process" in which divine guidance and human freedom meet and create a "single line

stretching from a definite beginning (creation) through an identifiable middle (incarnation) to an expected end (kingdom or
redemption)."[51] "The Book weaves the unified story of the
interaction between God and self."[52] The demise of the classical
vision means the end of the God whose Word set all things in
order and thus of everything that follows from it; namely, the
other tenets of the "logocentric" universe—the self, history,
and the Book. "With the death of God, a dark shadow falls over
the light that for centuries illuminated the landscape of the
West."[53]

Taylor's own "constructive" (my term) proposal[54] is accomplished without the substantive employment of inherited
Western symbols. God is "writing," he says, the self is "trace,"
history is "erring," and the Book is "text." "Writing is an
unending play of differences that establishes the thoroughgoing
relativity of all 'things.' This complex web of interrelations is the
divine milieu."[55] The "trace," which emerges with the disappearance of the mastery-driven self, "concretely embodies the
ceaseless interplay of desire and delight."[56] History is "erring"[57]—"rootless and nomadic (originless), . . . excentric [sic]
and exorbitant (centerless), . . . purposeless and aimless (endless)."[58] Text is "free interpretation, which has given up every
dream of conclusive certainty," extending "through an endless
process of multiplication, pluralization, and dispersal."[59]

Whether or not Taylor's "erring" is entirely rootless and purposeless, it certainly is eccentric and exorbitant. But it is also
valuable. It exposes the illusion of canonical finality in a radical
way, and with blatant excess it posits as a corollary the centrality
of play and the constancy of negotiation in tradition. And,
indeed, much that Taylor says constructively concerning the
nature of self, history, and even book coheres with the portrayal
of tradition and its habitation developed here. But Taylor, who
effectively challenges the "dyadic foundation" of Western theology,[60] is himself drawn to exclusionary opposites in a degree
that undermines the adequacy of his views. In his analysis of

book and text, for example, he can only juxtapose the sheer giveness that he attributes to the former with the sheer arbitrariness that he finds in the latter. Or, to recall the analogy of Chapter 3, when he peers into our cultural night sky Taylor can see planets (books) and constellations (texts) but never galaxies. Certainly after the reflections of the preceding chapters Taylor's description of "book," as it applies to the Christian canon, seems more than a bit dubious.

> The idea of the book is the idea of a totality. . . . A book is . . . a living whole in which all parts are integrally related as members of a single organism. Inasmuch as the book forms an ordered totality, it is, like history, logocentric. Although characterized in many different ways, the logos of the book invariably constitutes the principle of preestablished harmony, which forms the structural foundation of the volume's unity and coherence.[61]

With this view of canon before him, Taylor's own re(de)constructive proposal cannot, must not employ inherited symbols. They are complicit in the canon's totalization. God is dead. Thus the book is closed, and its symbols are silenced.

Taylor's radical theology, or a/theology, is valuable not only for its focus on creativity, but also for its immensely important disclosure of the alliance between the dominant discourses of Western history and the forms of Western oppression. Even so, if the preceding study (including its analysis of critiques of canon that depend upon Derrida and Foucault) is correct, he and other theologians of imagination are also one-sided, having failed to take the power of the past with sufficient seriousness. Christian history, for them, is valuable as a record of mistakes to be exposed, analyzed, and avoided, but not, except in this important instructional sense, as a positive resource useful in theological construction today.

According the view defended here, however, the Christian past is not only useful therapeutically, it is essential constructively in an effective and enduring theological vision. No effort has been made to deny the importance of material—constructive or critical—drawn from other traditions, secular and religious. Nothing has been said to restrain an ingenuity that soars beyond the confines of a particular canonical inheritance or a creativity that seeks to enlarge it. Nor has the imperative to expose and critique inherited structures of oppression been minimized. The point, instead, is that these alien materials, these imaginative leaps, these expansive visions, and these critical archaeologies, as substantive and transforming as they could turn out to be, are not likely to have an abiding effect except as they are integrated back into the reconstruction of Christianity's inherited resources. It may well be, as Audre Lorde insists, that the master's house cannot be dismantled by using the master's tools.[62] But whatever we wish to do with the house we inherit, and whatever the tools we use, we can succeed only by working on, precisely, that house—because to say that humans are historical means that our futures are built through the reconstruction of our pasts. For all their imagination, the radical theologians fail to imagine the radical potential of the canonical house in which they dwell. They fail to understand and explore the capacity of a tradition to become what it has not yet been, to say "all those things that are not yet spoken."[63]

But if the radical thinkers neglect the resourcefulness of tradition, they also neglect its power. Canons have enough diversity to bring forth radical novelty and enough unity to exercise enormous power. A canon is a rich and diverse field of play in which the canon, too, is an effective player. So effective, indeed, that it is naive—in fact, dangerous—to speak as if gods simply die, conceptions of self and world simply disappear, histories ever just end, and canons can merely be closed. For good and ill, gods, ideas, histories, and canons live on and on, encountering new and often resistant circumstances, undergoing transformations, and exercising their power over and through those who live in their gravitational fields. It diminishes their power little if those who live within their pull pretend otherwise, and their power in its pernicious forms only does more damage when they are so neglected. But if inattention to the resourcefulness of tradition can enhance its negative potential, it can also diminish its potential for good. Traditions are not only culprits; they also have goods to give—judgments and alternatives, as yet unnoticed, worthy of consideration, capable of transformation. To neglect tradition is to neglect its power for good as well as ill.

For these reasons theologies that seek to proceed free of the boundaries of particular traditions seem at best naive and at worst dangerous. Just as important, however, if the analysis of tradition offered here has merit, radical theologies are likely to enjoy little of the impact they might seek on cultural and religious traditions. They do not deal with the symbols that still dominate, if sometimes only as a whisper, the cultural and religious scene, the symbols that must be negotiated creatively if viable alternatives are to be discovered, lasting change is to occur, and worthy achievements are to be sustained.[64] Thus, even though these radical theologies are valuable for their emphasis on creativity, they are, taken alone, doomed to cultural and religious impotence by their neglect of tradition.[65]

Radical theologies deny the constitutive importance of inheritance and conservative theologies deny the constitutive importance of innovation. Liberal theologies acknowledge in some measure the importance of each, but they do so in much too restricted a fashion. Liberal theologies, at least in their current forms, are usually diminished theologies of character and imagination.

Liberal Christian theology shares with radical thinkers the judgment that the adjudication of truth claims is contemporary and contextual. For liberalism the norms of reflection are to be hammered out and applied piecemeal and tentatively across the span of our varied communities of contemporary discourse. But if liberal Christian theology has thus rejected the normativeness of the biblical inheritance, it has retained, albeit in a more intuitive than carefully reasoned way, a sense of past's peculiar importance. Hence, as American humanists of the early twentieth century were quick to observe,[66] theological liberalism has retained a vestige of conservative conviction: For liberal theologians the Christian canonical inheritance remains somehow uniquely compelling. Given this fact, liberal theology has had to wrestle with the problem of canon more seriously than either of the previous alternatives that either accept or reject canon wholesale.

Liberal theology begins with an acknowledgment of the irreducible diversity of the biblical canon—indeed, liberal scholarship demonstrated that diversity. But liberal theology also wishes in some way to take the biblical inheritance seriously. Its strategy for doing so has been to identify amid the canonical diversity a core of some sort that is taken to have unique relevance or significance.[67]

In perhaps the most systematically accomplished version of this strategy Schubert Ogden posits as the norm of all distinctively Christian reflection the "earliest apostolic witness." Ogden's assumptions are that all Christian theology is to be an "elaboration [of] the assertion that 'Jesus is the Christ' "[68] and that the norm for this elaboration

> cannot be the writings of the New Testament as such but can only be the earliest traditions of Christian witness accessible to us today by historical-critical analysis of these writings, . . . [which] form critics generally speak of as the earliest layer of the synoptic tradition. . . . [Hence] the "canon within the canon" to which all theological assertions must be appropriate is the meaning to be discerned in the . . . Jesus-kerygma of the apostolic community.[69]

Rosemary Ruether focuses on what she identifies as the "prophetic-liberating" or "prophetic-messianic" strand in Scripture, to which four themes are essential: (1) God's defense and vindication of the oppressed; (2) the critique of dominant systems of power and their powerholders; (3) the vision of a new age to come in which . . . God's intended reign of peace and justice is installed in history; and (4) finally, the critique of ideology, or of religion, since ideology in this context is primarily religious."[70] Ruether says this tradition within the Bible is normative, but she means by this that it is the principle in terms of which the rest of the Bible is to be evaluated and accepted or rejected.[71] What legitimizes the prophetic-messianic strand is the fact that there is a correlation between it and the feminist critical principle, that is, the feminist critique of sexism.[72]

In a somewhat different approach Gordon Kaufman privileges what he believes to be the four terms of Christianity's categorial scheme. He writes:

> A world-view . . . is given its full character and meaning by a complex pattern of words and symbols, liturgical practices and moral claims, behavioral patterns and institutional structures, stories and myths. . . . But . . . the basic structure and character of every world-view is determined by a few fundamental categories which give it shape and order. . . . The basic configuration of defining terms . . . I call its categorial structure.[73]

Christianity's categorial structure is composed of God, humanity, world, and Christ,[74] the last term of which provides the definitive understanding of the other three.[75] Within these parameters the theologian is to engage in a "comprehensive assessment and reconstruction of the Christian world-view."[76]

In a still different, and potentially more radical, vein John Cobb postulates as normative for Christian theology a particular christological construal in which "Christ" is the principle of creative transformation embodied and revealed in Jesus. To be faithful to Christ is to participate

> in the historical movement that owed its decisive impetus to Jesus but lives now in responsiveness to the living Christ

within it. This movement is not bound to preserve any specifiable doctrine, even of Jesus, although its identity is constituted by the primacy of its memory of that history of which Jesus is the center, and its healthy continuance depends on constant reencounter with Jesus and with the earliest witness to his meaning for the church.[77]

"The uniqueness and universality of Christ," Cobb concludes, "opens us radically to the achievements of other faiths, traditions, or Ways." Cobb's norm, in other words, entitles the Christian, as Christian, to move beyond the Christian canon to any symbolic space, ancient or modern, where creative transformation is being made manifest.[78]

Each of these liberal positions is significantly different—each has a different core, differently justified, accorded a different status, and put to a different purpose.[79] Yet all identify some core, some element or elements, as the interpretive center of Christian faith. That, certainly, is not problematic. But what usually follows in liberalism is the virtual disappearance of the remainder of the Christian symbolic complex. The elevated core takes on a life of its own and the rest of the symbolic system (or at least its substantive content[80]) disappears almost entirely. The core is not the interpretive center around which the remainder of the canonical reservoir is reconstructed; it is the summation of Christianity that reduces all other canonical voices to silence. Why? Often, it seems, because the interpretive core is assumed to have an intrinsic privilege that makes the rest of the canon extraneous.[81] Liberal theologies are usually developed as if they capture and explicate a uniquely valid summation of Christianity beside which the remainder of the canon can be, and largely is, relegated into oblivion.[82]

We have contended, of course, that canons are essentially diverse and that their claim to "normativity"[83] is tied to that diversity. Canons have no *intrinsically* privileged construal or adequate summation. Indeed, canonical diversity and fluidity is such that, although offering a particular construal for a particular circumstance is inescapable, in the nature of the case no single rendering, however complex, can finally get a fix on canon. Each interpretation of canon more or less ably develops and defends, in the arenas of its contemporary communities of discourse, a specific way of understanding the canon. Each such proposal reflects the play of several forces, including the interpreters and their specific situations of power, insight, and interests, as well as the "gravitational pull" of the canon itself in that time and place. But no interpretation—whether a construal of the whole or a summation of its core—finally "gets it right," not simply because of the inevitable deficiency of the interpreter but also, and far more important, because canons are not the kind of things that can be gotten right. Hence any liberal effort to identify some intrinsically privileged core, which renders the rest of the canon extraneous to theological construction, is illicit.

Moreover, the elevation of a core in a manner that expels the rest of the canon is, from liberalism's standpoint, systematically gratuitous.[84] Conservatism's rigid handling of the canonical whole is a function of its doctrine of canonical unity. Radical theology's dismissal of the canonical whole is driven by the same doctrine when coupled with the radical's valorization of creativity. But liberalism's affirmation of creativity in tandem with its recognition of canonical diversity should—or, at least, could—make the entire canon a fertile site of its imaginative reconstructions. (For that reason "constructive historicism" should be viewed as a revision of liberalism, not as a fourth type in addition to the liberal, conservative, and radical positions.) Thus, liberal neglect of the full range of canonical resources in theological construction is quite unnecessary.[85]

Most important, however, the affirmation of an authentic core to the exclusion of the rest of the canon in so much of liberal theology is quite unfortunate, for it curtails imagination and limits character. It does the latter, obviously, by taking from the canon only that which is judged to be "pure," rather than seeing the need to wrestle with and reorder the whole canon in terms of the core that is said to be central to it. The supposedly authentic core of the inheritance is elevated, and the remainder drops from view. The quaint, presumably misguided voices within tradition are shunted aside like an odd uncle at a family wedding. The outcome is more harmonious but less "interesting" than it might have been, for the purification of character impoverishes imagination. As much as liberal theology lauds human creativity, it has ignored or excluded from genuine conversation one of the major goads of Christian creativity—the full range of the canonical inheritance including its problematic forms. As a consequence, liberal Christian theology has looked, and sometimes fairly lunged, toward voices beyond its own tradition for vital stimulation and material. These conversations—for example, with philosophy, science, political theory, and other religions—may be enormously beneficial and for some purposes they have been absolutely essential. But, because liberalism has tolerated only the "purest" symbols of tradition as material with which to work, its conversations with voices from beyond the Christian mythic inheritance have increasingly provided not only the catalyst, but also the content, of liberal Christian theological construction. As a result liberal theology is in grave danger of becoming in disguise what radical theology is openly—creativity without the substance of inherited symbols. The result would be the same: conclusions that are important, but culturally and religiously ineffective.[86]

WHAT THEOLOGIES ARE AND DO

Theology should return to traditions. Not, of course, to traditions as they were understood by the Enlightenment mentality that uncritically dismissed them or by the counter-Enlightenment mind that uncritically embraced them, but to traditions as they persistently show themselves to be—dynamic and diverse streams of being and meaning that mold and are molded, continue and create, save and destroy. Theology should be the critical analyst and creative conveyor of the vast conceptual resources, actual and potential, of religious traditions. In thus critically and creatively reconstructing the past, a theology is a tradition's caregiver.[87] That, indeed, is the vocation of theology.

The Task of Theology

The theological vocation can be clarified by construing theological caregiving, diachronically, as a threefold activity. The first activity is to inquire into the varied meanings of the doctrines and beliefs, implicit and explicit, ingredient in a particular religious mythos, both in relative isolation and in their actual and possible relationships. This is a systematic task. It is not an effort to force every conceptual particle into some neat whole; it is an exploration of conceptual interactions throughout the symbolic complex. When theologians fuse Christian discourse about salvation with holistic conceptions of personal and social realities, the entire soteriological complex in Christian thought takes on quite novel meanings.[88] When theologians tie the healing power of Jesus to the faith present in communal solidarity, the relationship of christology and ecclesiology changes and the meaning of each is transformed.[89] This imaginative exploration of actual and possible relationships within the canonical complex is the systematic dimension of caring for tradition. It is an exploration of the possible interactions of its symbolic elements.

The second theological activity of theological caregiving is empirical or political. It is an examination of the ways the conceptual forms of a tradition, whether realized or as yet only dimly envisioned, are and might be related to actual and possible modes of life. What difference do these ideas make in particular forms of life, and what difference does life make to these ideas? These are the questions of political or empirical inquiry in theology. Feminist analyses of gender-specific names for deity are

examples of this kind of inquiry, as are feminist proposals of
alternative languages for referring to God.[90] So, too, was the
work of process thinkers, around midcentury, when they asked
what the affirmation of God's timelessness implied about the
worth of an essentially "timeful" nature and history and the
humanity embedded there.[91] Still earlier, in the first decades of
this century, the theologians of the early Chicago school under-
took the same kind of task when they examined the socio-historical functions of virtually the full range of Christian doctrine
throughout Western history.[92]

The third part of caring for tradition theologically is evalua-   3.
tive. In what ways can these complexes of ideas, in interaction
with other ideas and with social realities, be assessed, according
to what criteria, by whom, and how do they fair in such an
evaluation? Answering these questions is manifestly a tenuous
business for it necessarily involves a two-level, dialectical debate,
both about the criteria to be applied as well as their proper
application to specific circumstances. Negotiations about criteria and their application go hand in hand. On these issues the
current study has taken only a most general, but already a divi-
sive, position. The view here espoused—in fact, the view that
underlies the study itself, as was indicated in the Introduction—
is that the evaluative claims of theologian must be open to pub-   so,
lic debate and vulnerable to criticism from all of the communities   Hauerwas
of contemporary discourse that collectively constitute the public sphere. In this respect, at least, I side with those who speak of
theology as public discourse and those who emphasize the revisionary element in theological reflection,[93] even if I also maintain that what these theologians bring into the public arenas,
and what they subject to the revisionary process, is often far too
slight of "character."

However, if reflection on the evaluative task produces the
sharpest divisions within the field of theology, it also reveals the
pervasively evaluative character of caring for tradition. The theologian's judgment as to what meanings are possible within a

complex of religious ideas depends on what she or he is able to see, which in turn depends partly on what she or he thinks to be important. Prior to the Marxist attack on Christian otherworld-liness, for example, establishment theologians were familiar with the motifs and images that liberationists later made central to their theological constructions, but they neglected them, claiming that they were of only tertiary importance. A judg-ment of importance is an evaluation.

A theologian's assessment of empirical consequences, the sec-ond activity identified, depends on a prior identification and appraisal of the relevant empirical evidence. And what is deemed relevant and how it is construed are evaluations. Claims in the 1950s and 1960s that the church was dead and religious-ness was dying due to the stultifying character of orthodox Christian belief (variations on the theme were numerous) proved to be wrong because the evidence was misread. (At least when measured in terms of demonstrable survivability, which was the point at issue, the church and religion were not even ill!—whether or not they should have been.) The evidence was misread because the ecclesiastical and religious situations were interpreted through the evaluative lenses of the "secularization" hypothesis that minimized whatever countered the investigator's expectations.

Clearly, then, evaluation is already at work in systematic and empirical analysis; neither is separable from the other or from questions of proper criteria and modes of evaluation. Thus nei-ther, like the explicitly evaluative task, is free of the fallibility and messiness of constant adjudication in our ever-changing and varied communities of contemporary discourse. Each—systematic analysis, empirical analysis, and evaluation—is a con-structive activity rooted in the creativity of theologians in com-munities. And therefore each is conducted with risk, without reassuring guidelines or guarantees.

The Authority of Theology

The risk of theological caregiving is even more evident when theology is viewed, synchronically, as the negotiation with/in canon of continuity and change, order and disorder, the center and the margin, the actual and the imagined, the system and the antisystem, and all the other polarities in terms of which our intellectual wars are customarily framed. That each pole presupposes and in some sense requires the other is obvious. The problem is in deciding whether either should be favored, whether either somehow minimizes risk. Theology has generally privileged the former poles—that which has been established, that which, in the words of Vincent of Lerins (434 CE), "has been believed everywhere, always, and by all." What is ordinarily questioned about this formulation, with good reason, is its supposition that anything has received such universal assent. The more basic issue, however, is its preference for that which *has been*. This preference, as we have said repeatedly, is profoundly misguided for at least two reasons. First, repetition is never as it seems. As Whitehead has said, "you can make a replica of an ancient statue [but not] of an ancient state of mind."[94] And, indeed, the ancient meaning of a statue is now as misty as the innermost thoughts and feelings of the mind that once viewed it. Similarly, ancient doctrines, ideas, symbols, narratives, and rituals can never simply be replicated; their reproduction is always their transformation. Second, repetition, even to the degree that it is possible, is not intrinsically preferable, it offers no guarantees. At least if cultural and religious efficacy, to say nothing of moral adequacy, are the issues, the tradition must be appropriated creatively, imaginatively, with playful freedom. That, of course, has been a basic claim of the entire study.

This claim, however, should not be interpreted as a valorization of change, disorder, the margin, and so on. The repeated insistence here that creativity, imagination, construction is inescapable, and that it is good, is a claim about the character of the theological process, not necessarily about its consequence. In our creativity we can largely reclaim, or we can largely reconstruct, our pasts. But if relative repetition cannot be privileged neither can relative novelty. This judgment runs counter to recent French thought that, from Maurice Merleau-Ponty through Michel Foucault to Julia Kristeva, has privileged change—deconstruction, decentering, "depresentation"—and thus, in a curious way, has made change authoritative.[95]

In Merleau-Ponty, who stressed the plentitude and vitality of "wild Being," the valorization of change was fundamentally optimistic. Foucault's subsequent focus on the abusive and oppressive effects of the dynamic substratum of human being showed that a much more sober analysis would be required. Kristeva might be interpreted as attempting to strike the needed balance between optimistic and pessimistic expectations of the outcomes of novelty in the cultural process, but even so relative change retains in her analysis a curious priority.

Kristeva identifies three elements or "energies" in the dynamic of the human self and human culture: the semiotic, which is the dimension of disruptive impulses expressed in laughter, music, poetry, rhythm, the erotic, and, generally, that which is powerfully affective; the symbolic, which is the mode of order and representation that gives personal and corporate identity through the shaping of the semiotic; and the "thetic," a third term that is (the human arbitration of the other two). Because the semiotic and the symbolic are both violent, so too, very often, is their "thetic" modulation. Kristeva avoids the pessimism of Foucault, however, by insisting that the cathartic function of the thetic need not always take the destructive forms that Foucault so powerfully exposes. "Poetic animality" and art, Kristeva says, are nonviolent and healthy ways of "infiltrating" and transforming the symbolic order.[96]

Though there are exceptions in her work, Kristeva tends to identify the thetic function as a "limit" primarily on the social-symbolic order, and again with some exceptions, she tends to valorize the dismantling or disruptive movements of the thetic over against its ordering ones. In other words, she allies the thetic more closely to the semiotic. To be sure, Kristeva notes that the poetic can degenerate into coopted triviality, on the one hand, or "unspeakable delirium," on the other.[97] But these possibilities seem for her less inevitable and certainly less ominous than the oppressive totalization to which symbolic orders are said to be prone. But why order is inherently more threatening than disorder is unclear from Kristeva's analysis, especially because Kristeva herself is so perceptive in identifying what she calls the *abject* that infects every system—the remainder within every established order that continues to be unaccounted for, that embodies its inadequacy and generates from within it the alternatives that will eventually undo it. No comparable limits or correctives intrinsic to disorder are identified. Why then is disorder, deconstruction, decentering, and so forth held to be relatively more innocent? Perhaps Kristeva assumes that order is somehow more firmly grounded and, hence, that the disordering impulse needs encouragement. If so, however, this assumption is unsubstantiated in her analysis, and it is challenged in the present one. Whether we are talking of canons or cultures or narratives or systems or traditions, the "abjective," to use Kristeva's term, always lies at its heart, never to be eradicated, its effects never finally to be denied.

Neither relative change nor relative continuation is entitled to privilege. Neither provides the theologian with a haven from risk; a preference for neither minimizes that risk. Indeed, a preference for either is unwarranted. The outcome of theological construction must always be carried into whatever the contemporary communities of evaluative inquiry, without special privilege because it changes or continues, because it orders or disorders, because it represents the center or the margin, because it proclaims the achieved or the imagined, because it is a system or a fragment. The only authorization of the theological reconstruction of a tradition is the tentative and fallible affirmation that, for some times and for some places, might be granted by contemporary communities of evaluation, in which communities the varied voices of the tradition itself are entitled to full but unprivileged participation.

If continuity no more than change can be valorized, tradition must be seen as formative rather than normative, as an "author" rather than an "authorizer" of theological constructions.[98] Hannah Arendt has shown that the idea of "authority" as that which norms or authorizes, a view we are rejecting, is rooted in Roman law.[99] Arendt writes: "At the heart of Roman politics stands the conviction of the sacredness of foundation, in the sense that once something has been founded it remains binding for all future generations." In Rome "religion meant *religare*: to be tied back, obligated, to the . . . foundations. . . . To be religious meant to be tied to the past."[100] In this context the now prevalent view of theological authority as norm was formalized. According to this view the theologian who takes the canonical past seriously is bound to conform to it.

We have seen, however, that a tradition is grounded in a diverse and dynamic canonical field with/in which individual and communal identities are constantly being created and re-created. For the theologian to honor such a field cannot mean to reduplicate it in whole or in part; to take seriously a canon can mean only to play with/in it and be played by it. More adequate for this undertaking than the Roman model is the concept of authority as "exousia," which in portions of the New Testament at least connotes the power and freedom given to the community of faith.[101] From this perspective the *authority* of a canon is the creative power it manifests and therefore enables in those who inhabit it, and the authority of a tradition is the power of its canon again and again *to author* reconstructions, conceptual and affective, that yield viable individual and communal identities.[102]

The Place of Theology

Theological construction is affective as well as cognitive and collective as well as individual. From several quite different analytical perspectives—among them, as we have seen,[103] Gadamer's admission of the noncognitive life of language, the radical empiricists' claim that we know fundamentally through the body, Merleau-Ponty's emphasis on the formative power of the concrete matrix within which body-subject and world are coformed, and recent ritual theory—we are compelled to take seriously the judgment that conceptual construction in theology has its wellsprings in the affective vitalities of communal practice. Theological imagination is formed in the emotional tones of patterned actions and felt relationships not fully rationalized. It is fired in fractious and amateurish communal debates where the issue seems to be nothing less than the validity of a way of life. It is fed by symbols vaguely grasped but tenaciously entertained in these communities. The difference theology will make is the difference it makes with these symbols to these affections in these communities.[104] Theological constructions not somehow vitally rooted in these collective vitalities will be, in the long run, of little consequence—rather like sophisticated analyses of human love divorced from the realities of concrete human intimacy.

But reflection on the relationship between loving and thinking about loving ought to warn us away from excessive simplification in understanding how theology is rooted in communal practice. Perceptive analysts of human intimacy, whatever their specific field, may draw on the dynamics of their own personal relationships now past or on those of others to whom the analysts are keenly sensitive. Moreover, their reflections will be informed by a massive body of statistics, qualitative studies, and theories—all of which are to some degree abstractions. In addition, the proper placement of those who engage in the disciplined study of human intimacy to their subject matter is not

readily reducible to a set of rules—only to commonsense judgments, for example, they should not be indifferent or hostile to
their subject matter as a whole, even if they are highly critical to
some of its forms; they must be "open" and "sensitive" to concrete instances of the subject matter; they must constantly submit their more abstract verities to these concrete instances. And,
finally, it should be clear that this particular inquiry, which
addresses the most unmanageable and subjective of human passions, is nevertheless a perfectly legitimate scholarly discipline.

The manner in which theology is to be rooted in the vital
affections of communal practice also cannot be governed by
fixed rules of method or practice, only by the fluid and debatable judgments of common sense. As we have seen, the need for
such rootage does not necessarily mean that each theologian
must be a believer in, or practitioner of, the tradition or traditions to which he or she gives care. It does mean, however, that
in the long run effective theology cannot be constructed in
indifference or hostility to the communal feelings and practices
that give such reflection its vitality, however critical it may be to
some of their forms; that theology must be "open" and "sensitive" to the lived dynamics of these communal realities; that its
constructions must constantly be submitted to examination in
terms of these communal vitalities and what they contribute to
them, and so forth.

It should also be clear that constructive theology, which traf-
fics in the most basic of human feelings and parochial visions, is
nevertheless a perfectly legitimate form of disciplined scholarly
consideration, even within the secular university.[105] Theologians
inquire into the varied meanings, implicit and explicit, ingredient in the mythic frameworks of particular religious traditions.
Historians and literary critics undertake similar inquiries into
different subject matters. Theologians examine the ways the
conceptual forms of a tradition are and might be related to
actual and possible modes of life. Political philosophers and
economists conduct parallel studies. Theologians ask how these

complexes of ideas, in interaction with other ideas and with social realities, can be assessed, according to what criteria, by whom, and how they fare in such an evaluation. Philosophers and, indeed, all scholars in the humanities ask these questions. Each of these other forms of scholarship is concerned to care about particular kinds of human thinking and acting, actual and possible, in specific cultural traditions. Each critically analyzes and, inescapably, contributes to the reconstruction of thinking about these behaviors and therefore to the continuation or change of the behaviors themselves. It would be quite odd if our citadels of scholarship should be open to such a reconstructive study of all of the other forms of human acting, hoping, and thinking—economic, political, sexual, social—save religion. And it would be odder still if they were open to the study of all other aspects of religions—histories, rituals, myths, canons, morals—save their beliefs; especially because these other aspects cannot be understood except in relation to each other and to the dynamic and polyphonic sphere of beliefs!

However, it must be no less clear that theology, which ought to be a part of and at home in the academy, should also be rooted in the vitalities of practicing religious communities. Much as literary criticism must be connected to communities of writers (and often the critic will be a writer), political science to politics (and often the scholar will be politically active), anthropology to living communities (and often the investigator will be one of the people being studied), and analyses of human relationships to concrete human interaction (and often . . . !), so, too, a theology somehow must have living interaction with practicing religious groups—and often, of course, the theologian will be one of their number.

THEOLOGY'S CONSENT

The theologian—as analyst, critic, and artist—is a tradition's caregiver. Her or his task is to try to discern the varied conceptual possibilities ingredient within a tradition's lived realities, to formulate and elaborate these potentialities, to evaluate them in relation both to the practice of the communities that house them, often unknowingly, and the critiques of the critical discourses that surround them, thus to advocate some conceptual possibilities over others, and finally, to serve as he or she can the integration of these reconstructions back into communal feeling, practice, and articulation.

It is in light of this task that theology will "consent" to tradition: Theology accepts as a starting point what a tradition has been and is, accepts as a goal what it might be and should become, and accepts as an obligation the advocacy of that potential realization. If a tradition is right for the time, theology will sustain and enhance it. If a tradition becomes shallow, its hidden depths will be uncovered, explored, and proclaimed. If it becomes silent, the tradition will be made to say what it can. If it feigns uniformity, the tradition's diversity, actual and potential, will be held up to view. And whenever the tradition is wrong, consent means to condemn it, to challenge it, and to work for its transformation. Theology is the creative reconstruction of inherited symbols, the construction of a tradition's future from the resources of its past.

There is ample precedent for this view of theology, certainly in American religious thought. Indeed, since this conception embraces both a conservative and a liberal conviction, it is not surprising that we can find this practice of theology in both camps. In the middle of the nineteenth century a conservative like Horace Bushnell was frankly saying that the time had come to revise orthodox doctrines for the needs of the new day.[106] From that point on the cause of theological reconstruction grew, among preachers at first and then in the academy. Charles Briggs expressed its spirit when he said, it is sufficient that the Bible gives us the material for all ages and leaves to us the noble task of shaping that material to suit the wants of our own time. But the "new theology," as it was called, finally came into methodological self-consciousness in the last decade of the nineteenth century and the first three decades of our own, as the "liberalism" of the so-called Chicago School and, further east, as the social gospel. Both were creative theological responses to the moral and spiritual challenges presented by science, democracy, and rampant social injustice. Walter Rauschenbusch said that reverence for the inherited form of our ideas is a kind of ancestor worship, and for his own time he reconstructed the Christian symbol system around the concept of the kingdom of God as a moral community initiated by and through Jesus. The Chicago theologians set out after a full-blown revisionism, centered in a variety of ways within the Christian symbol system but more or less unified in its attention to the social function of theological reconstructions, past and present. It is interesting that the labels sometimes applied to these liberal efforts were *evangelical* as well as *modernist*. Both terms were fitting, for these theologians believed that the future is to be created, and hence they were modernists, out of the resources of the past, and hence they were evangelicals. They believed in theology as the reconstruction of inherited symbols. Theirs was a constructive historicism.

What happened to their efforts is complicated story, but simply put, it is the story, first, of the debacle of their very optimistic revisions of Christian faith and, then, their own loss of nerve.[107] I do not think, however, that constructive historicism—or *evangelical modernism*, as one still might call it—is only history. If it has not exactly flourished for some time now in the dominant American theologies, it is beginning to emerge again in the reflections of the racial-ethnic, feminist, and class-identified theologians. Their emphasis on liberation, variously construed, is already a substantive and, one assumes, a lasting contribution to theology. But their way of doing theology may prove to be of equally abiding importance, because theirs is a turn—or a return—to what we have called *constructive historicism*. When James Cone proposes that Christ is Black and proceeds to revise the entire Christian schema accordingly, the meanings of Christ and salvation once again have been profoundly revised, and a venture in constructive historicism has been undertaken.[108] When Sallie McFague speaks of God as mother, lover, and friend and suggests that the world is God's body, that might be the beginning of a theological reconstruction as powerful as the invention of Mother Earth and an example of constructive historicism.[109] And—in what may be the most compelling example of constructive historicism on the contemporary scene—when Judith Plaskow assimilates Torah to Jewish memory, including the memory of women, the expansion of Torah that results promises to be as revolutionary as was its ancient constriction during the exile.[110]

These particular experiments in constructive historicism may or may not prove to be adequate for the needs of today and tomorrow. That remains to be seen. But they are the *kind* of theological construction that speaks to religious and cultural communities in a manner that can be forcefully heard, passionately argued, vigorously lived, and, thus, that might make a difference. Moreover, they might represent the first manifestation of a much broader revival of theologies that address effectively the realities of our time, by creatively reconstructing our canonical symbols.

Notes

PREFACE

1.   William Carlos Williams, "To Elsie" (from *Spring and All*, 1923), in *William Carlos Williams: Selected Poems*, ed. Charles Tomlinson (New York: New Directions, 1985), p. 53.

2.   Delwin Brown, "Struggle till Daybreak: On the Nature of Authority in Theology," *Journal of Religion*, 65 (1985): 15-32.

INTRODUCTION: CICERO'S CONSENT

1.   *De Finibus Bonorum et Malorum*, V, 25, 74, trans. H. Rackham, Leob Classical Library (Cambridge: Harvard University Press, 1983), pp. 476f.

2.   Rene Descartes, *The Philosophical Works of Descartes*, trans. Elizabeth S. Haldane and G. R. T. Ross (Cambridge: Cambridge University Press), vol. I, p. 90.

3.   The image is from Francis Bacon, *Novum Organum*, Aphorism xcv, in *The English Philosophers from Bacon to Mill*, ed. E. A. Burtt (New York: Random House, 1939), p. 67. I owe this and the preceding reference to a splendid study of modern culture by Donald A. Crosby, *The Specter of the Absurd: Sources and Criticisms of Modern Nihilism* (Albany: State University of New York Press, 1988), pp. 221, 229.

4.   For exceptions to the widespread claim that we now live in a "postmodern" and therefore "post-Enlightenment" age, see Jurgen Habermas, "Modernity—An Incomplete Project," in *The Anti-Aesthetic: Essays on Postmodern Culture*, ed. Hal Foster (Port Townsend, Wash.: Bay Press, 1983), pp. 3–15; and Stanley Rosen, *Hermeneutics as Politics* (New York: Oxford University Press, 1987).

5.   Hans-Georg Gadamer, *Truth and Method*, 2d rev. ed., trans. rev. Joel Weinsheimer and Donald G. Marshall (New York: Crossroad Publishing Co., 1989), pp. 269ff; *Philosophical Hermeneutics*, ed. David E. Linge (Berkeley: University of California Press, 1976), p. 9.

6.   Among philosophers this development is represented by Alasdair MacIntyre, *After Virtue*, 2d ed. (Notre Dame, Ind.: University of Notre Dame Press, 1984); by Paul Ricoeur, *Time and Narrative*, vol. 1, trans. Kathleen McLaughlin and David Pellauer (Chicago: University of Chicago Press, 1984); and, especially, by Gadamer, whose *Truth and Method* contributes significantly to the analysis of this volume, as is particularly evident in Chapter 2.

7.   For examples in religious studies, see Peter Slater, *The Dynamics of Tradition: Meaning and Change in Religious Traditions* (San Francisco: Harper and Row, 1978); and Joseph P. Cahill, *Mended Speech: The Crisis of Religious Studies and Theology* (New York: Crossroad Publishing Co., 1982).

Among theologians, a positive appraisal of the role of tradition is particularly evident in the work of the postliberal or "narrative" theologians. See, especially, Hans W. Frei, *The Eclipse of Biblical Narrative* (New Haven, Conn.: Yale University Press, 1974); and George A. Lindbeck, *The Nature of Doctrine* (Philadelphia: Westminster Press, 1984). The importance of tradition as the vehicle of narrative is evident, if sometimes implicitly, throughout the literature on narrative and theology. See, for example, Paul Nelson, *Narrative and Morality: A Theological Inquiry* (University Park: Pennsylvania State University Press, 1987); Terrence W. Tilley, *Story Theology* (Wilmington, Del.: Michael Glazier, 1985); Michael Goldberg, *Theology and Narrative: A Critical Introduction* (Nashville: Abingdon Press, 1981), and in several of the essays in *Why Narrative? Readings in Narrative Theology*, ed. Stanley Hauerwas and L. Gregory Jones (Grand Rapids, Mich.: Wm. B. Eerdmans Publishing Co., 1989).

Among public and revisionist theologians, see, respectively, Linell E. Cady, *Religion, Theology and American Public Life* (Albany: State University of New York Press, 1993); and David Tracy, *Blessed Rage for Order: The New Pluralism in Theology* (New York: Seabury Press, 1975), *The Analogical Imagination: Christian Theology and the Culture of Pluralism* (New York: Seabury Press, 1981; and *Plurality and Ambiguity: Hermeneutics, Religion, Hope* (San Francisco: Harper and Row, 1987. For a somewhat more explicitly postmodern appropriation of tradition, see Mark Kline Taylor, *Remembering Esperanza: A Cultural-Political Theology for North American Praxis* (Maryknoll, N.Y.: Orbis Books, 1990). A phenomenological theology in which tradition is crucial is developed by Edward Farley, *Ecclesial Man: A Social Phenomenology of Faith and Reality* (Philadelphia: Fortress Press, 1975); and *Ecclesial Reflection: An Anatomy of Theological Method* (Philadelphia: Fortress Press, 1982).

8. See William C. Placher, *Unapologetic Theology* (Louisville: Westminister/John Knox, 1989), pp. 17ff; and Ronald Thiemann, *Revelation and Theology: The Gospel as Narrated Promise* (Notre Dame; Ind.: University of Notre Dame Press, 1985), pp. 72ff. Placher offers David Tracy, Schubert Ogden, and Gordon Kaufman as examples of the first option, and Hans Frei, George Lindbeck, and David Kelsey as examples of the second. Placher calls theologies of the first type *revisionary* or *public* theologies and those of the second type *postliberal* or *narrative* theologies.

9 Thiemann, *Revelation and Theology*, p. 75.

10. Tracy, Ogden, and Kaufman, it should be observed, differ in a number of ways rather significantly among themselves. Moreover, as Placher admits in the case of Tracy and Kaufman (pp. 154ff), the insistence that the criteria of theology are public is not in fact always based on the assumption of universal standards of rationality.

11. For a "postmodern" defense of universal norms—a kind of "fallibilistic common-sensism," drawing on C. S. Peirce and A. N. Whitehead—see the Introduction to David R. Griffin, ed., *Founders of Constructive Postmodern Philosophy* (Albany: State University of New York Press, 1993).

12.   This is not, of course, intended to be a specific proposal concerning the proper adjudication of theological truth claims. However, I have discussed this general viewpoint in relation to the notion of "epistemological privilege," championed by liberation theologians, in "Thinking About the God of the Poor: Some Questions for Liberation Theology from Process Thought," *Journal of the American Academy of Religion* 57 (1989): 267–81.

13.   My view does not presuppose the sharp systematic distinction that some theologians make between the claims of revelation or tradition, on the one hand, and the claims of modernity, on the other. (This disjunction is presupposed by liberal or revisionist theologians such as Langdon Gilkey and David Tracy, postliberal or narrative theologians such as George Lindbeck, and evangelical theologians such as Clark H. Pinnock.) This systematic differentiation is inappropriate because the past already infuses the present, influencing and forming many of its elements. Hence a contrast within modernity itself is of necessity a contrast already involving the past, and a contrast between past and present necessarily involves already the past as efficacious in the present. (For a critique of the tradition–modernity distinction as a methodological device, see Francis Schussler Fiorenza, *Foundational Theology: Jesus and the Church* [New York: Crossroad Publishing Co., 1984], pp. 301ff; and Rebecca S. Chopp, "Practical Theology and Liberation," in *Formation and Reflection: The Promise of Practical Theology* [Philadelphia: Fortress Press, 1987], pp. 120–38.) It is obvious that informal distinctions, sometimes quite valuable for heuristic purposes, can be made between past and present, as, indeed, between various arenas of social location and, within many of these, between arenas of academic inquiry (e.g., philosophy and anthropology). But this is only to say that the boundaries between all lived contexts and all arenas of discourse are fluid, softened always both by causal interaction and by some overlapping of criteria.

14.   In Chapters 1 and 2 the term *tradition* will be used informally, reflecting something of the diversity and vagueness of general usage. In Chapter 3 the term will be given a technical meaning, to be employed thereafter.

CHAPTER 1. TECUMSEH, TORAHS, AND CHRISTS

1. This claim is both made and illustrated with respect to anthropology in the January 1985 issue of *Theology Today*, edited by Mark Kline Taylor whose contribution is entitled, "What Has Anthropology to do with Theology." Anthropological theories contribute significantly to Taylor's theological analysis in his book, *Remembering Esperanza: A Cultural-Political Theology for North American Praxis* (Maryknoll, N.Y.: Orbis Books, 1990). Linell E. Cady argues that theology, excessively focused on textual analysis, has ignored the concrete dimensions of religion made available to us in ethnography, history of religions, and the social sciences. See her essay, "Resisting the Postmodern Turn: Theology and Contextualization," in *Theology at the End of Modernity*, ed. Sheila Greeve Davaney (Philadelphia: Trinity Press International, 1991), pp. 81–98. In *Theology and Social Theory: Beyond Secular Reason* (Oxford: Basil Blackwell, 1990), John A. Milbank develops an important critique of social scientific theory. His purpose, however, is not to dismiss social scientific *data* as being irrelevant for theology, but to show, by an analysis of the theological and antitheological assumptions of modern social thought, that the secular theories by which these data are interpreted are inadequate and must be replaced.

2. Later I refer the reader to critical assessments of each of the three case studies used. Although these published assessments are predominantly positive, conversations with scholars in the fields from which each is taken make it clear that they are not uncontroversial. As I recall, however, in every single instance where the judgment was expressed that a particular thesis (whether that of Gill, Sanders, or Clebsch) is fallacious, that judgment was coupled with an observation to the effect that "there are, nonetheless, much better examples that make precisely the same point." If scholars agree for the most part that these three case studies represent the *type* of data one finds in studying the behavior of religious traditions, then the case studies themselves may properly be taken to *illustrate the kind of phenomena that our inquiry must consider* even if their own particulars are controversial and possibly incorrect.

3.   The story of Tecumseh given here is drawn from Gill's book, *Mother Earth: An American Story* (Chicago: University of Chicago Press, 1987).

4.   For positive to generally positive assessments of Gill's argument, see the reviews by Harold Harrod (*Journal of Religion* 68 [1988]: 625f); Barnard W. Sheehan (*Journal of the American Academy of Religion* 56 [1988]: 574–76); Curtis M. Hinsley (*American Historical Review* 94 [1989]: 836f); and Thomas McElwain (*Western Folklore* [1988]). Positive appraisals, but with some substantive reservations, are provided by Thomas Buckley (*History of Religions* [1989]); Christopher Vecsey (*American Indian Quarterly* 12 [1988]: 254–56), and William S. Lyon (*Shaman's Drum* 17 [1989]).

The review by J. Baird Callicott (*Religious Studies Review*, 15 [1989]: 316–19) is more mixed in judgment. Callicott, like some other reviewers, thinks Gill's distinction between metaphor and belief is too rigid, but Baird agrees with Gill "that there has been some Indian myth-making going on in the twentieth century" (p. 319).

For negative reviews, in order of increasing intensity, see Jordan Paper (*Studies in Religion* 17 [1988]); the Editor (*Meeting Ground* 18 [1988]: 5); Ake Hultkranz (*Ethnohistory* 32 [1990]: 73f); Ward Churchill (*American Indian Culture and Research Journal* 12 [1988]: 49–67, published with Gill's reply, pp. 69–84); and M. Annette Jaimes and George A. Noriega (*The Bloomsbury Review* [1988]). The reviews by Churchill and by Jaimes and Noriega, though almost entirely ad hominem, are very significant because they show quite painfully the political connotations that Gill's thesis is perceived to have by many Indian people.

One of the most interesting critiques of Gill's book is provided in an interview with Russell Means (*Bloomsbury Review* [1988]). Means challenges Gill's claim that Indians came only recently to a belief in the earth as goddess by contending that Indians still do not hold to such a belief. The notion of Mother Earth, Means says, was only an "approximation in the English language" that an Indian would employ "to try to explain [to non-Indians] the way he or she related to the Earth." Means denies that there is, or ever was, an Indian concept of Mother Earth. About the Lakota he adds: "There's *nothing* in our tradition which remotely resembles some sort of 'earth goddess'. . . . What we are acknowledging in the concept which has become known in English as Mother Earth is an elemental force of nature, . . . [the fact that] the earth itself gives birth to and nurtures all life." While Gill and Means disagree about the presence of a Mother Earth belief among Indians today, they apparently agree about the nonexistence of that belief, as such, among Indians before the nineteenth century.

    5.   Gill, *Mother Earth*, p. 29.

    6.   Gill's animus is directed at the shabby scholarship of his predecessors and thus his most persistent criticism, in my judgment, is about scholarship: On the basis of the evidence available to them and us, White historians were not entitled to the conclusion they reached about a belief in Mother Earth among Indians. This strong emphasis, as well as some of Gill's own statements about Indian views made in the passive voice (e.g., "dependent upon" [p. 130], and "has now been appropriated" [p. 146]) can be taken to suggest that the emergence of the concept of Mother Earth among Indians was more of a simple Indian response to White scholarship and White needs than Gill's written account, taken as a whole, either says or legitimately implies. As I read it, on its constructive side Gill's argument about the emergence of Mother Earth is a claim about the creativity and agency of Native American traditions.

    7.   Gill, *Mother Earth*, p. 14.

    8.   Ibid., pp. 105f.

    9.   Ibid., p. 129.

   10.   Ibid., pp. 64.

   11.   Ibid., p. 50.

   12.   The story of the transformation of the Torah given here is drawn from James Sanders, *Torah and Canon* (Philadelphia: Fortress Press, 1972).

   13.   For critical assessments of Sanders's thesis, see the reviews by Bruce Vawter (*Catholic Biblical Quarterly* 34 [1972]: 536f) and Brevard S. Childs (*Interpretation* 27 [1973]: 88–91), and the discussion in James Barr, *Holy Scripture: Canon, Authority, Criticism* (Philadelphia: Westminster Press, 1983). Vawter says that Sanders "deals convincingly with the question of the "limits of the Pentateuch" (p. 536).

Childs agrees that the Torah was revised as Sanders claims and that historical factors affected this revision, though he disagrees with Sanders both about the theological interpretation given to this change by Israel and about the theological interpretation we should give to their hermeneutical process. Barr says Sanders's "point about the placing of Deuteronomy within the Torah, and the consequent separation between the Torah and the story thereafter, is . . . a point of importance . . . [and, he adds by implication, of scholarly] solidity" (p. 157). Earlier in the book, however, Barr expresses the view that "many of the details of [Sanders's] reconstruction . . . seem speculative to me" (p. 52, note 3; cf pp. 51f).

14.   William A. Clebsch, *Christianity in European History* (New York: Oxford University Press, 1979).

15.   Ibid., p. vi. Clebsch's insistence upon different Christs and different Christianities receives remarkably little complaint in the critical literature. Martin Marty, after observing that Clebsch's categories of delineation, while obviously an historian's impositions, are nonetheless well-grounded, points to some of the variety Clebsch missed (*Religious Studies Review* 8 [1982]: 128f). A positive estimate of the book is also offered by Belden C. Lane (*Religion in Life* 49 (1980): 107f); and Joseph A. LaBarge (*Horizons* 8 (1981): 146f). In his review essay, "Three Views of Christianity" (*Journal of the American Academy of Religion* 50 [1982]: 97–109), Peter Slater compares Clebsch's study of Christianity with that of Ninian Smart (*In Search of Christianity*, New York: Harper & Row, 1979). One might expect Smart to find Christianity rather more unified than does Clebsch because Smart approaches the topic from the perspective of the varied world religions. In fact, Slater says, there is more unity in Clebsch's interpretation of the Christian data than in Smart's (p. 105). Even the review by Donald K. McKim, an evangelical scholar, offers no objections to Clebsch's discovery of many "Christs" and "Christianities" (*Christianity Today*, 25 [February 6, 1981]: 58f). For reviews that appear to contest Clebsch's methodology rather than his conclusions, see Josef L. Altholz (*The Christian Century* 96 (1979): 824f); and James Hastings Nichols (*Church History* 51 (1982): 85f).

John W. O'Malley (*Religious Studies Review* 8 1982]: 129–33) says he finds "more continuity" in Christianity than Clebsch allows (p.

132). O'Malley's criticism is coupled with his own methodological claim that Clebschs secular approach, which O'Malley at first affirms, necessarily entails "some loss of sensitivity for . . . [what] one professes to study." O'Malley seems to suggest that the continuity of Christianity is evident only to those who are sensitive to it by virtue of their prior "spiritual affinity."

16.   Clebsch, *Christianity in European History*, p. 104.

17.   Ibid., p. 242.

18.   Ibid., p. 242.

19.   An account that takes up where Clebsch left off might well identify the beginning of a sixth period, one in which "Christ" and "Christianity" are undergoing yet another transformation through the liberating aspirations of those heretofore excluded and oppressed. From this standpoint it might also uncover vibrant alternatives in earlier Christian history heretofore suppressed.

20.   It should be noted that other claims about the process of continuity and change in religious traditions will emerge in subsequent discussion. One, not necessarily suggested by the examples cited in this chapter, is that neither continuity nor change is inherently good. Either can be destructive as well as beneficial.

CHAPTER 2.
MEDIATING THE PAST AND PRESENT

1.   Richard E. Palmer, *Hermeneutics: Interpretation Theory in Schleiermacher. Dilthey, Heidegger, and Gadamer* (Evanston, Ill,: Northwestern University Press, 1969), p. 164.

2.   Hans-Georg Gadamer, *Truth and Method*, 2nd rev. ed., trans. rev. Joel Weinsheimer and Donald G. Marshall (New York: Crossroad Publishing Co., 1989).

3.   Ibid., p. 41

4.   Ibid., p. 43, emphasis deleted.

5.   Or, to adapt a sentence from Palmer, art was left without a function in society except to embellish, and the artist without a purpose except to entertain (see Palmer, *Hermeneutics*, p. 167).

6.   Gadamer, *Truth and Method*, p. 97.

7.   Ibid., p. 100.

8.   Crucial to Gadamer's discussion of the experience of art is an extended argument to the effect that the appreciative self comes into being through a social process of "formation, education, or cultivation" (ibid., p. 9). An essential part of this formation is an openness to the other, the alien. The process of openness entails the self's movement from itself into the alien, but also the self's return to itself that, however, always changes the self in the process (ibid., p. 14). The vocation of the human spirit is this perpetual alienation, return, and therefore perpetual transformation. In a discussion of tact, common sense, taste, and judgment Gadamer argues that this process is communally formed and re-formed. Far from issuing into a kind of subjectivistic aestheticism, the aesthetic process is a mode of knowing and a source of truth—or more precisely, it is a socially formed mode of knowledge that yields claims to truth. Art is experienced as an assertion of meaning (ibid., p. 92). Art is an interpretation of our existence, which by presenting its interpretive challenge calls us to the interpretive task (ibid., p. 95).

9.   Ibid., p. 97.

10.   Ibid., p. 101. For Gadamer's discussion of play, see pp. 101–134. A critical analysis of Gadamer's view of play is provided later.

11.   Ibid., p. 103, 104f.

12.   Ibid., p. 104; cf p. 106.

13.   Ibid., p. 109ff.

14.   Ibid., p. 109f.

15.   Ibid., p. 171.

16.   Ibid., p. 118.

17.   Ibid., p. 114.

18.   Ibid., p. 126ff.

19.   Ibid., p. 137.

20.   Richard J. Bernstein, *Philosophical Profiles: Essays in the Pragmatic Mode* (Philadelphia: University of Pennsylvania Press, 1986), p. 96.

21.   The general character of Gadamer's view is evident at the outset of his analysis in his contrasting appraisals of Schleiermacher and Hegel regarding what it means to understand the past. Schleiermacher views understanding as the reconstruction of the past (*Truth and Method*, 165–69). "This view of hermeneutics," Gadamer says, is as futile and "nonsensical as all restitution and restoration of past life" (ibid., p. 167; see 173–242 for Gadamer's extended critique of Schleiermacher and the historical school that followed him). Gadamer sides with Hegel who realized that "the essential nature of the historical spirit consists not in the restoration of the past but in [its] *thoughtful mediation with contemporary life*" (ibid., p. 168f).

22.   Ibid., p. 270.

23.   See ibid., p. 265–300. Cf "The Universality of the Hermeneutical Problem" in *Philosophical Hermeneutics* (Berkeley: University of California Press, 1976), p.9: The historicity of our existence entails that prejudices, in the literal sense of the word, constitute the initial directedness of our whole ability to experience. Prejudices . . . are simply conditions whereby we experience something. . . . This formulation certainly does not mean that we are enclosed within a wall . . . [as if to declare that] 'Nothing new will be said here.' [But] is not our expectation and our readiness to hear the new also necessarily determined by the old that has already taken possession of us?

24.   Ibid., p. 272.

25.   Ibid., p. 273.

26.   Ibid., pp. 281f.

27.   Ibid., pp. 282f.

28.   Ibid., p. 300, cf pp. 300–307.

29.   Ibid., p. 301 and passim. In the Foreword to the second revised edition Gadamer says that the term *wirkungsgeschichtliche Bewusstsein* "is used to mean at once the consciousness effected in the course of history and determined by history, and the very consciousness of being thus effected and determined (ibid., p. xxxiv).

30.   Ibid., p. 300.

31.   Ibid., p. 301.

32.   Ibid., p. 300.

33.   Ibid., pp. 166f.

34.   Ibid., p. 357.

35.   Ibid., p. 290, emphasis deleted.

36.   Ibid., p. 295. Gadamer says. "every experience worthy of the name thwarts an expectation" (ibid., p. 356).

37.   Ibid., pp. 361f.

38.   Ibid., p. 361.

39.   Ibid., pp. 378f, 383ff, 438ff.

40.   Ibid., pp. 362ff.

41.   Ibid., p. 367.

42.   Ibid., pp. 299f, 362–379.

43.   Ibid., p. 363.

44.   Ibid., pp. 367f.

45.   Ibid., p. 302; cf pp. 302-307.

46.   Ibid., p. 306.

47.   Bernstein, *Philosophical Profiles*, p. 98. Cf Gadamer, *Truth and Method*, pp. 373, 463f, 472f.

48.   Bernstein, *Philosophical Profiles*, pp. 284f, note 30.

49.   See Paul Ricoeur, *Interpretation Theory: Discourse and the Surplus of Meaning* (Fort Worth: Texas Christian University Press, 1976).

50.   Gadamer, *Truth and Method*, pp. 296, 373, 462.

51.   Ibid., p. 375.

52.   Ibid., p. 461.

53.   Ibid., p. 462.

54.   Ibid., p. 397.

55.   Gadamer does not adequately address the criteria for distinguishing creative from destructive, true from false, potentialities

inherent in a tradition, and some of his statements—e.g., about achieving "a discipline that *guarantees* truth" (ibid., p. 491, emphasis added)—are manifestly un-Gadamerian.

Richard Bernstein is correct to observe that Gadamer "is employing a concept of truth that he never fully makes explicit" and to suggest that "what Gadamer himself is appealing to is a concept of truth which comes down to what can be argumentatively validated by the community of interpreters who open themselves to what tradition says to us. . . . We judge and evaluate competing claims to truth by the standards and practices that have been hammered out in the course of history" (*Philosophical Profiles*, pp. 107, 108).

Jean Grondin argues to a similar conclusion about Gadamer's functional view of truth. Grondin contends, too, that Gadamer's famous appeal to "temporal distance" as the key to distinguishing true and false prejudices (*Truth and Method*, p. 298) is simply indefensible, a point Gadamer himself has acknowledged in the most recent edition of *Truth and Method* (see p. 298, note 228). (This is not to find fault with Gadamer's basic point about temporal distance: "Time is no longer primarily a gulf to be bridged because it separates; it is actually the supportive ground of the course of events in which the present is rooted" [ibid., p. 297; cf pp. 296–300 for Gadamer's discussion of temporal distance].)

Grondin writes: "If one follows the postmetaphysical spirit of *Truth and Method*, it would be illusory to hope to discover something such as an absolute criterion that allows one to distinguish true from false prejudices. . . . The finitude that tries to test its prejudices benefits from a resource other than temporal distance. And this is *dialogue*" ("Hermeneutics and Relativism," in *Festivals of Interpretation: Essays on Hans-Georg Gadamer's Work*, ed. Kathleen Wright [Albany: State University of New York Press, 1990], p. 57.)

56.   Ibid., p. 373.

57.   Ibid., pp. 276–77 emphasis deleted.

58.   Ibid., p. 277.

59.   Ibid., p. 284.

60.   Ibid., p. 304.

61.   See note 8.

62.   Gadamer, *Truth and Method*, p. 306.

63.   Ibid., pp. 275f.

64.   See, especially, John D. Caputo, *Radical Hermeneutics: Repetition. Deconstruction, and the Hermeneutic Project* (Bloomington: Indiana University Press, 1987), pp, 108–15; see, too, Caputo's, "Gadamer's Closet Essentialism: A Derridean Critique," in *Dialogue and Deconstruction: The Gadamer-Derrida Encounter*, ed. Diane P. Michelfelder and Richard E. Palmer (Albany: State University of New York Press, 1989), pp. 258–64.

65. In this judgment I differ sharply from John Caputo, who writes that Gadamer "offers us the most liberal possible version of a fundamentally conservative idea" (*Radical Hermeneutics*, p. 115). My view, in contrast, is that Gadamer fails to develop the more "liberal" alternative implicit within his own framework, But neither do I think that Gadamer's view is "conservative," in the sense Caputo apparently intends to give to that term, when he characterizes the "sole function" of the hermeneutical tradition to be to "elucidate the Book, to help pass it on, and in so doing to remain as faithful to the original . . . as possible." "Hermeneutics," Caputo says, stems from a religious subordination to an original text and conceives itself as humble commentary [that] wants to be transparent and ultimately dispensable, superfluous" (p. 116). I do not find Gadamer's position, to say nothing of the development of it I am proposing, to be described in this characterization of hermeneutics.

66.   Gadamer, *Truth and Method*, p. 101.

67.   Ibid., pp. 110ff.

68.   Richard J. Bernstein, *Beyond Objectivism and Relativism* (Philadelphia: University of Pennsylvania Press, 1983), p. 121.

69.   Gadamer, *Truth and Method*, p. 105.

70.   Ibid., p. 105.

71.   Gadamer, *Philosophical Hermeneutics*, p. 53.

72.   Gadamer, *Truth and Method*, p. 103.

73.   Gadamer, *Philosophical Hermeneutics*, p. xxiii.

74.   Analyzing the phenomenon of play allows us to understand, better than did Gadamer, the participant's agency, the power she or he has creatively to transform tradition. This point is central to the discussion of later chapters. The disadvantage of an appeal to "play" is the association the English term has with frivolity and even triviality. Playing with and within tradition, as we shall see, is always serious, sometimes "deadly" so because it is a struggle against aspects of traditions that oppress and destroy. The agential dimension of the experience of play is crucial to the current analysis, and, in fact, this dimension allows us to make room conceptually for the possibility of successful struggles against abusive traditions.

75.   Jonathan Z. Smith, "Sacred Persistence: Towards a Redescription of Canon," in *Imagining Religion: From Babylon to Jonestown*, (Chicago: University of Chicago Press, 1982), p. 52.

76.   Carol Gilligan, *In a Different Voice: Psychological Theory and Women's Development* (Cambridge, Mass.: Harvard University Press), pp. 9–10.

77.   Whether this is so, and how, is crucial to the theory of tradition developed in the next chapter.

78.   The inclusion of both of these points in a hermeneutical understanding is a particular concern of Mark Kline Taylor in his *Remembering Esperanza: A Cultural Political Theology for North American Praxis* (Maryknoll, N.Y.: Orbis Books, 1990), p. 57f.

79.   Gadamer, *Truth and Method*, p. 389. See: "Language is the universal medium in which understanding occurs. . . . All understanding is interpretation, and all interpretation takes place in the medium of a language . . ." (ibid., p. 389, emphasis deleted). "Being that can be understood is language" (ibid., p. 474, emphasis deleted). "Man's relation to the world is absolutely and fundamentally verbal in nature" (ibid., pp. 475f).

80.   Ibid., p. 401.

81.   Ibid., p. 403.

82.   Ibid., p. 114. Cf the earlier edition, *Truth and Method* (New York: Seabury Press, 1975), p. 102.

83.   Gadamer, *Philosophical Hermeneutics*, p. 38.

84.   Gadamer, *Truth and Method*, p. 426 emphasis deleted.

85.   Cf Gadamer, *Truth and Method*, p. 276; see p. 40 in this chapter.

86.   See, especially, William James, *Essays in Radical Empiricism*, published as vol. I in combination with *A Pluralistic Universe* (New York: Longmans, Green and Co., 1947); John Dewey, *Experience and Nature* (Chicago: Open Court Publishing Co., 1926), and *Art as Experience* (New York: Capricorn Books, 1958), chapters 3, 4, 5, 11, and 12; Alfred North Whitehead, *Symbolism: Its Meaning and Effect* (New York: Macmillan Publishing Co., 1927), *The Function of Reason* (Princeton, N.J.: Princeton University Press, 1929), *Modes of Thought* (New York: Macmillan Publishing Co., 1938), and *Process and Reality*, corrected edition, ed. David Ray Griffin and Donald W. Sherburne (New York: Free Press, 1978), Chapters 4, 7, and 8; and Bernard E. Meland, *Faith and Culture* (New York: Oxford University Press, 1953), and "The Appreciative Consciousness" in *Higher Education and the Human Spirit* (Chicago: University of Chicago Press, 1953), Chapter 5.

For historical accounts of radical empiricism, and the best current applications of it to the understanding of religion, see William Dean, *American Religious Empiricism* (Albany: State University of New York Press, 1986), passim but especially pp. 20–39 and 92–99; William Dean, *History Making History* (Albany: State University of New York Press, 1986), passim but especially chapter 4; and Nancy Frankenberry, *Religion and Radical Empiricism* (Albany: State University of New York Press, 1987), Chapters 3, 4, and 5.

87.   Parallels to this aspect of radical empiricism are evident in Michael Polanyi's concept of "tacit knowledge" (see *Personal Knowledge: Towards a Post-Critical Philosophy* [New York: Harper and Row, 1964] and *The Tacit Dimension* [Garden City, N.Y.: Doubleday Books, 1966]) and, shorn of its particular ontology, in Martin Heidegger's doctrine of "attunement" (see, e.g., *The Will to Power as Art*, "Nietzsche," vol. 1 (New York: Harper & Row, 1979).

Parallels may also be seen in a number of recent contributions to metaphor theory. Examples of these include the following:

Paul Ricoeur, principally *The Rule of Metaphor* (Toronto: University of Toronto Press, 1977), but also, e.g., "Creativity in

Language," *Philosophy Today*, 17 (1973): 111; "The Metaphorical Process as Cognition, Imagination, and Feeling," *Critical Inquiry*, 5 (1978): 143–59; and *Essays on Biblical Interpretation* (Philadelphia: Fortress Press, 1980), p. 101: "My deepest conviction is that poetic language alone restores to us that participation-in or belonging-to an order of things which precedes our capacity to oppose ourselves to things taken as objects opposed to a subject."

George Lakoff and Mark Johnson, *Metaphors We Live By* (Chicago: University of Chicago Press, 1980); Mark Johnson, "Introduction, Metaphor in the Philosophical Tradition," in Johnson, ed., *Philosophical Perspectives on Metaohor* (Minneapolis: University of Minnesota Press, 1981), pp. 3–47; and Mark Johnson, The Body in the Mind: *The Bodily Basis of Meaning, Imagination, and Reason* (Chicago: University of Chicago Press, 1987).

Frank Burch Brown, *Transfiguration: Poetic Metaphor and the Languages of Religious Belief* (Chapel Hill: University of North Carolina Press, 1983), especially Chapters 6 and 7, the argument of which employs a Whiteheadian analysis of experience for interpreting poetic metaphor and religious language.

Phillip Stambovsky, *The Depictive Image* (Amherst: University of Massachusetts Press, 1988), especially Chapter 2, in which Whitehead's concepts of "perception in the mode of causal efficacy' and "perception in the mode of presentational immediacy" are applied to the analysis of metaphor.

88.   Whitehead, *Symbolism*, p. 43.

89.   Ibid., pp. 43f. Cf *Process and Reality*, p. 176.

90.   Whitehead, *Process and Reality*, p. 113.

91.   Ibid., p. 81.

92.   Ibid., pp. 119f.

93.   Ibid., p. 178. For a more extended discussion of Whitehead's doctrine of causal efficacy, see Nancy Frankenberry, *Religion and Radical Empiricism*, pp. 160–65.

94.   Radical empiricism must offer a plausible hypothesis as to how the preconscious and preconceptual experience that it posits might give rise to sensation and reflection. Whitehead's theory of concrescence (see *Process and Reality*, Part III) is one way to give an

account of such an emergence. Whitehead's theory is summarized by Donald W. Sherburne in *A Key to Whitehead's Process and Reality* (New York: Macmillan Publishing Co., 1966), Chapter 3, and more extensively, in *A Whiteheadian Aesthetic* (New Haven, Conn.: Yale University Press, 1961).

95.   Whitehead, *Process and Reality*, p. 119.

96.   Ibid., pp. 162f.

97.   Ibid., p. 163.

98.   The interpretive character of all experience, however "primitive" or basic, has been a cardinal doctrine of the American tradition since, at least, the work of Charles Sanders Peirce, William James's somewhat misleading talk about "pure experience" notwithstanding. (According to Nancy Frankenberry, however, James's doctrine of pure experience means simply that "everything real must be experienceable and everything experienced must be real" [*Religion and Radical Empiricism*, p. 105].) For Peirce's views on the interpretive character of human experience, see "Concerning Certain Faculties for Man" and "Some Consequences of Four Incapacities" in *Collected Papers of Charles Sanders Peirce*, ed. C. Hartshorne, P. Weiss, and A. Burks (Cambridge, Mass.: Harvard University Press, 1935), vol. 5, para. 213–263 and 264–317, respectively. For introductions to Peirce see Michael L. Rapaso, *Peirce's Philosophy of Religion* (Bloomington: Indiana University Press, 1989), and, more briefly, two articles by William L. Power, "*Homo Religiosus*: From a Semiotic Point of View" in *International Journal for Philosophy of Religion* 21 (1987): 65–81, and Peircean Semiotics, Religion, and Theological Realism" in *New Essays in Religious Naturalism*, ed. Creighton Peden (Macon, GA.: Mercer University Press, 1993).

99.   Whitehead, *Process and Reality*, p. 121. See *Process and Reality*, p. 162: The organic philosophy holds that consciousness only arises in the late derivative phase of complex integrations. . . . [Conscious] prehensions are late derivatives in the concrescence of an experient subject. . . . [M]ost of the difficulties of philosophy are produced [by the neglect of this fact]. Experience has been explained in a thoroughly topsy-turvy fashion, the wrong end first. In particular,

emotional and purposeful experience have been made to follow upon Hume's impressions of sensation."

100.   For one of the more influential developments of the ecological potential of process philosophy, with its radical empiricist presuppositions, see Charles Birch and John B. Cobb, Jr., *The Liberation of Life: From Cell to Community* (Cambridge: Cambridge University Press, 1981). See, too, Jay McDaniel, *Of God and Pelicans: A Theology of Reverence for Life* (Philadelphia: Westminster/John Knox, 1990) and, more briefly, my " 'Respect for the Rocks': Toward a Christian Process Theology of Nature," *Encounter* 50 (1989): 309–21.

101.   In order to find obvious examples of the pure mode of causal efficacy," Whitehead writes, "we must have recourse to the viscera and to memory" (*Process and Reality*, pp.1121f). With respect to the viscera, his point is that we have an awareness (not located in the five senses) of our bodies as the "starting point for our knowledge of the circumambient world (ibid., p. 81; cf pp. 122, 178f, 312). By *memory*, here, Whitehead refers to the inheritance of our immediately past experiences in the present moment of experience (ibid., pp. 120, 129, 166f). In both cases, Whitehead argues that we have a persistent, if dim, awareness of our connectedness with things that has been obscured in modern philosophy since Descartes and Hume, who followed the Greeks in wrongly taking visual experience to be the model for what it means to perceive the world (cf, e.g., ibid., p. 117).

102.   As Frankenberry observes: "The doctrine of causal efficacy . . . provides an elemental base in human experience for designating the most deeply creative transformations associated with religion. It is an insistence on the centrality of the body and the fact that consciousness, even when dominant in human experience, is in organic association with bodily, visceral, affective processes which either enhance conscious attention or frustrate and attenuate it. It points also to the fact that images, concepts, and theories alone do not enlighten or liberate, redeem or destroy. More profoundly, lives are created and re-created in terms of organic physical energies of nature which are most intimately experienced with the body" (*Religion and Radical Empiricism*, p. 164f).

103.   Radical empiricism, it should be said, has no special utility with respect to the adjudication of competing truth claims. Radical empiricism does lead us to the important supposition that there is a "givenness" that constrains us and our knowledge claims to some degree (cf Dean, *American Religious Empiricism*, pp. 77–85). But the contention that "radical empiricism locates its own . . . confirmability criterion . . . [in the] felt qualities of lived experience" (Frankenberry, *Religion and Radical Empiricism*, p. 106) is, at best, misleading. In the assessment of competing knowledge claims, the radical empiricist is no more able than anyone else to appeal to an experiential given undefiled by an interpretive framework that includes in particular the grid imposed by linguistic convention.

Both Nancy Frankenberry and William Dean are inadequately clear on this issue, it seems to me. Generally, Frankenberry's analysis is properly guarded. Because "we cannot compare interpretations with anything that is not itself a product of another interpretive framework," Frankenberry observes "any appeal to lived experience is relative to the theory available" (p. 131). She then makes this observation the basis for her criticism of a tendency in Bernard Meland (like William James before him) to somehow privilege "felt experience" for the adjudication of truth claims (pp. 136–44). At the conclusion of her book, however, Frankenberry says, "justification terminates ultimately not with beliefs about felt qualities of experience but with the felt qualities themselves" (p. 188), as if these experiences could be separated from the beliefs (interpretive frameworks) that we hold about them.

In *History Making History* Dean maintains that radical empiricism enables one to ground pragmatism in empirical awareness (p. 84), to have an experiential criterion of value (p. 87), and to offer reasons for one's normative judgments (p. 93). These statements, because they are made in the context of Dean's critique of the indifference of the "new historicists" to the need for criteria (see p. 82f), might be read as saying that radical empiricism produces the criteria that Rorty et al. require. It does not. But if Dean means only that radical empiricism enables us to give an account of how criteria, and the values that they presuppose, come into being or "grow from a historical tradition" (p. 83), then his point is well taken.

Radical empiricism is warranted, if at all, only insofar as it is useful in filling out an account of how humans are related to their larger environments. The effective interaction of humans and their worlds that we call *knowledge* is one form of this relationship. Another is the emergence of human valuation in relation to the natural and historical contexts of our lives. The employment of the radical empiricist hypothesis in the fourth chapter, to illuminate the relationship of individuals and religious traditions, is an extension of each of these intertwined relationships between humans and their larger environments.

104.   Gadamer, *Truth and Method*, p. 434.

105.   Ibid., p. 432.

CHAPTER 3. CULTURE AND CANON

1.   Stanley Fish, "Consequences," in *Against Theory: Literary Studies and the New Pragmatism*, ed. W. J. T. Mitchell (Chicago: University of Chicago Press, 1985), p. 128.

2.   See, e.g., the essays by Steven Knapp and Walter Benn Michaels, Stanley Fish, and Richard Rorty in Mitchell, ed., *Against Theory*, ibid. (The other essays in this volume defend theory against Knapp and Michaels.) See, too, Paul de Man, "The Resistance to Theory," *Yale French Studies* 63 (1982): 3–20.

3.   Interestingly, the critiques of theory, method, and canon are parallel arguments, claiming either on moral or philosophical grounds that each is somehow totalitarian. Hence the critique of theory will be discussed more fully, if only implicitly, later in relation to the concept of canon. What is said about canon can be applied mutatis mutandis to an evaluation of theory (and, though the issue is not discussed here, method).

4.   Cornel West, "Theory, Pragmatisms, and Politics" in *Consequences of Theory*, ed. Jonathan Arac and Barbara Johnson (Baltimore: Johns Hopkins University Press, 1991), p. 36. The contributors to this volume are "left-liberal" thinkers, in disciplines as diverse as religion, history, philosophy and literary theory, who applaud the desire of antitheorists to criticize illusion and oppression,

but who find their wholesale opposition to theory ironically complicit in the same failings.

5.   The burden of the essays in *Consequences of Theory* is that the abolition of theory is not in fact an effective cure for the quite demonstrable destruction theory has wrought in Western culture.

6.   See Robert Neville, *Reconstruction of Thinking* (Albany: State University of New York Press, 1981), pp. 23–27.

7.   For a more systematic rendering of this general point, see ibid., Chapter 2 and passim.

8.   Ibid., pp. 23–27.

9.   See Alfred North Whitehead, *Process and Reality*, corrected edition, ed. David Ray Griffin and Donald W. Sherburne (New York: The Free Press, 1978), p. 259. The technical category about which Whitehead was speaking, a *proposition*, includes what is here meant by theory.

10.   See Nikolaus Lobkowicz, *Theory and Practice: History of a Concept from Aristotle to Marx* (South Bend, Ind.: University of Notre Dame Press, 1967); Jurgen Habermas, *Theory and Practice* (Boston: Beacon Press, 1973); Richard Bernstein, *Praxis and Action: Contemporary Philosophies of Human Activity* (Philadelphia: University of Pennsylvania Press, 1971); Matthew Lamb, *Solidarity with Victims: Toward a Theology of Social Transformation* (New York: Crossroad Publishing Co., 1982); Rebecca Chopp, *Praxis and Suffering: An Interpretation of Liberation and Political Theologies* (Maryknoll, N.Y.: Orbis Books, 1986), and Clodovis Boff, *Theology and Praxis: Epistemological Foundations* (Maryknoll, N.Y.: Orbis Books, 1987).

11.   Clifford Geertz, *The Interpretation of Cultures* (New York: Basic Books, 1973), pp. 12f; cf Chapters 1 and 2. For discussions of ways in which anthropology today may be moving in a post-Geertzian directions, see Paul Rabinow, "Representations Are Social Facts," in *Writing Culture: The Poetics and Politics of Ethnography* (Berkeley: University of California Press, 1986), pp. 241ff. For a post-Geertzian move in religious studies, see Caroline Walker Bynum, "Introduction: The Complexity of Symbols," in *Gender and Religion: On the Complexity of Symbols*, ed. Caroline Walker Bynum, Stevan Harrell, and Paul Richman (Boston: Beacon Press, 1986), pp. 9ff.

12. This historical discussion is especially dependent on Raymond Williams, *Marxism and Literature* (Oxford: Oxford University Press, 1977), pp. 11–20. See also James Clifford, *The Predicament of Culture: Twentieth-Century Ethnography, Literature, and Art* (Cambridge, Mass.: Harvard University Press, 1988), pp. 92ff and 230ff, and Geertz, *Interpretation of Cultures*, pp. 249ff.

13. Williams, *Marxism and Literature*, p. 14.

14. For more on the relationship of art and culture, see Clifford, *Predicament of Culture*, pp. 215–51.

15. Giambattista Vico, *The New Science*, trans. T. Bergin and M. Fisch (Ithaca, N.Y.: Cornell University Press, 1948), quoted in Williams, *Marxism and Literature*, p. 16.

16. Williams, *Marxism and Literature*, p. 17, emphasis added.

17. Ibid., p. 17.

18. Clifford, *Predicament of Culture*, p. 230.

19. Clifford, ibid., p. 232.

20. Ibid., p. 235.

21. Ibid., p. 273; cf pp. 92f.

22. Ibid., pp. 337f.

23. Ibid., p. 274.

24. Ibid., p. 275.

25. Ibid., p. 273.

26. Ibid., p. 46.

27. Ibid., p. 339.

28. Ibid., pp. 117f.

29. Ibid., p. 341. Clifford here cites Marshall Sahlins, *Islands of History* (Chicago: University of Chicago Press, 1985).

30. See Roy Wagner, *The Invention of Culture*, rev. and expanded ed. (Chicago: University of Chicago Press, 1981).

31. Ibid., p. 4.

32. Ibid., p. 52. See pp. 10ff, 35ff, and passim for Wagner's view that both the concept of *culture* and that which the concept is about, i.e., culture, are inventions. Wagner's view is at best ambiguous and

probably inconsistent. Alongside the rhetorical flair of his "invention-alism" (e.g., p. 140: "We create nature, and tell ourselves stories about how nature creates us!") there is a hearty realism in Wagner's actual analysis, as if he thinks he is describing "what is the case." (Cf pp. 30, 40, 50, 58, 75, 126ff, and 137.) Wagner's apparent equivocation may reflect his unsystematic terminology, but it also may stem from the thrust of what is simply bad logic. In an astonishing passage Wagner announces that the step from the findings . . . that man 'interprets'. . . his surroundings through his own categories, to the conclusion that man creates his realities[,] . . . is *a necessary and inevitable one.*" (p. 150, emphasis added; cf p. 143).

However Wagner wishes to characterize his own view, I think his position is best understood as a form of interactionism. (See 52, 69, 104, 137.) In his specific analyses, Wagner's emphasis on the inventive or creative character of both cognition and culture is balanced by his sense that invention emerges in an interaction with something that is there apart from the act of creativity. And, given his idea that this dialectical process may even have analogues at the animal level (p. 52), Wagner's view can hardly be the simple "idealism" that he sometimes represents it to be.

33.   See Marshall Sahlins, *Islands of History*, p. vii (cf pp. viiff), and *Historical Metaphors and Mythical Realities: Structure in the Early History of the Sandwich Islands Kingdom* (Ann Arbor: University of Michigan, 1981), pp. 3ff.

34.   Sahlins, *Islands of History*, p. x.

35.   Ibid., p. vii; *Historical Metaphors*, p. 153. His view of cultural structures as complexes of possibilities is remarkably similar to Ricoeur's view of texts and Gadamer's (implicit) view of traditions (see Chapter 2), as well as J. Z. Smith's understanding of myth (see his *Map Is Not Territory: Studies in the History of Religions* [Leiden: E. J. Brill, 1978, p. 308).

36.   Sahlins, *Islands of History*, 148. Sahlins offers no systematic explication of what he means by *empirical realities* or *worldly circumstance*, though he sometimes refers to *nature* in this connection (see later). Sahlins seems to be assuming only that the world is not exhausted by our "cultural schemes" or symbol systems and that this

"more" is often, indeed regularly, resistant to these interpretive systems. He never suggests or implies that we can have access to these "empirical realities" independent of interpretive categories, nor does he deny that what is resistant to our categories at any one point might not also be infected with other, alternative categories. Sahling's fundamental point is that our cultural schemes are always at risk and frequently defied.

37.   Sahlins, *Historical Metaphors*, p. 67; cf *Islands of History*, pp. ix, 138, 145, 148, 149.

38.   Sahlins, *Islands of History*, p. viiif; *Historical Metaphors* p. vii.

39.   Sahlins, *Historical Metaphors*, p. 67; *Islands of History*, pp. ix, 138, 145, 148, 149.

40.   Sahlins, *Islands of History*, p. ix.

41.   Ibid., p. 140.

42.   Ibid., p. 153.

43.   Sahlins, *Historical Metaphors*, p. 7.

44.   Sahlins, *Islands of History*, p. 152.

45.   Ibid., pp. 144f, 153.

46.   Ibid., p. 149; cf p. viii.

47.   Ibid., p. 152; cf p. viii.

48.   Ibid., p. ix; cf pp. 148f.

49.   Clifford, *Predicament of Culture*, pp. 14f.

50.   Ibid., p. 145.

51.   Ibid., p. 10.

52.   Geertz, *Interpretation of Cultures*, Chapters 1 and 2. I prefer to speak of actions as having a place rather than having a meaning, for two reasons. First, *meaning* tends to be exclusively cognitive, leading us to ask "What do they mean?" when we should (also) ask, "What do they do?" In addition, *meaning* obscures the power and control inherent in symbol systems (cf, too, ibid., p. 46), whereas reference to the place and thus *the placing* of actions suggests the dimension of power.

53.   Cf Geertz, *Interpretation of Cultures*, p. 250.

54. Clifford, *Predicament of Culture*, pp. 338f.

55. Geertz, *Interpretation of Cultures*, p. 46.

56. The broader uses of "tradition"—e.g., as whatever is handed down or the process of handing down, as that which is inherited and received as being of special value, etc.—are entirely legitimate. But, for the sake of clarity, from this point on *tradition* will be used in the stricter sense of the term here being developed.

57. It is not hard to imagine, though, how the special character of the divine source, in the religious view, could be subtly transferred to the human sources of the classics, in the secular view, with results that are racist and classist.

58. See Arnold Krupat, *The Voice in the Margin: Native American Literature and the Canon* (Berkeley: University of California Press, 1989), pp. 22ff. A good deal of the following is dependent on Krupat's discussion, though it differs in important respects from some of his conclusions. In particular, Krupat's defense of a canon's inherent dynamism is coupled with his curious assumption, never defended, that the religious approach, and thus presumably religious canons as well, are antithetical to such dynamism (see, e.g., p. 26). That judgment, I shall argue, is simply unwarranted.

59. The desire to demonstrate the uniqueness of the biblical canon in order to justify claims about the Bible's unique function was the intellectual motive behind the development of Christian fundamentalism. See Ernest R. Sandeen, *The Roots of Fundamentalism: British and American Millenarianism 1800–1930* (Chicago: University of Chicago Press, 1970); George M. Marsden, *Fundamentalism and American Culture: The Shaping of Twentieth Century Evangelicalism: 1870–1925* (New York: Oxford University Press, 1980), and Marsden, ed., *Understanding Fundamentalism and Evangelicalism* (Grand Rapids, Mich.: Wm. B. Eerdmans Publishing Co., 1991). Much of the crisis and creativity in contemporary conservative Christian scholarship stems from the recognition that Christian scriptures do in fact have the kind of "human" characteristics that liberals have long claimed, and thus do not have the kind of uniqueness that much of previous conservative theology had alleged.

60. Krupat, *Voice in the Margin*, p. 23.

61. Frank Kermode, "Institutional Control of Interpretation," *Salmagundi* 43 (1979): 72–86. As evidence of the ambiguity of this analysis it should be noted that Kermode nevertheless defends canon. For a critique of this view and Kermode's use of it, see Charles Altieri, *Canons and Consequences: Reflections on the Ethical Force of Imaginative Ideals* (Evanston, Ill.: Northwestern University Press, 1990), pp. 22ff, 59ff.

62. Krupat, *Voice in the Margin*, p. 29.

63. Cf: "What is in the text? That question assumes that at some . . . level what is in the text is independent of and prior to whatever people have said about it, and that therefore the text is stable, even though interpretations of it may vary. I want to argue that there always is a text . . . but that what is in it can change, and therefore at no level is it independent of and prior to interpretation" (Stanley Fish, "Natural Circumstances, Literal Language, Direct Speech Acts, the Ordinary, the Everyday, the Obvious, What Goes Without Saying, and Other Special Cases," in *Interpretive Social Science: A Reader*, ed. Paul Rabinow and William M. Sullivan [Berkeley: University of California Press, 1979], pp. 245f).

64. Christopher Norris, *Derrida* (Cambridge, Mass.: Harvard University Press, 1987), p. 15. Cf Jacques Derrida, *Margins of Philosophy*, trans. Alan Bass (Chicago: University of Chicago Press, 1982), pp. 3–27.

Frank Lentricchia argues that Derrida himself cannot properly be employed in support of American deconstructionism, which seeks to "legitimize a genuine idealism narcissistically preoccupied with an endlessly self-generated textuality" (in *After the New Criticism* [Chicago: University of Chicago Press, 1980], p. 171). See, too, a defender of Derrida, Christopher Norris (in *The Context of Faculties: Philosophy and Theory After Deconstruction* [London: Methuen, 1985 and *Derrida* [Cambridge, Mass.: Harvard University Press, 1987]), and a critic of Derrida, Alex Callinicos (in *Against Postmodernism: A Marxist Critique* [New York: St. Martin's Press, 1990]), who make the same point.

65. See Stanley Fish, "What Makes an Interpretation Acceptable?" in *Is There a Text in This Class?* (Cambridge, Mass.:

Harvard University Press, 1980). Fish argues rightly that "disagreements are not settled by the facts, but are the means by which the facts
are settled" (p. 338). From this he infers wrongly that the facts are
whatever we settle them to be, for from the fact that "in disagreements we determine what we take the facts to be" it does not follow
that "the facts are what we take them to be."

My reasons for wanting to keep distinct the results of our determination (what we decide) and the objects of our determination (what
we decide about) have nothing to do with finding a basis for justifying
one interpretation over another. The reasons, instead, are three. First,
the collapse of the two is simply not required by the logic offered in
support of it, Roy Wagner to the contrary notwithstanding (see note
32). Second, if we should dispense with, say, the meaning of a play in
itself because we obviously cannot get beyond our interpretations of
the play to the play itself, we should also dispense with the interpretations others offer of the play because we obviously cannot get beyond
our interpretations of their interpretations to their interpretations
themselves—which I take to be absurd. Third, and most important, I
think being able to maintain the relative autonomy of the other (play,
language of the other, "object" of nature, canon, etc.) is essential for
an interactive realism, the utility of which I attempted to demonstrate
in Chapter 2 regarding Gadamer and will address again, later, with
respect to the efficacy of religious traditions. Marshall Sahlins was
implicitly making this point when he insisted that "the worldly circumstances of human action are under no inevitable obligation to
conform to" our interpretations of them (*Historical Metaphors*, p. 67).

66.   This view of text as a vast but not infinite complex of interrelated possibilities is indebted to Ricoeur, of course, but it is also similar to what Gadamer seems to presuppose about tradition (see pp. 38f)
and what Sahlins assumes about the nature of cultural structures (see
p. 64).

67.   Altieri, *Canons and Consequences*, pp. 12f. I believe Altieri asks
precisely the right question. His general alternative, however, seems
dubious to me in two respects. First, he seems to think postulating the
"purposive activity" of the text would be aided by resuscitating the
notion of "authorial presence" (p. 12). Second, his overall analysis

tends to minimize, though it does not explicitly deny, the adaptability of canons (see, e.g., pp. 52ff).

68.   For an extensive list of references to recent anti- and post-deconstructionism in literary criticism, see the Introduction to Altieri, *Canons and Consequences*, esp. notes 2 and 3 (on pp. 319f).

69.   West's comment is reported in Krupat, *Voice in the Margin*, p. 52. About Foucault's project, West observes that it allows for "revolt and rebellion" but never for "reform and revolution" (see *The American Evasion of Philosophy: A Genealogy of Pragmatism* [Madison: University of Wisconsin Press, 1989], p. 226.)

70.   Elizabeth Fox-Genovese, "Gender, Race, Class, Canon," *Salmagundi* 72 (1986) : 133.

71.   Krupat, *Voice in the Margin*, p. 29.

72.   Allon White, The Struggle for Bakhtin: Fraternal Reply to Robert Young, *Cultural Critique* 8 (1987–88): 233. Altieri makes a similar point when he writes "so long as we freely spin out undecidable textual possibilities we can claim to explain nothing but our ability to generate textual meanings. . . . We cannot . . . claim to interpret anything more than the potential for constructing certain meanings" (*Canons and Consequences*, p. 13).

73.   Fox-Genovese, "Gender, Race, Class, Canon," p. 133.

74.   Krupat, *Voice in the Margin*, p. 27.

75.   Krupat notes that, generally, the effort to retain but humanize the concept of canon seems far more urgent among "feminist critics and those . . . who are interested in marginalized and subordinated traditions" than among "male, anglophone, progressive" literary critics (*Voice in the Margin*, p. 48, note 14). Frank Kermode makes a similar point in *History and Value* (Oxford: Clarendon Press, 1988), p. 114.

Those who inhabit structures of privilege, it could be argued, can well afford to dismiss the notion of canon because "their" canon is already well ensconced in power anyway. Dispensing with the concept of canon, as a defensible locus of normative possibility, will not disestablish the hegemony of the dominate world-view; it will only remove any moral basis for the continuation of that already well-established hegemony. But dismissing canon will also deny to competitive world-views, which by definition lack the power to institute themselves, any right to claim a superior moral basis for challenging hegemony. Hence, for good pragmatic reasons insurgents are not likely to want to abolish canon; "the canon," as Kermode says, is more likely to be "what the insurgents mean to occupy . . . " (*History and Value*, p. 114).

It does not follow, however, that canon is properly taken as a basis for adjudicating differences, in the way that both Krupat and Kermode seem to imply. What a canon can and cannot do is discussed in the next chapter. Still, the claim that the wholesale dismissal of the concept of canon in fact serves the class interests of the privileged seems undeniable. (For a discussion of "deconstructionism's complicity with bourgeois interest," see Altieri, *Canons and Consequences*, pp. 2ff. Cornel West, in *American Evasion of Philosophy*, pp. 206ff, provides a similar analysis of Richard Rorty's neopragmatism, which, he says, only kicks the philosophic props from under liberal bourgeois capitalist societies; it requires no change in our cultural and political practices.")

76.   Cornel West maintains that "the use of universal discourse by the privileged to mask oppression is a modern affair enacted by the European bourgeoisies" in *Philosophical Fragments* (Grand Rapids, Mich.: Wm. B. Eerdmans Publishing Co., 1988), p. 210.

77.   None of this is meant to deny that power interacts with and permeates social relations including, especially, the social practice called *truth*—"a system of ordered procedures for the production, regulation, distribution, circulation and operation of statements (Michel Foucault, "Truth and Power" in *Power/Knowledge* [New York: Pantheon Books, 1980], p. 133). It is meant to deny any reductionism that sees social relations only in terms of the power-laden interests of specific hegemonies.

Cf Foucault, *The Order of Things* (New York: Vintage Press, 1973) and *The Archaeology of Knowledge* (New York: Harper and Row, 1976), esp. pp. 215–37. For a general introduction to Foucault, see Herbert Dreyfus and Paul Rabinow, *Michel Foucault Beyond Structuralism and Hermeneutics* (Chicago: University of Chicago Press, 1983). For an application of Foucault to anthropology, see Paul Rabinow, "Representations Are Social Facts: Modernity and Post-

Modernity in Anthropology," in *Writing Culture: The Poetics and Politics of Ethnography*, ed. James Clifford and George E. Marcus (Berkeley: University of California Press, 1986); For a critique of Foucault, see Altieri, *Canons and Consequences*, pp. 28ff, 59ff.

78.   Cf, for example, the Clebsch study discussed in Chapter 1.

79.   See John Dominic Crossan, *In Parables: The Challenge of the Historical Jesus* (New York: Harper and Row, 1973), and *Cliffs of Fall: Paradox and Polyvalence in the Parables of Jesus* (New York: Seabury Press, 1980); and Mary Ann Tolbert, *Perspective on Parables: An Approach to Multiple Interpretations* (New York: Seabury Press, 1980). The tensive, polyphonic character of this literature is nicely illustrated in the New Testament parable of the unjust steward (Luke 16:1–13), which is successively followed by six distinct summary statements, each showing a different way the parable might be interpreted. (See Willlam G. Doty, *Contemporary New Testament Interpretation* [Englewood Cliffs, N.J.: Prentice-Hall, 1972], p. 123).

80.   See, e.g., Douglas A. Knight, *Rediscovering the Traditions of Israel* (Atlanta: Scholars Press, 1975); the essays in *Tradition and Theology of the Old Testament*, ed. Douglas A. Knight (Philadelphia: Fortress Press, 1977), esp. those by Michael Fishbane, Walter Harrelson, and Douglas Knight, Robert Laurin, and Walther Zimmerli; Joseph Blenkinsopp, *Prophecy and Canon* (Notre Dame, Ind.: University of Notre Dame Press, 1977), and *Wisdom and Law in the Old Testament* (New York: Oxford University Press, 1983); Michael Fishbane, *Biblical Interpretation in Ancient Israel* (Oxford: Clarendon Press, 1985); and James A. Sanders, *Canon and Community* (Philadelphia: Fortress Press, 1984), and *From Sacred Story to Sacred Text* (Philadelphia: Fortress Press, 1987).

81.   See Walter Brueggemann, "Trajectories in Old Testament Literature and the Sociology of Ancient Israel," in Norman Gottwald, ed., *The Bible and Liberation* (Maryknoll, N.Y.: Orbis Books, 1983), pp. 303–33.

82.   See Elizabeth Schussler Fiorenza, *In Memory of Her: A Feminist Theological Reconstruction of Christian Origins* (New York: Crossroad Publishing Co., 1983), and Dennis R. MacDonald, *There Is*

No Male and Female: The Fate of a Dominical Saying in Paul and Gnosticism (Philadelphia: Fortress Press, 1987).

83.   See, e.g., James M. Robinson and Helmut Koester, eds., *Trajectories Through Early Christianity* (Philadelphia: Fortress Press, 1971); Ernst Kasemann, "The Problem of a New Testament Theology," *New Testament Studies* 19 (1973). 235–45; James D. G. Dunn, *Unity and Diversity in the New Testament* (Philadelphia: Westminster Press, 1977); and Gerhard Hasel, *New Testament Theology: Basic Issues in the Current Debate* (Grand Rapids, Mich.: Wm. B. Eerdmans Publishing Co., 1978).

84.   See David Kelsey, *The Uses of Scripture in Recent Theology* (Philadelphia: Fortress Press, 1975), and J. Severino Croatto, "Biblical Hermeneutics in the Theologies of Liberation," in *Irruption of the Third World: Challenge to Theology*, ed. Virginia Fabella and Sergio Torres (Maryknoll, N.Y.: Orbis Books, 1983), pp. 140–67.

85.   See Clark Pinnock, *The Scripture Principle* (San Francisco: Harper and Row, 1984), pp. 71f and passim.

86.   See Krupat, *Voice in the Margin*, 163ff. About Leslie Marmon Silkos *Storyteller* (New York: Seaver Books, 1981), Krupat writes: "Having called herself a storyteller, [Silko] thus places herself in a tradition of tellings, suggesting . . . that the stories to follow . . . cannot strictly be her own. . . . There is no single, distinctive, or authoritative voice in Silko's book nor any striving for such a voice (or style). . . . *Storyteller* is presented as a strongly polyphonic text, in which the author defines herself . . . in relation to the voices of other storytellers Native and non-native. . . . "

87.   The quotation is from Krupat, *Voice in the Margin*, p. 164. See also Dennis Tedlock, *Finding the Center: Narrative Poetry of the Zuni Indians* (Lincoln: University of Nebraska Press, 1978).

88.   Mary Midgley, *Beast and Man: The Roots of Human Nature* (New York: Meridian Books, 1980), p. 295.

CHAPTER 4. CANON, CHAOS AND ORDER

1.   I owe this use of "galaxy" to Sam D. Gill. who, however, gives it a more technical meaning. See "One, Two, Three: The Inter-

pretation of Religious Action," in *Native American Religious Action: A Performance Approach to Religion* (Columbia: University of South Carolina Press, 1987), pp. 147–72.

2. This use of the term is taken from Donald Pease, in "Toward a Sociology of Literary Knowledge," *Consequences of Theory*, ed. Jonathan Arac and Barbara Johnson (Baltimore: Johns Hopkins University Press, 1991), p. 121.

3. Jonathan Z. Smith, "Sacred Persistence: Towards a Redescription of Canon," in *Imagining Religion: From Babylon to Jonestown* (Chicago: University of Chicago Press: 1982), p. 51.

4. To indicate both sides of this dynamic I usually speak of playing or negotiating *with/in* canon.

5. Cf Paul Lauter, *Canons and Contexts* (New York: Oxford University Press, 1991), p. 169: "canons are socially constructed *by* people and *in* history, . . . they have always changed and can be changed."

6. Charles Altieri, *Canons and Consequences: Reflections on the Ethical Force of Imaginative Ideals* (Evanston, Ill.: Northwestern University Press, 1990), p. 33.

7. It might be maintained, for example, that canon is "canonically" interpreted only under the guidance of a particular group (e.g., a specially authorized body), or through a particular process (e.g., communal commentary or exegesis), or with a particular attitude (e.g., openness to divine guidance).

8. Cf Harry Y. Gamble, speaking of the biblical canon: "What needs special recognition . . . is that the canon is pluralistic in principle," in "Canon—New Testament," *The Anchor Bible Dictionary*, vol. 1, ed. David Noel Freedman (New York: Doubleday Books, 1992), p. 859. On the pluralism or internal diversity of the biblical canon, also see, e.g., James A. Sanders, Canon—Hebrew Bible," *Anchor Bible Dictionary*, vol. 1, pp. 847f; Sanders, *From Sacred Story to Sacred Text* (Philadelphia: Fortress Press, 1987); and Donn F. Morgan, *Between Text and Community* (Minneapolis: Augsburg Press, 1990), pp. 6f and passim.

9. Sanders, "Canon—Hebrew Bible," p. 843.

10.   See Gamble, "Canon—New Testament," p. 859.

11.   In this vein James Sanders speaks of the Bible as a "monotheizing literature in spite of the fact that it is not, strictly speaking, monotheistic (see "Canon—Hebrew Bible," pp. 843–45). For Sanders, this means simply that "the Bible as canon induces the belief that there is moral fiber to the universe despite all the obvious and evident injustice" (p. 850). As we shall see, except perhaps at a level of extreme generality (the confidence that there is "moral fiber to the universe," after all, might well be a useful working definition of "religiousness" as such!), the complex and dynamic "gravitational pull" of a canon throughout its history defies singular descriptions, even though proposing such descriptions or construals in and for particular times and places is part of what it means to inhabit a canon.

12.   Altieri, *Canons and Consequences*, p. 27.

13.   The position developed here on the normativeness of canon differs somewhat from that in my "Struggle till Daybreak: On the Nature of Authority in Theology," *Journal of Religion* 65 (1985): 15–32. In that article I spoke of the canon as a whole as formative but not as normative in any sense. Obviously, I have modified that position. In view of the diversity within canon, however, my present position still leads me to speak of the "authority" of a canon as its power to *author* identity rather than as its entitlement to *authorize* belief and action. Authorizing is a task fallibly conducted through critical examination in the arenas of contemporary discourse.

14.   In *The Voice in the Margin: Native American Literature and the Canon* (Berkeley: University of California Press, 1989), pp. 51f and passim, Arnold Krupat proposes "heterodoxy" as a principle for organizing an American literary canon. I am proposing that religious canons do not need to be so organized; in fact, they already are heterodoxies!

15.   *Negotiation* and *play*, used interchangeably to this point, can be distinguished, informally, as different though interrelated forms of contestation. *Negotiation* can be used to refer to the dominantly cognitive dimension of the process of contestation (e.g., in theology), whereas *play* can be taken to indicate the affective and predominantly noncognitive dimension of that process (e.g., in ritual).

16.   Cf Gamble "although [canon] requires a limitation and speci-
fication of its meaning to exercise a normative function, it nevertheless resists the absolutizing of any particular appropriation . . . "
("Canon—New Testament," p. 859).

17.   The term *size* comes from Bernard Loomer. See his "The
Size of God," in *The Size of God: The Theology of Bernard Loomer in
Context*, ed. William Dean and Larry E. Axel (Macon, Ga.: Mercer
University Press, 1987).

18.   On the adaptability of canon, see, esp., James Sanders,
"Adaptable for Life: The Nature and Function of Canon," in *From
Sacred Story to Sacred Text*, pp. 9–39, and "Canon—Hebrew Bible,"
pp. 847f.

19.   This is Robin Horton's conclusion (a reversal of his earlier
view) about the privilege granted to the past in African traditions.
"An item of [inherited] belief is legitimated," he writes, "*not just*
because it is certified as having come down to us from the ancients;
but *ultimately* because the beliefs of the ancients, in general, are
thought to have proved their worth down through the ages as instru-
ments of explanation, prediction, and control. To put it in a nutshell,
beliefs are accepted, not just because they are seen as age-old, but
because they are seen as time-tested." (See Robin Horton, "Tradition
and Modernity Revisited," in *Rationality and Relativism*, ed. Martin
Hollis and Steven Lukes [Cambridge, Mass.: MIT Press, 1984], p.
240. Horton's earlier article was "African Traditional Thought and
Western Science," *Africa* 37 [1967].)

20.   The role of canon in the creation and recreation of individual
and corporate identity is a central theme throughout James Sanders's
work on canon. See *Torah and Canon* (Philadelphia: Fortress Press,
1972); *Canon and Community* (Philadelphia: Fortress Press, 1979);
From Sacred Story; and Canon—Hebrew Bible," pp. 846–51. (As
Sanders rightly observes, incidentally, to attribute to canon an existential function is not necessarily to subscribe to an existentialist philosophy. See *From Sacred Story*, p. 153.)

21.   Altieri, *Canons and Consequences*, p. 10.

22.   Raymond Williams, *Marxism and Literature* (Oxford: Oxford
University Press, 1977), p. 130.

23.   Ibid., p. 118.

24.   Ibid., p. 118 emphasis deleted. Williams describes the hegemonic as "a whole body of practices and expectations, over the whole of living: our senses and assignments of energy, our shaping perceptions of ourselves and our world. It is a lived system of meanings and values—constitutive and constituting—which as they are experienced as practices appear as reciprocally confirming" (p. 110).

25.   Ibid., p. 118.

26.   Alasdair MacIntyre, *After Virtue: A Study in Moral Theory*, 2nd ed. (Notre Dame, Ind.: University of Notre Dame Press, 1984), p. 216. For MacIntyre's broader argument, as it relates to his view of tradition, see pp. 201–225.

27.   Ibid., p. 216.

28.   Williams, *Marxism and Literature*, p. 130.

29.   Dennis Tedlock and Arnold Krupat, as we saw in Chapter 3, contend that stories have a tendency to dissimilate. The transformation of stories into story into narrative—a process implicit in MacIntyre's analysis and in much of the "narrative theology" that allies with him—resists this possibility and obscures the inherently conflictual consequences of the diversity of stories within canon.

30.   Cf Roy Wagner's comment on effective cultural change: "the innovator remains committed to the Culture he is precipitating and innovating against . . . " (*Invention of Culture* [Chicago: University of Chicago Press, 1981], p. 68).

31.   This perception, however, may be mistaken, and the mistake may be prompted by the organic notion of cultural forms with which cultural theory has operated until quite recently. The fractured and unwieldy character of cultural forms in general, and of canons in particular, make it likely that canonical processes will constantly be in need of "repair," i.e., negotiation, even without significant external challenge. (Marshall Sahlins seems to doubt that external challenge is the greater impetus for change. See his *Islands of History* [Chicago: University of Chicago Press, 1985], pp. viiif; and *Historical Metaphors and Mythical Realities: Structure in the Early History of the Sandwich Islands Kingdom* [Ann Arbor: University of Michigan, 1981], p. vii.)

32.   Whether the material drawn upon is "really" canonical is, at this level of analysis, a moot point. Just as for the reader a particular text is in part the history of its interpretations as they affect the reader, so, too, a canon is in part the history of its interpretations through communal celebration, imagination, and explication as they impinge upon the adherent. Pressing the question of what is "really" canonical occurs, or may occur, as a strategy within the process of negotiating canon, but not in the process of characterizing that negotiation.

33.   Thus, according to the studies discussed in Chapter 1, Christ as savior and model of righteousness is continuously reconfigured (Clebsch), Torah is relocated (Sanders), and historic Indian sensibilities are focused and elevated (Gill). The cultural theories considered in Chapter 3 lead to the same conclusion.

34.   Sahlins, *Islands of History*, p. ix.

35.   Caroline Walker Bynum, "Introduction: The Complexity of Symbols," in *Gender and Religion: On the Complexity of Symbols*, ed. Caroline Walker Bynum, Stevan Harrell, and Paula Richman (Boston: Beacon Press, 1986), pp. 15f.

36.   Wagner suggests that "Americans and other Westerners" try to predict, rationalize, and order" their world, whereas "tribal, religious, and peasant peoples" try to change it—"to knock the conventional off balance" (Wagner, *Invention of Culture*, pp. 887f).

37.   Altieri, *Canons and Consequences*, p. 21.

38.   Cf Frank Kermode, *History and Value* (Oxford: Clarendon Press, 1988), pp. 144f: "[Canon] is a highly selective instrument, and one reason why we need to use it is that we haven't enough memory to process everything. The only other option is not a universal reception of the past . . . but a Dadaist destruction of it."

39.   See Chapter 3, pp. 64f.

40.   See Chapter 3, pp. 69–72.

41.   See this chapter, pp. 75–77.

42.   See Chapter 2, pp. 39–45.

43.   Jonathan Z. Smith, *Imagining Religion: From Babylon to Jonestown* (Chicago: University of Chicago Press, 1982), p. 57; cf pp. 53–65. My understanding of Smith has benefited greatly from an

unpublished essay by Sam D. Gill, "No Place to Stand: Jonathan Z. Smith and Religion," though my assessment of the place of continuity and change in Smith's view of ritual differs somewhat from Gill's, in whose work the disjunctive or "abductive" function of ritual is made primary. (See, e.g., *Native American Religious Action: A Performance Approach to Religion* [Columbia: University of South Carolina Press, 1987], especially "Disenchantment: A Religious Abduction," pp. 58–75; and *Beyond 'The Primitive': The Religions of Nonliterate Peoples* [Englewood Cliffs, N.J.: Prentice-Hall, 1982].) I am sure that Sam Gill, more than anyone else, is responsible for my appreciation of the role of ritual in tradition.

For primary sources for work on ritual in religious studies, see Ronald Grimes, *Beginnings in Ritual Studies* (Washington, D.C.: University Press of America, 1982), and *Research in Ritual Studies: A Programmatic Essay and Bibliography* (Metuchen, N.J., and London: American Theological Library Association and Scarecrow Press, 1985), as well as the volumes of *Journal of Ritual Studies*. Perhaps the most important recent work in ritual theory within the context of religious studies is that of Catherine Bell, especially *Strategic Practices: Ritual in Thought and Action* (Oxford: Oxford University Press, 1992).

44.   Smith, *Imagining Religion*, p. 59.

45.   Ibid., p. 59; Smith is quoting from D. Zelenin, *Kult ongonov v Sibiri* (Moscow-Leningrad, 1936), as translated in G. Welter, *Le Culte des idoles en Siberie* (Paris, 1952).

46.   Smith, *Imagining Religion*, p. 60f.

47.   Ibid., p. 63, italics removed.

48.   Ibid., pp. 62, 63, respectively.

49.   See "To Put in Place," in Jonathan Z. Smith, *To Take Place* (Chicago: University of Chicago Press, 1987), pp. 47–73, where Smith discusses the views of Paul Wheatley, Roy Rappaport, Clifford Geertz, and others.

50.   Smith, *To Take Place*, p. 110.

51.   Jonathan Z. Smith, *Map Is Not Territory* (Leiden: E. J. Brill, 1978), p. 309.

52. Smith, *Imagining Religion*, p. 63, italics removed; cf Smith, *To Take Place*, p. 109.

53. See *To Take Place*, pp. 55ff. It should be apparent that the maintenance of the status quo can sometimes be desirable, either because the values inherited are worthy of perpetuation or because the most likely alternatives are, at least for the time being, more destructive than the given state of affairs. Thus in this discussion "the ideal" and "alternative possibility" are not simply equated, though both stand as alternatives to the status quo, the former being a subset of the latter.

54. Smith, *Map Is Not Territory*, p. 309. The locative map is a "conservative" (p. 293) one that "guarantees meaning and value through structures of congruity and conformity" (p. 292, cf pp. 308f). For the utopian map there is "terror and confinement in interconnection, correspondence, and repetition. The moments of disjunction become coextensive with finite existence and the world is perceived to be chaotic, reversed, liminal. Rather than celebration, affirmation and repetition, man turns in rebellion and flight to a new world and a new mode of creation" (p. 309).

55. Gill, "No Place to Stand" (unpublished).

56. For an account and critique of this view, see Joseph Fontenrose, *The Ritual Theory of Myth* (Berkeley: University of California Press, 1971).

57. Victor Turner, *Dramas. Fields, and Metaphors: Symbolic Action in Human Society* (Ithaca, N.Y.: Cornell University Press, 1974) p. 57.

58. See Clyde Kluckhohn, "Myths and Rituals: A General Theory," *Harvard Theological Review* 35 (1942): 45–79. See, however, Mary Douglas: "Implicitly I find myself returning to Robertson Smith's idea that rites are prior and myths are secondary in the study of religion," in *Natural Symbols* (New York: Pantheon Books, 1970), p. 30.

59. A. R. Radcliffe-Brown, *The Andaman Islanders* (Glencoe, Ill.: The Free Press, 1965), p. 157.

60. See Emile Durkheim, *The Elementary Forms of the Religious Life* (New York: The Free Press, 1915). Cf, too, Bobby C. Alexander,

Victor Turner Revisited: Ritual as Social Change (Atlanta: Scholars Press, 1991), pp. 3, 27ff.

61. Clifford Geertz, "Ritual and Social Change: A Javanese Example," in *The Interpretation of Cultures* (New York: Basic Books, 1973), p. 143; cf pp. 142–69.

62. Victor Turner, *From Ritual to Theatre: The Seriousness of Human Play* (New York: Performance Art Journal Publications, 1982), p. 79. See Alexander, *Victor Turner Revisited*, pp. 13–26, for a discussion of Turner's definitions and for critiques of them. In his earliest definitions and for long thereafter Turner associated ritual with beliefs "in mystical beings or powers" (e.g., *The Forest of Symbols: Aspects of Ndembu Ritual* [Ithaca, N.Y.: Cornell University Press, 1967], p. 19). The potential significance of Turner's eventual replacement of these beliefs with beliefs in "invisible . . . powers," to be discussed later in this section, is not considered by Alexander in his generally superb study. My view, incidentally, is that *ritual*, like *religion*, refers to a family of phenomena related variously, with the result that no definition will cover all the plausible members of the family. This view is argued for, though in ways I do not find wholly persuasive, by Jack Goody in "Against 'Ritual': Loosely Structured Thoughts on a Loosely Defined Topic" (in *Secular Ritual*, ed. Sally F. Moore and Barbara G. Myerhoff [Amsterdam: Van Gorcum, 1977], pp. 25–35).

63. Alexander, *Victor Turner Revisited*, p. 17.

64. Victor Turner, *The Ritual Process* (Chicago: Aldine, 1969), p. 95; cf pp. 94–130. See, too, Victor Turner, "Variations on a Theme of Liminality" in *Secular Ritual*, pp. 36–52.

65. Turner, *Dramas, Fields, and Metaphors* p. 238.

66. See especially Turner, *Ritual Process*, pp. 125–165, and *Dramas, Fields, and Metaphors* pp. 231–271.

67. For references, see Alexander, *Victor Turner Revisited*, pp. 1f.

68. See, e.g., Victor Turner, *The Drums of Affliction: A Study of Religious Processes Among the Ndembu of Zambia* (Oxford: Clarendon Press, 1968), p. 7.

69.   For a discussion of the variety of ways that ritual promotes change, according to Turner, see Alexander, *Victor Turner Revisited*, pp. 45–66.

70.   See Turner, *The Forest of Symbols*, p. 95.

71.   Turner's assimilation of ritual to liminality is criticized by Ronald Grimes (*Beginnings in Ritual Study*, p. 155), and Caroline Walker Bynum ("Women's Stories, Women's Symbols: A Critique of Victor Turner's Theory of Liminality," in *Anthropoloqy and the Study of Religion*, ed. Robert L. Moore and Frank E. Reynolds [Chicago: Center for the Scientific Study of Religion, 1984], pp. 105–25). Bynum writes: "If women's communities [in the Western European Middle Ages] . . . were institutionalized liminality in Turner's sense, that liminality was imaged as continuity with, not as reversal of, the women's ordinary experience" (p. 117). Grimes suggests that "ritual studies should be grounded in hermeneutics," not liminality (p. 155), a point with which I agree if hermeneutics is understood as indicated in Chapter 2.

72.   Moore and Myerhoff, *Secular Ritual*, p. 17.

73.   See earlier, p. 183, note 30.

74.   Therefore, see Moore and Myerhoff, *Secular Ritual*, p. 5: "One of the least disputable contentions of this book [a collection of conference essays] is that a balance should be sought between these two ways of looking" at the function of ritual.

Catherine Bell (see "Ritual, Change, and Changing Rituals," *Worship* 61 [1989]: 31–41) holds that ritual can serve either continuity or change because it is "not intrinsically concerned with either (p. 34). For Bell (see "The Ritual Body and the Dynamics of Ritual Power," *Journal of Ritual Studies* 4 [1990]: 299–313), ritual addresses "a contradiction between the cultural order and the conditions of the historical moment" (p. 310) "without becoming explicit either in personal consciousness or social discourse" (pp. 301f). She adds, "It does not see what it does to this situation, which is to redefine it" (p. 310). Bell's blanket exclusion of consciousness from the ritual process is excessive, hinging on a dualism she herself rejects (p. 300), and probably it is more than she intended because Bell later refers to the "*relative* unconscious" of the ritual process (p. 310, emphasis added).

75.   Cf Catherine Bell's observation that among ritual theorists today "there is a temptation to swing from the pole of considering rites powerless to the opposite extreme of characterizing ritual as all-powerful . . . " (in "The Ritual Body," p. 300).

76.   Answers to these questions are likely to be even more speculative, and thus more tentative in character, than an inquiry, such as the foregoing, into what ritual is and does. But seeking plausible answers, i.e., hypotheses, is necessary if we are seriously to challenge the supposition, deeply ingrained in the modern Western mind and pervasive in its scholarship, that ritual is dispensable or secondary (or at least it ought to be) to the ongoing development of healthy, informed, and "enlightened" traditions.

77.   Meredith B. McGuire ("Religion and the Body: Rematerializing the Human Body in the Social Sciences of Religion," *Journal for the Scientific Study of Religion*, 29 [1990]: 283–296) offers a wonderful "creation tale" in which God, in the process of preparing for the creation of human beings, requests and receives elaborately detailed plans for humans and projections of human behavior from the "top angel social scientists of religion" in heaven. God is much impressed, except for one small detail: "Colleagues," she says, "these ideas are very promising. . . . [But] what if—I mean, try to imagine for a moment, just what if these humans had *bodies*???" More recent research has shown that God's angelic consultants also included a number of theologians and philosophers.

78.   See McGuire, "Religion and the Body," and Scott Heller, "The Human Body and Changing Cultural Conceptions of It Draw Attention of Humanities and Social-Science Scholars," *The Chronicle of Higher Education* (June 12, 1991), pp. A4, A8f.

79.   See George Lakoff's, *Women, Fire, and Dangerous Things: What Categories Reveal About the Mind* (Chicago: University of Chicago Press, 1987), in which it is argued that categories are grounded in "our collective biological capacities and our physical and social experiences" (p. 267) rather than in the supposedly common properties of the objects classified.

80.   See, e.g., Iris Marion Young, *Throwing Like a Girl and Other Essays in Feminist Philosophy and Social Theory* (Bloomington: Indiana

University Press, 1990), which locates the source of "feminine bodily comportment, motility, and spatiality" in the "particular situation of women as conditioned by their sexist oppression in contemporary society" (p. 153). See, esp., Part III ("Throwing Like a Girl," "Pregnant Embodiment," "Women Recovering Our Clothes," and "Breasted Experience"). See, too, the special issue of *Hypatia*, 6 (Fall 1991) on "Feminism and the Body."

81.   See Mark Johnson, *The Body in the Mind: The Bodily Basis of Meaning, Imagination, and Reason* (Chicago: University of Chicago Press, 1987), which seeks to demonstrate that the "structures of our bodily experience work their way up into abstract meanings and patterns of inference" (p. xix) by means of imagination, which is taken to be "central in . . . all meaning, understanding, and reasoning" (p. ix). Cf, too, George Lakoff and Mark Johnson, *Metaphors We Live By* (Chicago: University of Chicago Press, 1980).

82.   In "Body Works: Knowledge of the Body in the Study of Religion," *History of Religions*, 30 (1990): 86–99, Lawrence E. Sullivan notes that, in spite of the very different conceptions of the human body they are working with, there is among the scholars he reviews impressive agreement that "the body lies at the center of [a] cultural worldview" (p. 99), and among the religions represented in these studies even more remarkable agreement that the body has a knowledge of the world that is "transmitted in a critical apprenticeship or in a critical ritual experience—that is, a bodily experience—rather than through the transmission of narrative, doctrine, or discourse" (p. 87). Sullivan asks whether it might not be appropriate to allow these other cultures to be more than objects studied by our methods, but also resources to be heeded in answering questions about "the different modes of knowing and the relations among them" (p. 87).

83.   Bell, "The Ritual Body," p. 300.

84.   Merleau-Ponty, *The Structure of Behavior* (Boston: Beacon Press, 1963); first published as *La Structure du comportement* in 1942.

85.   Gary Brent Madison, *The Phenomenology of Merleau-Ponty* (Athens: Ohio University Press, 1981), p. 19.

86. Merleau-Ponty, *The Phenomenology of Perception* (London: Routledge and Kegan Paul, 1962); first published as *Phenomenologie de la perception* in 1945.

87. I wish to acknowledge the indebtedness of my discussion of Merleau-Ponty to the work of Diane Prosser MacDonald, whose 1993 Ph.D. dissertation at the University of Denver and Iliff School of Theology is entitled "Transgressive Corporeality: The Body, Poststructuralism, and the Theological Imagination."

88. See, esp., Merleau-Ponty, *Phenomenology of Perception*, pp. 3–63.

89. See ibid., passim, but especially pp. 98–153 and 299–409. Cf Maurice Merleau-Ponty, "The Primacy of Perception and Its Philosophical Consequences," in *The Primacy of Perception*, ed. James M. Edie (Evanston, Ill.: Northwestern University Press, 1964), pp. 12–42.

90. Ibid., p. 150.

91. Ibid., p. 82.

92. Ibid., p. 148.

93. See Patrick Burke, "Listening to the Abyss" in *Ontology and Altarity in Merleau-Ponty*, ed. Galen A. Johnson and Michael B. Smith (Evanston, Ill.: Northwestern University Press, 1990), pp. 81–97.

94. Merleau-Ponty, *Phenomenoloqy of Perception*, pp. 211, 430.

95. Ibid., pp. 174–199.

96. Merleau-Ponty demonstrates the same interrelationship of natural processes and human meanings in his analysis of desire and love in "The Body in Its Sexual Being" (see *Phenomenology of Perception*, pp. 154–73).

97. Merleau-Ponty, *Phenomenology of Perception*, p. 197, cf pp. 196f.

98. Ibid., p. xiii. The bulk of Merleau-Ponty's last major writings (and his judgment on his earlier work—see pp. 159, 211) appear in *The Visible and the Invisible* (Evanston, Ill.: Northwestern University Press, 1968); first published an *Le visible et l'invisible* in 1964.

99. Maurice Merleau-Ponty, "Eye and Mind," in *Primacy of Perception* p. 172, cf pp. 159–90 (first published as "L'Oeil et l'esprit" in 1961).

100. For a critical analysis of Merleau-Ponty's notion of *flesh*, see Madison, *Phenomenology of Merleau-Ponty*, pp. 168–265.

101. Ibid., pp. 49f.

102. Merleau-Ponty, *Phenomenology of Perception*, p. 190.

103. Ibid., p. 193.

104. Ibid., p. 190.

105. See ibid., pp. 177ff on speech, pp. 184ff on gesture.

106. See ibid., pp. 189f.

107. See ibid., pp. 186ff, 369–409.

108. Maurice Merleau-Ponty, *Signs* (Evanston, Ill.: Northwestern University Press, 1964), p. 80.

109. See, e.g., ibid., p. 81, and *Phenomenology of Perception*, pp. 388ff.

110. Merleau-Ponty, *Phenomenology of Perception*, 166.

111. Ibid., p. 189.

112. Ibid., p. 291: "We must recognize as anterior to 'sense-giving acts' . . . 'expressive experiences' . . . ; as anterior to the sign significance . . . , the expressive significance . . . , and finally as anterior to any subsuming of content under form, the symbolical 'pregnancy' of form in content."

113. Ibid., p. 296: "The lived is certainly lived by me. . . . But I can experience more things than I represent to myself. . . . That which is merely lived is ambivalent; there are feelings in me which I do not name."

114. Ibid., p. 298: "The consciousness of the world is not *based* on self-consciousness. . . . There is a world for me because I am not unaware of myself: and I am not concealed from myself because I have a . . . pre-conscious possession of the world."

115. Ibid., p. 298.

116. Ibid., pp. 187, 188.

117.   In *The Body's Recollection of Being* (London: Routledge and Kegan Paul, 1985), David Michael Levin proposes just such a "radicalization" of Merleau-Ponty. The task now, according to Levin, is a therapeutic one; namely, to retrieve the primordial sense of our bodily "inherence in the field of Being as a whole" (p. 67), which is, he says, preconceptual, precognitive, prereflective, or even preontological—his terms vary. Toward that end Levin begins to "adumbrate . . . a process by virtue of which we go into the innermost body of felt experience in order to *develop* an inborn potential for opening to the presencing of Being as such, and *redeem* thereby the primordial claim on our existence that our inherence in Being has already laid out" (p. 78).

118.   Merleau-Ponty, *Visible and the Invisible*, p. 147.

119.   Levin, *Body's Recollection of Being*, p. 5.

120.   Whitehead's only extended discussion of ritual, in *Religion in the Making* (New York: Macmillan Publishing Co., 1926), pp. 20–23, is quite unsystematic.

121.   The best formal statement of Whitehead's cosmology is his *Process and Reality*, corrected ed., ed. David Ray Griffin and Donald Sherburne (New York: Free Press, 1978). For a more accessible entre into Whitehead's thinking, see *Science and the Modern World* (New York: Macmillan Publishing Co., 1925) and *Adventures of Ideas* (New York: Free Press, 1933). The earlier critical interpreters of Whitehead's general philosophical viewpoint were William A. Christian, Ivor Leclerc, and Charles Hartshorne. The more important recent interpreters include John B. Cobb, Jr., Lewis S. Ford, David R. Griffin, George Lucas, and Donald W. Sherburne. The journal *Process Studies* is devoted to specialized studies in Whiteheadian philosophy.

122.   Alfred North Whitehead, *Modes of Thought* (New York: Macmillan Publishing Co., 1938), pp. 188f.

123.   See Chapter 2, pp. 49–52.

124.   The term is from Turner's later definition of ritual. See page 95 and note 62.

125.   Interest in the impact of speaking vs. writing on what is thought and communicated has mushroomed since the publication of

Albert Bates Lord's 1949 doctoral dissertation on the oral epic tradition of Yugoslavian singers, as *The Singer of Tales*, (Cambridge, Mass.: Harvard University Press, 1960). (For accounts of this development, see John Foley, *The Theory of Oral Composition: History and Methodology* [Bloomington: Indiana University Press, 1988]; and Jean-Pierre Vernant, "The Reason of Myth," in his *Myth and Society in Ancient Greece* [Sussex: Harvester Press, and Atlantic Highlands, N.J.: Humanities Press, 1980].) Among the most important studies on the general topic, see Walter J. Ong's *Orality and Literacy: The Technologizinq of the Word* (New York: Methuen, 1982), and Jack Goody's *The Interface Between the Written and the Oral* (New York: Cambridge University Press, 1987), both of which argue that orality is more creative than literacy. See, too, William Graham's *Beyond the Written Word: Oral Aspects of Scripture in the History of Religion* (New York: Cambridge University Press, 1987), which contends that the more influential transition was not that from orality to literacy, but from oral and chirographic cultures to typographic ones. Graham argues that oral and chirographic modes allow for more holistic religious expression. However, Paul Ricoeur, in *Interpretation Theory: Discourse and the Surplus of Meaning* (Fort Worth: Texas Christian University Press, 1976) and elsewhere, contends that writing has greater meaning potential than does orality. Jacques Derrida, too, values writing over orality. See his *Speech and Phenomena* (Evanston, Ill.: Northwestern University Press, 1973); *Of Grammatology* (Baltimore: Johns Hopklns University Press, 1976), and *Writing and Difference* (London: Routledge and Kegan Paul, 1978).

Drawing on the work of Michel Foucault, however, one might deny all such "essentialist" interpretations of the function of orality and literacy, but hold nonetheless that each becomes tied historically to particular power/knowledge constructs and, thus, that overturning either is essential to undermining the patterns of reasoning and power enjoyed by the dominant group that employs them. See Foucault, *The Order of Things: An Archaeology of the Human Sciences* (London: Tavistock Publications, 1979), and *Power/Knowledge* (New York: Pantheon Books, 1980). Werner H. Kelber's work on the shift from oral traditions in the early Christian movement to the written gospels could be placed in this interpretative context. Kelber, in *The Oral and the Written Gospel* (Philadelphia: Fortress Press, 1983) argues that Mark was written to displace the authority of an oral tradition in order to create a new christology.

For introducing me to many of these materials, and for much of this note, I am indebted to Diane Prosser MacDonald.

126.   Levin, *Body's Recollection of Being*, p. 347.

CHAPTER 5. IMAGINATION AND CHARACTER

1.   The discussion of the preceding chapters can presumably stand on its own as a theoretical analysis of the nature of religious tradition. As such it contributes to the genre of "religious studies" scholarship that seeks, among other things, to understand religions as more or less integrated systems and not simply as elements of and functions within some construal of the larger social fabric. As acknowledged in the Preface, however, this particular study of tradition is motivated by an interest in what it implies about theological construction. This final chapter, which remains in a sense pre- or metatheological, examines those implications.

2.   For representative literature dealing, directly or indirectly, with the cultural marginality of theology, see David Tracy, *Blessed Rage for Order: The New Pluralism in Theology* (New York: Seabury Press, 1975), Chapters 1–3, *The Analogical Imagination* (New York: Crossroad Publishing Co., 1981), esp. pp. 3–46, and *Plurality and Ambiguity* (San Francisco: Harper and Row, 1987); Max Stackhouse, *Public Theology and Political Economy: Christian Stewardship in Modern Society* (Grand Rapids, Mich.: Wm. B. Eerdmans Publishing Co., 1987); Ronald F. Thiemann, *Constructing a Public Theology: The Church and the Pluralistic Culture* (Louisville: Westminster/John Knox, 1991); Richard John Neuhaus, *The Naked Public Square: Religion and Democracy in America* (Grand Rapids, Mich.: Wm. B. Eerdmans Publishing Co., 1984); Robert Bellah, *The Broken Covenant* (New York: Seabury Press, 1975), and especially Linell E. Cady, *Religion, Theology and American Public Life* (Albany: State University of New York Press, 1993), which provides a comprehensive analysis of the literature and the issues.

3.   See the Preface and Chapter 1.

4.   See Chapter 1.

5.   In Chapter 4, *tradition* was defined more narrowly to have a necessary relationship to canon—the negotiation of identity within, and with, the dynamic space of canon.

6.   See Chapter 2.

7.   See Chapter 3.

8.   See Chapter 4.

9.   I will not undertake to define or characterize what is meant by *religious.* In this regard, all that is necessary for the present argument is the assumption that there is something, or better, some set of more or less related things, usefully distinguished as being "religious."

10.   When used in this sense, the term *normative* (and its variations) will henceforth be placed in quotation marks. This sense differs, of course, from the more common understanding of the normativeness of a canon, according to which there is a particular canonical meaning—whether that of the whole canon, or of some privileged element within the whole—to which the believer, as such, is obliged to conform (e.g., because the truth of this meaning is presupposed, or because conforming to it is what it means to be a believer).

11.   See the Preface.

12.   These terms are used here solely to indicate different ways of balancing the interplay of inheritance and creativity in theological construction. They do not correlate precisely with the substantive theological positions that ordinarily are given the same labels. More important, the terms here represent points along a continuum rather than distinct alternatives.

13.   I have already acknowledged the contribution of Sheila Greeve Davaney, an Iliff colleague, to my constructive proposal, but I should here add specifically that my discussion of current theologies in this chapter has benefited enormously from her analyses, published and unpublished. Of course, Davaney is not responsible for, nor does she always agree with, the judgments expressed here.

14.   Clark H. Pinnock, *The Scripture Principle* (San Francisco: Harper and Row, 1984). Portions of this analysis of Pinnock's book are adapted from my "Rethinking Authority from the Right: A Critical Review of Clark Pinnock's *Scripture Principle*," *Christian Scholar's Review* 19 (1989): 66–72.

15.   Pinnock, *Scripture Principle*, 62.

16.   Ibid., p. 194.

17.   Ibid., pp. 71f.

18.   Ibid., p. 194.

19.   Ibid., p. 45; cf pp. 181f.

20.   Ibid., p. 191; cf pp. 169f.

21.   Ibid., pp. 172, 193, 204.

22.   Ibid., p. 186.

23.   Ibid., p. 208; cf p.109.

24.   Ibid., p. 69.

25.   Ibid., p. 69.

26.   See, for example, his statement in Clark H. Pinnock and Delwin Brown, *Theological Crossfire: An Evangelical/Liberal Dialogue* (Grand Rapids, Mich.: Zondervan Publishing House, 1990), p. 45 and passim.

27.   George A. Lindbeck, *The Nature of Doctrine: Religion and Theology in a Postliberal Age* (Philadelphia: Westminster, 1984). This description of Lindbeck is taken in part from Sheila Greeve Davaney and Delwin Brown, "Postliberalism," in *The Encyclopedia of Modern Christian Thought* (Oxford: Basil Blackwell, 1993), pp. 453–456.

28.   Lindbeck, *Nature of Doctrine*, p. 18.

29.   It should be noted, first, that Lindbeck is using *liberalism* in a narrower sense than will be employed in this chapter and, second, that Lindbeck's characterization of liberal theology, even in his more specific sense, is questionable. Certainly it seems inaccurate to posit "experiential-expressivism" as the common basis of nineteenth and twentieth century liberal theology in America. (See Delwin Brown and Sheila Greeve Davaney, "Liberalism: USA," in the *Encyclopedia of*

Modern Christian Thought [Oxford: Basil Blackwell, 1993], pp. 325–330, including the bibliography provided there.)

30. Lindbeck, *Nature of Doctrine*, p. 16.

31. Ibid., pp. 17, 47.

32. Ibid., p. 129.

33. Ibid., pp. 82f.

34. Ibid., p. 81.

35. Ibid., pp. 94, 92.

36. Ibid., p. 94.

37. Ibid., p. 81.

38. By this term Lindbeck means that his theory should stand or fall independent of particular Christian theological assumptions. (Although the term *pretheological* is used only to characterize Chapter 2 of *The Nature of Doctrine*, it is not until Chapter 6 that Lindbeck discusses the implications of his view for Christian theology.)

39. There certainly are other differences, the chief among them having to do with Lindbeck's purely intramural view of truth seeking, and the primacy that he gives to language.

On the first issue, Lindbecks view contrasts with my position, set forth in the Introduction, that the theologian, whenever possible, is obligated to give reasons beyond his or her immediate context, and that such reason giving is possible, in spite of the absence of effective rules of universal validity, because there are criteria that overlap perspectival or contextual boundaries. Why this is so has become evident during the course of the discussion: The boundaries of cultures, traditions, and subtraditions are always flexible (revisable from within) and porous (permeable from without).

In contrast to Lindbeck's assertion of the primacy of language, I have argued, drawing principally on radical empiricism, that within our awareness language and experience are inextricably intertwined and that from a theoretical standpoint primacy ought to be given to historically formed strands of experience or, following Merleau-Ponty, dynamic patterns of being. Doing so, I have said, takes our understanding of the power of tradition beyond language (whether as conceptual analysis or as narrative) and thus better accounts for the efficacy in traditions of that which is not primarily conceptual, e.g., ritual action. (I shall return to this point in discussing the location of theology.)

40.   For a recent critique of Lindbeck's attempt to identify abiding "regulative principles," see David J. Bryant, "Christian Identity and Historical Change: Postliberals and Historicity," *Journal of Religion* 73 (1993): 31–41.

41.   See Rita Nakashima Brock, "And A Little Child Will Lead Us: Christology and Child Abuse," in *Christianity, Patriarchy. and Abuse: A Feminist Critique*, ed. Joanne Carlson Brown and Carole R. Bohn (New York: Pilgrim Press, 1989), pp. 42–61; and Brock, *Journeys by Heart: A Christology of Erotic Power* (New York: Crossroad Publishing Co., 1991). For a womanist interpretation of Jesus as cosufferer and friend, see Jacquelyn Grant, *White Women's Christ and Black Women's Jesus* (Atlanta: Scholars Press, 1989).

42.   James H. Evans, Jr., *We Have Been Believers: An African-American Systematic Theology* (Minneapolis: Fortress Press, 1992), pp. 6f. Evans says these folk stories are rooted in the African tradition of the epic hero (see pp. 80ff).

43.   One can imagine that in the psyche of the Indian people confronted by the European invasion there was a strong conservative voice (see Chapter 1). It would rightly have called upon the Indian nations to arm themselves with the symbols of their forebears. But it would also have insisted that they be precisely the same symbols, understood in the same relationships, used in the same way. The conservative voice would have argued that the inheritance means one thing, is based on one deposit of truth, houses one revelation, or has one grammar. And had this voice prevailed, Mother Earth would not have been born.

44.   My discussion of Mark C. Taylor has benefited from the Ph.D. dissertation of Carol Wayne White, "Towards A Postmodern Hermeneutical Theological Discourse" (Iliff School of Theology and the University of Denver, 1993).

45.   Mark C. Taylor, *Erring: A Postmodern A/Theology* (Chicago: University of Chicago Press, 1984), pp. 4, 19ff; and *Altarity* (Chicago: University of Chicago Press, 1987), pp. 3–33.

46. I say "in a certain fashion" because Taylor criticizes the, one might say, "naive constructivism" that supposes that although the creator God has died the creative human subject remains intact and can simply step in to take God's place. See Mark C. Taylor, *Deconstruction in Context* (Chicago: University of Chicago Press, 1986), p. 4.

47. Carl Raschke, *Theological Thinking* (Atlanta: Scholars Press, 1989), p. 105.

48. Taylor, *Erring*, p. 10.

49. Ibid., p. 7.

50. Ibid., p. 7.

51. Ibid., p. 7

52. Ibid., p. 7.

53. Ibid., p. 20.

54. What Taylor offers is not to be understood as another constructive system to replace those that have now failed us. Taylor holds, following Derrida, that systems are not reflections of the nature of things so much as strategies of exclusion and repression. (See, e.g., Jacques Derrida, *Writing and Difference* [Chicago: University of Chicago Press, 1981].) Indeed, the pretense of a system to reflect the nature of things, which he terms the *economy of representation*, leads to the "economy of domination" (see Taylor, *Erring*, pp. 25ff). The categories of the established system inevitably proceed to govern or rule the remainder of the conceptual domain, invading or colonizing all that stands as "other" to it (ibid., pp. 28f).

Throughout Taylor's work Hegel's system is paradigmatic of the system's insatiable drive toward domination. But lest one think that Hegel or even system as such is the problem, it should be clear that Taylor suspicions all efforts to create what might be called organic and comprehensive conceptualities, even in narrative form. According to Taylor, narrative, being a storied ordering of things, "arises from the need to achieve a position of mastery"; it "reflects the effort to ease the trauma of dislocation by weaving scattered events into a seamless web. . . . Historical narrative serves such . . . ends by familiarizing the strange and settling the unsettled" (ibid., pp. 69, 71). Thus Taylor writes that his own reflections "will, of necessity, be unsettled and unsettling. Repeatedly slipping through the holes in the system within which it must, nevertheless, be registered, such thought is perpetually transitory and nomadic. It is neither simply this nor that, here nor there, inside nor outside. . . . [Such writing] can, therefore, be described as *erring*" (ibid., p. 11).

In chapter 3 I argued against the notion that "theory" (including, by implication, system, narrative, etc.) necessarily has the totalitarian character that Taylor, following Derrida, attributes to it. (Nor do I think there is much evidence that an anti- or asystematic stance is on balance markedly more free of dogmatism or more tolerant of difference.)

55.   Ibid., p. 118.

56.   Ibid., p. 15.

57.   On "erring," see Taylor, ibid., pp. 11f. In fact, Taylor uses the term in reference to all four categories, and another prominent metaphor used to replace history is *mazing grace*.

58.   Ibid., p. 157.

59.   Ibid., p. 180.

60.   Ibid., pp. 8f.

61.   Ibid., p. 77. The quotation is from Jacques Derrida, *Of Grammatology* (Baltimore: Johns Hopkins University Press, 1976), p. 18.

Taylor's insistence on canonical uniformity is even more problematic than the views of Pinnock and Lindbeck, for whom the fissures within canon are somewhat too obvious for their theological comfort. But Taylor's contrasting claim that text, in distinction from book, is "irreducibly contextual"—helplessly subject, as it were, to the endless play of interpretation—is equally questionable. It fails to recognize the gravitational pull of a canonical galaxy or, shifting metaphors, the power of a game to play those who play it. Significantly, in *Interpretation and Overinterpretation* (Cambridge: Cambridge University Press, 1992), Umberto Eco, one of the guiding figures for American poststructuralism, challenges the view that a textual message can mean anything the interpreting context purports to see in it (p. 43 and passim). "I have the impression," he says, "that, in the course of the last decades, the rights of the interpreters have been overstressed" (p. 23).

62.   See Audre Lorde, "The Master's Tools Will Never Dismantle the Master's House," in *This Bridge Called My Back: Writings by Radical Women of Color*, ed. Cherrie Moraga and Gloria Anzaldua, (Watertown, Mass.: Persephone Press, 1981), pp. 98–101.

63.   From Rainer Maria Rilke, *Das Stundenbuch*: "Ich glaube an alles noch nie Gesagte."

64.   Post-Christian feminism—for example, in the work of Mary Daly, Carol P. Christ, Sharon D. Welch, and Daphne Hampson—might also be interpreted as a version of what I have called *radical theology*. Like Taylor, it joyously affirms the legitimacy and power of creativity, it (often more perceptively than Taylor) locates and confronts the hegemonic vectors of classical Christian theology, and it understands these inherited categories to be part of a singular systematic (patriarchy) that must be renounced on behalf of the theological (or "thealogical") task at hand. Thus also like Taylor, from my standpoint, post-Christian feminism misreads the nature of canon; namely, the power of its pluralistic potential to subvert the dominations that it has itself fostered.

Post-Christian feminism, however, differs from Taylor's deconstructive project in that (1) it often moves rather forthrightly toward the development of comprehensive constructive perspectives, and (2) it recognizes the power of inherited resources to create and sustain individual and communal identity. Thus it is a constructive historicism to a degree that Taylor's work is not. For many women this creative employment of symbols inherited from extra-Christian resources has been life-giving. If the argument of the preceding chapters is correct, however, the manifest vitality of these extra-Christian symbols would likely have more lasting efficacy in the broader cultural and religious arenas if they were integrated into the reconstruction of Christianity's inherited symbolic resources, there to subvert and transform the dominant construals of those resources at the same time that they capitalize on their power. Post-Christian feminists might well reply, like Taylor, that the inherited Christian symbol system is incapable of such transformation (a view challenged throughout this discussion), and that, in any case, they are not seeking broad cultural and religious efficacy.

65.   One can imagine that the Indians confronted by White usurpation of their land heard from radical voices (see Chapter 1). They would have called upon the Indians to be creative, to dare new ways of thinking, new forms of sight. But they would have insisted that creativity means utter originality, something that is clean of the past. The radicals would not have countenanced a reconstructed Indian symbol. They would have required something totally new— perhaps a theory of property rights imported from eighteenth century France. In any case, had the radicals prevailed Mother Earth would not have been born.

66.   See, e.g., Albert Eustace Hayden, *The Quest of the Ages* (New York: Harper and Row, 1929), and John Dewey, *A Common Faith* (New Haven, Conn.: Yale University Press, 1934).

67.   In early twentieth century liberal theologies this core, e.g., the teachings of Jesus, was also said to be normative, but that claim was usually equivocal because liberals had difficulty deciding whether the core was normative because it was Jesus' teachings or because it happened to conform to the best of modern knowledge. There is little doubt that "modern knowledge" was the real norm then; it certainly is for liberalism now, though in a much more tentative, plural, and functional sense than in earlier forms. Claims are to be tested and at best tentatively validated in the multiple arenas of contemporary discourse. Thus "modernity" provides the proper context (and with that a diversity of operative and vulnerable assumptions), but not a set of privileged conclusions.

68.   Schubert M. Ogden, "The Point of Christology," *Journal of Religion*, 55 (1975): 376.

69.   Schubert M. Ogden, *On Theology* (San Francisco: Harper & Row, 1986), pp. 64f. The apostolic witness, it should be noted, is the standard for testing the "Christianess" (or "appropriateness"), not the truth (or "credibility"), of theological claims.

70.   Rosemary Radford Ruether, *Sexism and God-Talk: Toward a Feminist Theology* (Boston: Beacon Press, 1983), p. 24.

71.   Ibid., p. 23.

72.　See Rosemary Radford Ruether, "Feminist Interpretation: A Method of Correlation," in *Feminist Interpretation of the Bible*, ed. Letty M. Russell (Philadelphia: Westminster Press, 1985), pp. 112–17.

73.　Gordon D. Kaufman, *The Theological Imagination: Constructing the Concept of God* (Philadelphia: Westminster Press, 1981), p. 102. For a discussion and critique of Kaufman's position, see Sheila Greeve Davaney, "Directions in Historicism: Language, Experience, and Pragmatic Adjudication," *Zygon* 26 (1991): 199–218.

74.　Kaufman, *Theological Imagination*, pp. 109–20.

75.　Ibid., p. 116.

76.　Ibid., p. 122. This involves three tasks: clarifying and articulating more fully the four terms of the categorial scheme, bringing the scheme into relationship with contemporary human experience, and assessing the viability of the fourfold scheme (pp. 120f).

77.　John B. Cobb, Jr., "Response to Pannenberg," in *John Cobb's Theology in Process*, ed. David Ray Griffin and Thomas J. J. Altizer (Philadelphia: Westminster Press, 1977), p. 187. The full development of Cobb's christology is found in *Christ in a Pluralistic Age* (Philadelphia: Westminster Press, 1975).

78.　The Christian is supposed to maintain a memory of this historically grounded entitlement, according to Cobb, but the reason for this exception is unclear because, presumably, the entitlement to pursue creative transformation might also be granted elsewhere.

79.　The first two differences are obvious. As to status, Ogden, for example, grounds the primacy of the apostolic witness in the logic of biblical authority whereas Kaufman's categorial scheme is said to be a purely contingent emergent in history. With respect to purpose, Ogden and perhaps Ruether regard the cores they identify as constituting the essence of Christianity; Cobb and Kaufman deny that Christianity has an essence, but they nonetheless present, respectively, creative transformation and the categorial scheme as the marks of authentic Christian identity.

80.　Kaufman's practice is less to dismiss elements of the canon than to employ certain of its major motifs (the four categories) at such an abstract level that they lack substantive canonical content.

81.   In *Types of Christian Theology* (New York: Yale University Press, 1992), Hans Frei traces this feature of liberal theology to Kant (pp. 58f).

82.   Happily, there are exceptions, e.g., Ruether's *Sexism and God-Talk*, and, to some degree, Kaufman's recent *In Face of Mystery: A Constructive Theology* (Cambridge, Mass.: Harvard University Press, 1993), Chapters 21–29.

83.   For the meaning of *normativity* here, see note 10.

84.   The relative neglect of canonical reconstruction in Ogden, Ruether, Kaufman, and Cobb may in part have individual vocational explanations—the decision to concentrate on methodological issues (Ogden and Kaufman) or on pressing social issues (Ruether and Cobb). But, in some cases (perhaps most!), it may also stem from what could be called a *thin* version of historicism. According to Kaufman, for example, *historicism* means, first, that humans "are shaped by" history and, second, that humans have "some control over the processes of historical change" (*In Face of Mystery*, p. 127; cf pp. 103–6 and passim). In this there is no recognition of a third dimension of historicism, which is the claim that an effective shaping of the future, Kaufman's second element, *requires* the creative employment of what has shaped us, Kaufman's first element.

Interestingly, Cobb could offer a systematic reason for neglecting the task of canonical reconstruction. In principle, Cobb's christological premise exempts the Christian from giving attention to inherited resources unless they happen to be the site of transformative creativity. From the standpoint of the theory of tradition developed in this book, however, creativity is not effectively transformative except as it imaginatively employs inherited resources. If this material claim were coupled with Cobb' christology, the drift toward the radical position inherent in Cobb's formal premise would then be checked.

85.   This is most nearly acknowledged by Kaufman, who says that the first task of Christian reconstruction is to "clarify further and articulate more fully" the categorial scheme, "with the help of" concepts such a "sin, fall, salvation, church," etc. (*Theological Imagination*, pp. 120f). Until *In Face of Mystery*, however, Kaufman's work has been devoted primarily to methodological question and what he identifies

as the second task of Christian theology today; namely bringing "the categorial scheme . . . into relationship with contemporary human experience . . ." (p. 121). In this project, as we have said, the four categories are basically thematic motifs without substantive content.

86. One can imagine that among the Indians of the nineteenth century there were liberals (see Chapter 1). They would have embraced the feminine earth as the pure core of Indian faith, they would have joined in its elevation as deity, and extolled it as their norm. So far so good. But were they like the liberals of today, at their hands the rest of the symbolic complex would have withered and virtually disappeared. Grandfather-Grandmother, the Four Winds, Coyote, Changing Woman, the Uwanami and Kachinas, the vision quest, the masks and pipes, and so on would have become, at best, interesting antiquities, relics of an ancient orthodoxy, contaminated by past inadequacies, unsuitable for retrieval, reconstruction, and renewal. Mother Earth would been born, only to live a life of sterile solitude and sidle eventually into irrelevance.

87. In thinking of theology as "caregiving" I depend primarily on the work of the philosopher Milton Mayeroff, *On Caring* (New York: Harper and Row, 1971), the ethicist Nel Noddings, *Caring: A Feminine Approach to Ethics and Moral Education* (Berkeley: University of California Press, 1984); and Nancy J. Brown, my wife, whose research in this area first made me aware of these writers and the massive amount of material now appearing on this topic. In all of this work, it should be said, "caring" is not serving; it is a dynamic, reciprocal relationship in which the integrity of "carer" and "cared for" is to be protected, and the development of each is to be promoted.

88. One result, of course, is "liberation theology," the classic example of which is Gustavo Gutierrez, *A Theology of Liberation* (Maryknoll, N.Y.: Orbis Books, 1973).

89. See Brock, *Journeys by Heart*, esp. pp. 66–70. In effect, Brock assimilates christology to ecclesiology. For a fuller development of this kind of move, see the writings of John Knox, especially "On the Meaning of Christ," in *Jesus: Lord and Christ* (New York: Harper and Row, 1958), pp. 193–276.

90.   This literature is voluminous, but one of the most influential examples is Sallie McFague, *Models of God* (Philadelphia: Fortress Press, 1987), esp. Part II. For a summary of the literature, see Anne E. Carr, *Transforming Grace: Christian Tradition and Women's Experience* (San Francisco: Harper and Row, 1988), esp. pp. 134–157.

91.   See the works of Charles Hartshorne, especially *Man's Vision of God and the Logic of Theism* (Chicago: Willett, Clark, 1941); *The Divine Relativity: A Social Conception of God* (New Haven, Conn.: Yale University Press, 1948); and *Philosophers Speak of God* (Chicago: University of Chicago Press, 1953), pp. 1–25, 499–514.

92.   See Shirley Jackson Case, *The Evolution of Early Christianity: A Genetic Study of First Century Christianity in Religion to its Religious Environment* (Chicago: University of Chicago Press, 1914); and Shailer Mathews, *The Atonement and the Social Process* (New York: Macmillan Publishing Co., 1930), and *The Growth of the Idea of God* (New York: Macmillan Publishing Co., 1931).

93.   See, especially, the works of Linell E. Cady and David Tracy listed in note 2. (It should be clear that I find Tracy's notion of "classic" far too restrictive [and, paradoxically, too vague] as a designation of what is canonical for the Christian; and I do not hold to Tracy's earlier appeals to a universal form of experience ["limit-experience"], an approach he seems to have abandoned in *Plurality and Ambiguity*.)

94.   Alfred North Whitehead, *Science and the Modern World* (New York: The Free Press, 1925), p. 140.

95.   In this discussion I am indebted to the Ph.D. dissertation of Diane Prosser MacDonald, "Transgressive Corporeality: The Body, Poststructuralism, and the Theological Imagination" (Iliff School of Theology and the University of Denver, 1993).

96.   Julia Kristeva, *Revolution in Poetic Language* (New York: Columbia University Press, 1984), p. 79.

97.   Julia Kristeva, *Desire in Language: A Semiotic Approach to Literature and Art* (New York: Columbia University Press, 1980), p. 86.

98.   The following discussion of the authority of tradition is drawn from my article "Struggle till Daybreak: On the Nature of Authority in Theology," *Journal of Religion*, 65 (1985): 15–32.

99.   Hannah Arendt, "What Was Authority?" in *Authority* ed. Carl J. Friedrich (Cambridge, Mass.: Harvard University Press, 1958), pp. 81–112.

100.   Ibid., pp. 98f.

101.   See Werner Foerster, "Exousia," in *Theological Dictionary of the New Testament*, vol. 2, ed. Gerhard Kittel, trans. G. Bromiley (Grand Rapids, Mich.: Wm. B. Eerdmans Publishing Co., 1964), pp. 562–74.

102.   For a development of this view of the authority of canon, see Brown, "Struggle till Daybreak." In important ways my view parallels that of Elisabeth Schüssler Fiorenza, who writes "The Bible is not the controlling and defining 'court of appeals' for contemporary feminist theology and community but its *formative* root-model" (*Bread Not Stone: The Challenge of Feminist Biblical Interpretation* [Boston: Beacon Press, 1984], p. 88). For a comparison and critique of our views, see Charles Wood, "Hermeneutics and the Authority of Scripture," in *Scriptural Authority and Narrative Interpretation*, ed. Garrett Green (Philadelphia: Fortress Press, 1987), pp. 3–20.

103.   See Chapters 2 and 4.

104.   For my brief analysis of the repressed affections of the liberal church, see my comments in Pinnock and Brown, *Theological Crossfire*, pp. 183–86.

105.   I have developed this argument in "The Location of the Theologian: John Cobb's Career as Critique," *Religious Studies Review* 19 (1993): 3–6, and in "Constructive Theology and the Academy," *CSSR Bulletin* 22 (1993): 7–9. The propriety of theology in the university is also defended in several of the essays in *Theology and the University: Essays in Honor of John B. Cobb, Jr.*, ed. David R. Griffin and Joseph C. Hough (Albany: State University of New York Press, 1991).

106.   The material in this paragraph is taken from Brown and Davaney, "Liberalism: USA."

107. See Delwin Brown, "The Fall of '26: Gerald Birney Smith and the Collapse of Socio-Historical Theology," *American Journal of Theology and Philosophy* 2 (1990): 183–201.

108. See James H. Cone, *A Black Theology of Liberation*, 2d ed (Maryknoll, N.Y.: Orbis Books, 1987), and *God of the Oppressed* (New York: Seabury Press, 1975).

109. See Sallie McFague, *Models of God*, and *The Body of God: An Ecological Theology* (Minneapolis: Fortress Press, 1993).

110. Judith Plaskow, *Standing Again At Sinai: Judaism from a Feminist Perspective* (San Francisco: HarperCollins Publishers, 1991).

Index

74, 77, 82, 88, 93f, 109, 127, 129, 131, 144, 165, 183f. *See also* Negotiation.
Post-Christian feminism, 205f
Postliberal Theology, ix, 123–126, 152
Public Theology, 139, 153

Radical Empiricism, x, 49–53, 106–109, 166–168, 170f
Radical Theology, 127–132, 179
Raschke, Carl, 128
Rauschenbusch, Walter, 149
Revisionist Theology. *See* Public Theology.
Ruether, Rosemary, 133f, 207f
Ricoeur, Paul, 166f, 174, 178
Ritual, 3, 92–109, 187–192
  and embodiedness, 97, 99f, 103f, 106f
  and radical empiricism, 53, 106–109
  as conservative, 93f, 95–97
  as creative, 93f, 95–97
  as bearer of meaning, 101f, 106f
  as indispensable to tradition, 108f
  Merleau-Ponty on, 98–104
  Whitehead on, 102–106
  role in tradition, 108f
Revisionary Theology. *See* Public Theology.

Sahlins, Marshall, 64f, 174f, 178
Sanders, James, 16–18, 155, 157f, 184f
Schussler-Fiorenza, Elizabeth, 73
Smith, Jonathan Z., 92–94, 174, 187–189
Stambovsky, Phillip, 167
Sullivan, Lawrence E., 193

Taylor, Mark C., 127–130, 203f
Taylor, Mark K., 155, 165
Tedlock, Dennis, 186
Theology, 9–12, 120, 137–150
  as critical consent
    to tradition, 147f

as tradition's caregiver, 138, 147f, 209
authority of, 141–144, 184, 199
See constructive historicism
criteria of, 4–7, 11, 82, 90, 115, 119, 135f, 154
place (location) of, 145–147
task (vocation) of, 4, 117, 120, 138–140
Theory, 55–59, 171f
Torah, 16–19
Tracy, David, 153f, 198, 210
Tradition, ix, 1, 57, 67, 86–92, 97–100, 117, 119, 154, 176, 199
  affective dimension of, 46–54, 91f, 117
  and identity, 28f, 67, 83–86, 89, 144
  as complexes of possibilities, 38f, 40, 174, 178
  as canonical negotiation, 67, 90f, 114, 184
  canon of. *See* Canon.
  continuity and change in, 24–30, 112f
  destructive capacities of, 2, 114, 115f, 130
  effective change in, 24–30, 86f, 112f, 116f, 118, 125–127, 130–132, 136f, 187
  Gadamer on, 31–54, 113f
  negotiation in. *See* Negotiation
  play in. *See* Play.
  strict definition of, 67, 90, 114
  ten hypotheses on, 24–30, 112f
Turner, Victor, 95–97

Wagner, Roy, 63, 97, 173f, 178
West, Cornel, 56, 70f, 171f, 179f
Whitehead, A. N., x, 49–51, 58, 102–106, 172
Williams, Raymond, 61, 83, 173, 185f

Young, Iris Marion, 192f

- authenticated
- what holds it together
  dyadic 129